CANADA

Publisher:	Aileen Lau
Project Editor:	Vanita Jayaram
Assisting Editor:	Wong Ee Ling
	Catherine Khoo
Design/DTP:	Sares Kanapathy
	Sarina Afandie
	Michelle Ng
Production:	Brian Wyreweden
Illustrations:	Chua Teck Chai
Cover Artwork:	Susan Harmer
Maps:	Dicky Xie

Mary Ann Simpkins wishes to acknowledge the assistance of Craig Barran for his contributions to her work.

Published in the United States by
PRENTICE HALL GENERAL REFERENCE
15 Columbus Circle
New York, New York, 10023

ISBN 0-671-88278-3

Titles in the series:
Alaska - American Southwest - Australia - Bali - California - Canada - Caribbean - China - England - Florida - France - Germany - Greece - Hawaii - India - Indonesia - Italy - Ireland - Japan - Kenya - Malaysia - Mexico - Nepal - New England - New York - Pacific Northwest USA - Singapore - Spain - Thailand - Turkey - Vietnam

USA MAINLAND SPECIAL SALES
Bulk purchases (10+copies) of the Travel Bugs series are available at special discounts for corporate use. The publishers can produce custom publications for corporate clients to be used as premiums or for sales promotion. Copies can be produced with custom cover imprints. For more information write to Special Sales, Prentice Hall Travel, Paramount Communications Building, 15th floor, 15 Columbus Circle, New York, NY 10023.

Printed in Singapore

CANADA

Text by Mary Ann Simpkins

Project Editor
Vanita Jayaram

Prentice Hall Travel

New York London Toronto Sydney Tokyo Singapore

C O N T E N T S

C O N T E N T S

C O N T E N T S

CONTENTS

Natural Canada inspires with kaleidoscopic color from the sun-drenched

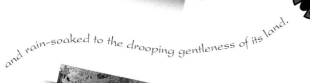

and rain-soaked to the drooping gentleness of its land.

Geese and goldenrod, heralders of spring, speck the countryside

in their homely browns, bits of black and dazzling white.

Quiet silhouettes against the shifting tides of Canadian waters startle the traveller into a musing wonderment of all that Canada has to offer

Canada's rich cultural and physical diversity are the reasons why it should be at the top of every tourist's list of countries they want to visit. There is something for everyone. For the nature lovers or people who just want to get away from it all, there are large areas of unspoiled wilderness which are popular with campers, whitewater rafters, hunters and anglers. Or you could enjoy the scenic and serene fishing communities on the coasts of the country.

Canada is filled with deep blue rivers and snow-capped mountains.

For the urban lovers there are vibrant and interesting cities. Quebec city with its old European-style buildings, Montreal for its *joie-de-vivre* (love of life), and for great music and other eclectic night-time pursuits, Toronto. Epicureans can delight in the variety of ethnic restaurants found in the major cities. Lovers can enjoy the mystical and romantic charm of the timeless Niagara Falls.

Introduction

1

Whitewater fun and excitement on the Rouge River.

"Canada" is thought to be derived from the Iroquoian word *"Kanata"*, meaning village or community. One of the earlier explorers, Jacques Cartier, picked this word up from the Indians who were living around what is currently known as Quebec City.

The sheer vastness of Canada, where the major cities are separated by thousands of kilometers, can sometimes be intimidating even to the most intrepid of travellers.

As the second largest country in the world, it spans six different time zones

and every region.

The Canadian climate with its long cold winters may seem unendurable to people from more moderate climates, but Canadians have adapted and made the best out of something that is beyond their control. Winter sports such as skating, skiing, tobogganing, curling and the national pastime of Canada, hockey, are popular winter sports and enjoyed by many. The snowmobile, a Canadian invention, is another adaptation to the Canadian winter, facilitating winter travel. It has displaced the dog sled and the horse drawn sleigh, but don't despair, if you have your heart set on taking a sleigh ride, they are still a popular form of family recreation.

Canada's dual colonization by first France and then England has produced a bilingual country with a largely British flavor and a minor, but significant, French tinge. In order for the country to function, the two cultures have had to learn to be flexible and responsive to each others' needs.

The immigration of large numbers of immigrants from around the world has added spice to this bicultural state. Immigration is now pegged at roughly one percent of the population. Flexibility and responsiveness to the needs of the minority have made Canadians skilled negotiators on the world stage, better able to grasp and sympathize with the plight of each side. Canada's population is dynamic, changing ever so slightly as immigrants bring new blood, vitality and hope for a better life.

and is more than 40 times the size of England. What may come as a surprise to some is that the city of Windsor, Ontario, is actually further south than Seattle, Detroit and even Boston.

The landscapes and climates of Canada are so dominating that they have played a large part in shaping the attitudes of the people living in each

Lady in a Loyalist outfit.

Despite sporadic and half-hearted efforts to assimilate French Canada – or *Qué becois* as they call themselves – they have kept their Latin identity.

Of course, this Latin temperament means French Canadians zoom around corners and down roads at high speeds and display more emotion in public than English Canadians, but French Canadians also spend more time enjoying themselves, with their families or socializing with friends in sidewalk cafes or late night bars.

To the rest of the world, it might seem that Quebec is always on the verge of going its separate way. But their separatist tendencies usually only come to the fore in response to some perceived slight from the rest of Canada.

English Canada has been quite flexible with Quebec, and now their culture and French language are quite secure. A further safeguard is their numerical superiority in Quebec and the championing of their constitutional and human rights by the Quebec provincial government.

The northern region of Canada is dominated by the Arctic tundra, home of the Inuit. The Inuit have been pulled along by the rest of Canada into the modern age and you won't find them living in igloos anymore. Instead, you might find them watching satellite television or zipping around on their snowmobiles visiting friends or checking on their trap lines.

The inhabitants of British Columbia, cut off from the rest of Canada by numerous mountain ranges, consider themselves a people apart, and this sentiment is reciprocated by other Canadians who think British Columbians are a little zany. Their isolation, location on the Pacific and a more moderate climate have made British Columbians the Californians of the North.

The sense of community, friendliness and conservatism of the prairies reflect its strong agricultural roots. You won't see cowboys or Indians chasing buffalo across the plains anymore. Nowadays, the only cowboys you are likely to encounter will be on a cattle ranch or at one of the many rodeos held across the West each year. As for Indians, they are found in most parts of Canada. After being kept out of society

Making the most of a fur coat and a long cold winter.

Because of time differences across the country and a population heavily weighted in Eastern Canada's favor, the West's sense of powerlessness manifests itself during national elections. As the polls close in the East, the election has often already been decided before the polls in the West have even closed.

Ontario is the economic engine of Canada and home to the two cities that Canadians love to hate – Ottawa for its political control and Toronto for its financial dominance. Of course, everyone pushes personal prejudices of Toronto aside when the baseball season comes around. The *Toronto Blue Jays* have won the last two World Series. Yet even Montreal, Toronto's financial and commercial rival, comes on board and

for so long, they are gradually becoming an integral part of it.

Prairie folk, along with their British Columbian neighbors, form yet another larger region within Canada. They are united by their feeling of isolation from Central Canada and have their own nucleus today.

Some two thirds of the population live in Central Canada, which is composed of Quebec and Ontario. The concentration of population means both provinces dominate the country economically and politically. Westerners feel they don't have any real say in running the country. Although there is no threat of Western separation, there is often some animosity towards Central Canada over this issue.

An Indian totem pole carving.

Fast Facts

Area: Canada covers an area of 9,970,610 square kilometers. It is the second largest country in the world, after Russia.

Highest Point: The highest point in Canada is Mount Logan in the Yukon at 5951 m.

Population: 27,647,000 (est. 1993)

Capital city: Ottawa is the capital of Canada. It has the fourth largest metropolitan population. Toronto is the financial center as well as Canada's largest city.

Government: Canada is a constitutional monarchy. The Head of State is the Queen of England, who is represented in Canada by the Governor-General. The Governor-General is largely a ceremonial post with no power to govern. Real power resides in the Prime Minister and his or her cabinet. The Prime Minister is the leader of the political party that commands the support of the majority in the House of Commons. The Commons is the lower house of Parliament and its members are elected by a popular vote. Elections must be held at least every five years.

The Senate is the Upper house of Parliament and its members are appointed by the Governor-General on the advice of the Prime Minister. Seats are allocated on a regional basis, with the largest provinces getting the most seats. Senators may hold their seats until they reach 75 years old. The Senate cannot veto legislation from the House of Commons.

Canada is also a federal state with 10 provinces. Each Province has its own elected legislative system.

Language: Canada has two official languages: English and French. However, Canada is a predominantly English speaking country and only 16 percent of the population can speak both languages. The French speaking population is concentrated in the province of Quebec. Quebec is the only province to have a French speaking majority.

People: Canada is an "immigrant" country made up of many different nationalities. Canadians of British or French backgrounds constitute the majority of the population. About 28 percent have a British background while 23 percent have a French heritage. About 16 percent of Canadians were born outside of their country. Over one million Canadians have aboriginal origins.

Religion: Most Canadians are Christians. About 46 percent of the population is Roman Catholic while 36 percent is Protestant.

Currency: The basic unit of currency is known as the Canadian dollar which is composed of 100 cents.

Economy: Canada has the seventh largest industrial economy in the world. Besides manufacturing, agricultural, minerals, fishing and forestry play major roles in the economy. Auto manufacturing is the single largest industry.

National flag: The Canadian flag consists of a stylized red maple leaf on a white background sided by two red vertical bands.

National Flower: Sugar Maple.

National anthem: The national anthem is "O Canada". There is both an English and a French version. A bilingual version is sometimes sung at major events.

---

uninhibitedly roots for the *Jays*.

Most immigrants head to Ontario and metropolitan Toronto in particular, which is a multicultural wonderland. The ethnic neighborhoods have lent spice to the city which used to be considered staid and colorless. In contrast, rural Ontario is heavily populated by Canadians of British stock.

The rocky beauty of the Maritimes is a land seemingly untouched by events in the rest of Canada. The people are more conservative than in Central Canada, more willing to accept things as they are. Here, life moves slowly, but steadily at its own pace.

Canada's economy doesn't revolve around the industrious beaver anymore,

Floral rhapsody in spring at Butchart Gardens.

as it once did in the 17th century, but Canada is still heavily dependent on its natural resources. Abundant mineral, agricultural, fish and forestry products still play a large role in the economy. These resources along with state of the art manufacturing facilities have pro-vided Canada with one of the world's richest economies. Telecommunications, space technologies, computer software and other information technologies are going to lead Canada right into the 21st century. The Canadians' tolerance has built a better society.

Canadian history, contrary to popular belief, doesn't begin with the arrival of the Europeans in the late 15th century. The land was already populated by an estimated 300,000 natives who are Indians whose ancestors had "discovered" Canada thousands of years earlier.

The Indians

A timber church built by the early 17th century missionaries.

The first North American inhabitants probably started arriving somewhere between 40,000 and 15,000 years ago. They came during the last ice age when much of the earth's water was stored in glaciers. The sea level dropped, revealing a land and ice bridge connecting Siberia and North America.

The Indians in the 15th century were not a homogeneous group. Besides having different physical attributes and customs they spoke 11 major languages and many more dialects. Some languages were as different

Indian Chiefs

An Indian woman at work at a tribal camp.

Pontiac

Pontiac, chief of the Ottawa, led an Indian uprising in 1763 against the British.

With the capture of Quebec during the Seven Years War, colonial settlers soon expanded westward into Indian territory, angering the Indian inhabitants. Fanning the flames of Indian hostility was the treatment they received at the hands of the British. British traders who flooded into the area were cheating the Indians. Another bone of contention was, unlike the French, the British didn't treat the natives with respect.

Pontiac's strategy was to get one tribe to attack the fort closest to it, then move in and wipe out the unprotected settlements. Of the (12) forts, eight were targeted. One of the more ingenious battles occurred when the Ojibaway and the Fox organized a game of lacrosse near Fort Michilimackinac. One player purposely flung the ball over the wall of the fort, and the Indians rushed in after it. The Indian women who were already inside the fort passed out weapons they had hidden beneath their clothing.

The fort was quickly taken and 70 British soldiers were killed. More than 2,000 civilians and soldiers were killed before the uprising was quelled the following year. Pontiac was later kicked out of his village after he signed a peace treaty with the British.

Joseph Brant

Joseph Brant was a Mohawk Chief who straddled both the Indian and White cultures. After fighting alongside the British during the Seven Years War, Brant's abilities were recognized by General Sir William Johnson who sent Brant off to an Indian school.

Later, Brant worked as an interpreter for Johnson and helped to translate several religious works into the Mohawk language.

as English is from Korean.

The population was unevenly scattered all across Canada. Most Indians lived in semi-permanent settlements along the coast of British Columbia, the St. Lawrence Valley as well as in Southern Ontario. Most of these settlements were not properly established and were in a constant state of flux.

Eastern Woodland tribes

The Iroquois were the dominant group in the Eastern Woodlands. Two mutually hostile Iroquoian confederations were formed in the lower Great Lakes area. The Five Nations, or the Iroquois Confederacy, was composed of the

The outbreak of the American Revolution in 1775 worried Brant who thought the Americans would kick his people off their lands. Travelling to London, he received assurances from King George III that the Indian lands would be protected. On his return, Brant fought in an Indian-Loyalist band throughout the war, where his military exploits became legendary.

After the war, Brant was shocked that Indian lands had been ceded to the Americans by the Treaty of Paris. In compensation, Brant received land for himself and his Indian allies along the Grand River in Ontario. Today's Brantford is named after him.

Tecumseh

Tecumseh, a Shawnee Chief, dreamed of establishing an Indian nation that would co-exist with white neighbors in North America. He built a settlement on the Tippecanoe River in Indiana, which was to be the capital of his new state. Tecumseh's dream dismayed the Americans, who, had no wish to see this "nation" come into being. In 1811, the Americans destroyed the town, killing many inhabitants.

Tecumseh fled to Canada, eventually allying himself with the British during the War of 1812, mainly because he admired and trusted Sir Isaac Brock. His support proved vital to the British during the first year of the war. In 1813, Tecumseh's bravery became legendary when he refused to retreat with the British forces. He died in the battle. Tecumseh was one of Canada's earliest and outstanding heroes.

Seneca, Mohawk, Cayuga, Oneida, and Onondaga. This group was pitted against the Huron Confederacy, which consisted of the Huron, Erie and the Neutral. The Iroquois lived in villages: some of which had 2,000 inhabitants. They depended heavily on the produce they grew, crops such as corn, beans, squash and sunflowers.

The Inuit

The predecessors of the Inuit arrived later than those of the Indians, roughly 4,000 years ago. By this time the land bridge had submerged and disappeared. The Inuit are thought to have crossed the narrow Bering Strait by boat or on frozen sea.

Later, waves of different Inuit groups spread east across the Arctic to Greenland. The Inuit were a nomadic people. Depending on the season, the Inuit would travel in search of fish, land and sea mammals.

The Vikings

The first recorded Europeans to land in Canada were the Vikings. Their discovery dates from around AD 986 when Bjarni Herjulfsson was blown off course as he was sailing on an expedition from Norway to Greenland.

Amazingly, he didn't even land. Bjarni just sailed up the coast until he had regained his bearings. Leif Ericsson hearing of this land, rich in timber, set sail a few years later. Leif landed on Baffin Island, Labrador and a place he named Vinland.

Soon, other Viking expeditions were launched and at least one settlement was established in Newfoundland. The settlement of Canada was short-lived, possibly due to hostile natives. Firearms would subsequently give later European

Traditional Scottish attire reflects Canada's rich history.

explorers a big advantage.

Beginning in the late 15th century, explorations by Europeans exploded. This was prompted by the European quest for an alternate route to the riches of the Far East and to advances in navigation and shipbuilding.

John Cabot

John Cabot, an Italian sailing for England, set off in 1497 to search for a Far Eastern route. Cabot is thought to have landed in Newfoundland, Cape Breton and Labrador.

Cabot became the first person to claim territory for England in the New World. Of greater consequence, Cabot's tales of the fish-rich waters off the coast of Newfoundland soon attracted large numbers of fishing vessels.

With his first voyage in 1534, Jacques Cartier discovered the St. Lawrence River basin and visited Indian settlements at the present-day sites of Montreal and Quebec City. Cartier's findings led to the growth French settlement in this area.

In 1576, the British were trying to find a North West route through the Arctic. Martin Frobisher was hired by a British company which he later helped bankrupt. Frobisher, thinking he had struck a rich source of gold, mined it and returned to England. Unfortunately for Frobisher and his company, the "gold" turned out to be fool's gold.

The Fur Trade

By the 16th century the main impetus behind voyages to the New World was the fur trade. There was an enormous demand for beaver pelts, which were used to make hat felt. French traders, bartering with the Indians, exchanged European goods for pelts. The French government began offering fur monopolies to companies who would bring over settlers for the colonies.

Samuel de Champlain

Samuel Champlain, a man of many talents, took part in a short-lived trad-

The Notre Dame Basilica – a legacy from Canada's French past.

ing settlement in Acadia (now Nova Scotia). After this failed, Champlain established Canada's first permanent settlement at Quebec in 1608.

Despite Champlain's attempts to increase settlement, Quebec grew very slowly. By 1627, Quebec had only less than 100 people, which included less than 12 women.

The Kirke Brothers

The French government started playing

Prairie Settlers

Scottish tenant farmers who were kicked off their land in Scotland, victims of the changing economy, were the first prairie settlers in Canada. It is a tradition that has continued into this century. Most of the people who settled in the prairies were fleeing from something - poverty, religious persecution, discrimination - the prairies held a promise of being free, the opportunity to own their own land.

Yet, at first settlement was slow. Lord Selkirk had brought the Scottish farmers to the confluence of the Red and Assiniboine Rivers, to what is now Winnipeg, in 1812. This was a rich farmland and, eventually, the Red River Settlement flourished, but few followed them and some of them just couldn't cope with the hardship. They fled to established centers.

In the late 1800s, the government anxious to settle the prairies, began to aggressively advertise for tough, hard working people. The government called for good, sturdy peasants, people from Central and Eastern Europe who had some experience in working the land.

They enticed them by offering homesteads, 160 acres of land for $10.00. The low-priced land came with rules everyone had to follow. They had to farm at least 10 acres of the land each year for three years. They had to build a house within three years. They had to live on the farm for six months of each year for three

a more active role in New France when it realized that the fur companies were more interested in profit than in settlement. So, in 1628, 400 settlers set sail. Unfortunately, while sailing, war broke out with England.

The would-be settlers were forced to return because a fleet of English privateers under the Kirke brothers blockaded the mouth of the St. Lawrence River. After capturing Quebec, the Kirke brothers, in 1629, expelled Champlain and his settlers.

Champlain and 200 settlers returned to Quebec in 1633 after the treaty of St. Germain-en-Laye gave back New France to the French. This provided some measure of stability for the settlers and they were able to live in comparative peace in their new settlements.

The Missionaries

Missionaries streamed into New France to convert the Indians to Christians.

years. If they complied with these conditions, after three years, they owned the land and received a deed to the land. The government insured people who met these conditions. Russian Doukhobours who obtained a homestead in 1899 in Saskatchewan lost their land because they refused to go along with the conditions. Thousands of people jumped at the government's offer. From 1901 to 1921, the number of Ukrainians in the three prairie provinces increased from 5,622 to 96,055. Some 116,000 Poles immigrated over a period of approximately 15 years. By 1914 all the good homesteading land had been taken, despite the hardships of settling this land.

Hailstones, grasshopper plagues and drought took their toll in the summer while in the winter, a family needed a sturdy house to withstand blizzards that could pile snow on the eaves. Fall was a busy time since food had to be preserved and stocked for the long winters. It wasn't unusual to have to walk 100 to 150 km to get into town.

It was a hard life but most of these settlers stuck it out and today some of their descendents are the business people and politicians who run Canada. The Governor-General of Canada, Ramon Hnatyshyn, is the grandson of Ukrainian settlers in Saskatchewan.

The Recollects arrived first, in 1615. The Jesuits, who would play a greater role, began arriving in 1625.

The Jesuits moved deep inland to live with the Indians. Many Hurons were hostile to the Jesuits, only tolerating their presence for the sake of the fur trade. The main effect the Jesuits had on the Indians was to indirectly help kill them by spreading diseases to which the Indians had never been exposed. Diseases such as small pox and measles ravaged the Indian population. By the

A Totem pole, symbol of Indian culture and heritage.

1640s the Huron population was reduced to half its former size.

The Hurons and the Iroquois

The bloodiest Indian wars in Canadian history broke out during the 1640s over control of the fur trade. The weakened Hurons were almost completely annihilated by the Iroquois. In the process, they also managed to slaughter a number of Jesuits.

The Iroquois then started killing French settlers and fur traders, bringing the fur trade almost to a halt. King Louis XIV ended this chaos in 1663 by taking direct control of New France and sent

A bequeathal of the missionaries in St John's Church.

Re-enactment of English-Canadians taking tea in their traditional cotton frocks.

1,000 troops who quickly restored order.

New France

French supremacy in the fur trade was very much threatened by the British establishment of the Hudson Bay Company in 1670. The company had received control of a large swath of land around Hudson Bay.

From the late 17th century and into the 18th century, fur traders kept on increasing the size of New France. New France soon extended west to the Prairies and south to encompass all of the Mississippi River basin area. This enlargement created more conflicts with the English colonists who wanted to expand westward.

The end of the 16th century saw the eventual loss of Acadia in 1713 and Quebec in 1763.

By 1681, the population of New France reached 10,000. Most French Canadians today are descended from this population.

By the 1730s, New France was exporting crops. The colony also started to build ships and produce iron. However, the mainstay of the economy was still the fur trade.

A series of European wars spilled over into North America starting in the late 16th century. There were a series of battles which marked this turbulent period in Canadian history. Peace was only regained much later.

The Treaty of Paris

During the Seven Years War, Quebec fell in 1759. The fall of Montreal the year after soon spelt the end of French rule for the entire 65,000 inhabitants of New France.

The Treaty of Paris in 1763 gave the British all French territory in New France except for the two tiny islands of St. Pierre and Miquelon which are off the coast of Newfoundland.

The British

After 1763, British Governor Generals allowed the French to retain many of their institutions, and French cultural, legal and political rights were officially recognized in the Quebec Act of 1774.

The Act was the result of prodding by Governor General Guy Carleton. The British government agreed with Carleton mainly because it already had its hands full with the rebellious American colonies.

The Act also allowed Quebec to retain all its land between the Mississippi and the Appalachians. This infuriated the colonies who wanted this land for expansion.

The American Revolution

In 1775, the Americans invaded Quebec before the American Revolution even began! They had hoped to bring their Northern neighbors onto their side and, failing that, to remove the Northern threat entirely.

The Americans captured Montreal along with a handful of forts and then laid seige to Quebec. They withdrew only when they were threatened by the arrival of a fleet of British ships.

The American Revolution had a major impact on British North America.

During and after the war about 45,000 loyal British subjects in America (Loyalists) emigrated to the Maritimes and a further 10,000 went to Quebec while the loss of the Mississippi basin greatly reduced the size of British North America. The British North American hold in the Mississippi was therefore considerably weakened.

Constitutional Act of 1791

The Constitutional Act of 1791 divided Quebec into Upper and Lower Canada, mainly along ethnic lines. Upper

A reminder of Canada's war-strewn past.

Canada, present-day Ontario, had a population of 20,000.

They were mostly Loyalists, while Lower Canada had 100,000 French and 7,000 English citizens. The Act attempted to placate both the English and French by giving them their own spheres of influence respectively.

The Act established an elected assembly in each province. The veto powers given to both lieutenant-governors and their executive councils would eventually lead to conflict.

The War of 1812

There were several reasons for the War of 1812 between the Americans and the British. One of them was that the Americans accused the British of arming the Indians in the Ohio Valley.

With the European Napoleonic War in full swing, the British Navy was searching American vessels sailing to Europe. The Navy would remove any British deserters it found and sometimes, in the process, took off American sailors as well. Other Americans clamored for war in order to annex Canada.

Most of the fighting took place in Upper Canada along the US border. In 1812, General Issac Brock, the Lieutenant-Governor of Upper Canada, stopped an invasion from Detroit and another one on the Niagara peninsula at Queenston Heights.

An advance party of 600 Americans

Samuel de Champlain

Samuel de Champlain is regarded as the father of Canada. Against all odds, Champlain succeeded in establishing the nucleus of New France at Quebec. Historian Marcel Trudel wrote that without Champlain's persistence, "there would not have been a New France."

The details of Champlain's earlier exploits are sketchy at best, but he is thought to have sailed, in some unknown capacity, to the West Indies in 1600.

Champlain, in the employ of fur traders, charted the St. Lawrence on his first voyage to New France in 1603. On his return to France he published a chronicle of his voyage titled *Des Sauvages*. This was the first of four books Champlain would write. His writings helped stir up interest in the colony.

Champlain was hired by the Sieur de Monts, a fur trader who had been granted the fur monopoly. Champlain was to undertake exploratory expeditions to search for a permanent settlement. In 1604 a settlement was established in Acadia which lasted for three years. Champlain spent his time looking for a passage to the Far East and charting the coasts of New England and the Maritimes.

By 1607, De Monts was not making enough money to continue the Acadian settlement, partly because he couldn't enforce his monopoly. Fishermen were trading up and down the coast. In 1608 at the urging of Champlain, de Mont sent Champlain to trade on the St. Lawrence. Here Champlain established the first permanent settlement in New France at Quebec. This was an intelligent move. The fur monopoly was easier to enforce in the narrow

St. Lawrence. Also many rivers flowed into the St. Lawrence. These rivers passed through heavily forested regions which were rich in fur.

Quebec didn't get off to an auspicious start. During the first winter 20 out of 28 men died from malnutrition and scurvy. Luckily for Champlain and his settlement, the spring heralded the arrival of French ships carrying supplies and more settlers. The rejuvenated colony was soon trading with the Indians for their furs.

Trade alliances with the Indians drew Champlain into conflicts against the Indians' foes. Champlain often helped the Huron and their allies defeat the Iroquois. These battles made the Iroquois bitter enemies of the French.

When Champlain wasn't taking care of business at Quebec, he travelled and explored New France. Champlain incorporated his observations with other fur traders and the Indians to produce a map of New France. The map, published in 1632, was a cartographic masterpiece that highlighted how far Champlain had extended European knowledge of New France.

Five years after the French had been evicted by the English Kirke brothers, a determined Champlain returned to Quebec with 200 settlers and a handful of Jesuit priests. Champlain died there in 1635.

Although he never saw the fruition of his dream, Champlain can be credited with pushing both the Crown and the fur companies to bring over settlers. Without Champlain's persistence, New France might have remained little more than a series of trading posts and would have eventually been annexed by the English colonists to the south.

---

crossed the Niagara River into Canada and onto the Heights. Brock was killed leading a charge but the Americans were defeated. Strangely enough, the New York militia just watched as the American forces were wiped out. They refused to come to their aid, saying their terms of service didn't include fighting

outside the United States.

In 1813 the Americans burned the government buildings in York (Toronto). The British retaliated the next year by burning nearly every government building in Washington, including the White House and the Capitol building.

The war developed into a stalemate

A glimpse of old Montreal through wrought-iron gates.

and peace was finally restored in 1814.

Rebellions in Canada

Trouble was again brewing in Canada during the 1830s. The colonists wanted a responsible government. They were upset that their legislation was being vetoed by non-elected representatives.

In Lower Canada, the French were further angered by the appointed officials being English-speaking. They felt that they should rightfully be represented by French-speaking officials.

These political problems led to several small rebellions in both provinces in 1837.

The government responded with the Act of the Union (1841) which combined Upper and Lower Canada into the Province of Canada. The new legislative assembly was to have 42 members from each former province and were to be given more autonomy.

The British were hoping that by having only one province, the French would be assimilated. The principal of responsible government was finally achieved in 1849 after the Governor General signed this legislation that he personally disagreed with.

Confederation

There were a number of factors behind the drive for Confederation: the need to

Pre-1915 architectural heritage.

pull together out of economic necessity and to lessen the chances of U.S. annexation, the British desire to cut colonial expenses, and the hope that the Union would break the political deadlock in the Province of Canada.

The British North American Act

The British North America Act establishing the Dominion of Canada was passed by the British Parliament on March 29, 1867, and the Dominion of Canada came into being on July 1.

The Dominion consisted of four provinces: Ontario, Quebec, New Brunswick and Nova Scotia.

Canada got a British-style of Parliament with the Queen as Head of State. It was not really a complete independence. The British Parliament still could veto legislation whenever it wanted.

Sir John A. MacDonald

The first Prime Minister was John A. MacDonald, one of the principal architects of confederation. Canada expanded quickly under MacDonald. The acquisition of Ruperts Land from the Hudson Bay company in 1869 increased the size of Canada sixfold and three new provinces were added – Manitoba in 1870, British Columbia in 1871 and Prince Edward Island in 1873.

Bringing Manitoba into confederation ended up dividing the country. The majority of people in Manitoba were Métis; part Indian and part European. Shortly before Manitoba was to become a province, Louis Riel seized control and formed a provisional government to negotiate its incorporation. Riel, a Métis, demanded political rights for the Métis, the establishment of French Catholic schools and the recognition of French as an official language in Manitoba. When a revolt broke out against Riel's government, an English-speaking Ontarian was executed. Ontarians called for Riel's blood while the French looked upon Riel as a hero for standing up for French culture. Riel was exiled and later granted amnesty. Unfortunately, Riel was hanged in 1885 for leading a Métis revolt in Saskatchewan. The execution made Riel a French Canadian martyr.

The building of a transcontinental railway was necessary to unite the entire country. Indeed, British Columbia entered confederation only when the government promised to build a railway. In 1885, the Canadian Pacific Railway linked British Columbia to the rest of Canada enabling better transport.

The government was spurred to settle the Prairies by fears of American annexation due to a number of factors (see box). Between 1871 and 1901, the prairie population increased tremendously from 75,000 to 420,000. By 1911 it was about 1,300,000. As a result, Alberta and Saskatchewan became provinces in 1905.

World War One

The British Declaration of War on August 4, 1914, automatically meant that Canada, as part of the British Empire, was also at war. The war turned out to be costly in terms of human casualties; 63,000 dead and 175,000 wounded.

The war once again strained national unity. Tensions between the English and French mounted when Conscription was introduced in 1917. Most of the English supported it while the French didn't.

Canada came out of the war stronger and more independent. Canada supplied the British with most of her food and also produced large quantities of munitions, airplanes and ships, which transformed Canada from an agricultural to an industrial society.

The Depression

The New York stock market collapse in 1929 hit Canada hard. Its export market declined by 67 percent between 1929 and 1933. Unemployment reached 27 percent in 1933. It was the worst year of the depression.

The prairie provinces fared the worst. The price of wheat, their only main product, plunged due to world overproduction.

To compound difficulties, many parts of the West were devastated by drought between 1933 and 1937.

Canada's growing independence was evident in 1939 when the British declared war on Germany. Unlike the World War when Canada would have automatically been at war, Canada waited a full week before declaring war on Germany.

When war was declared in September 1939, Prime Minister Mackenzie King promised that conscription would not be introduced. He didn't want to see the country split again over this issue. The wounds from the conscription crisis from the last war still festered between the English and the French.

The demand for large quantities of ships, airplanes, tanks, motor vehicles and weapons finally pulled Canada out of the depression. Most Canadian war production was destined for England, but since they couldn't afford the immense costs, Canada gave England several billion dollars worth of loans and grants which enabled them to purchase Canadian goods.

After the Federal government passed measures giving itself greater control of the wartime economy, the opportunistic Maurice Duplessis, the Premier of

Gothic-style Ottawa's ornate, high-domed Parliament.

25

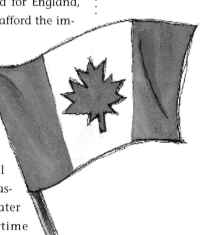

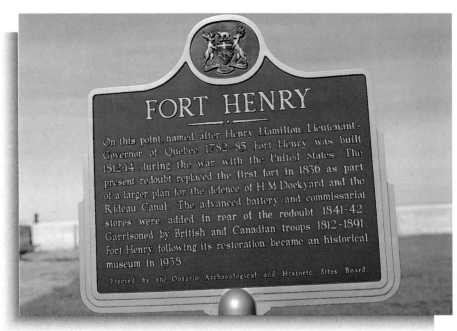

The Fort Henry sign at Kingston.

Quebec, called a surprise election, on the grounds that Quebec's autonomy was being threatened. This backfired on Duplessis when Federal cabinet ministers from Quebec threatened to resign if Duplessis was re-elected premier. The threat of no Quebec cabinet representation had its intended outcome: Duplessis lost the election.

By 1940, there were stronger calls from English Canada for a larger role in the war. The French, however, opposed this idea. Even though Germans occupied France, the French Canadians saw the war as being primarily British. To alleviate the pressure from English Canada, Prime Minister King called a plebescite in 1942 to release him from his no conscription pledge.

Not surprisingly, the French voted overwhelmingly against it. The reverse occurred with the English. Still, King held off introducing conscription for overseas service until 1944, when voluntary enlistment could no longer replace Canadian casualties. Animosity was minimized because the war was soon over and the number of conscripts sent overseas was relatively small.

More than one million Canadians out of a population of 11.5 million served in the armed forces. The 42,000 death toll was smaller than in World War I.

Post War

After the war, Canada became a much

A provincial parliament building – the stalwart domain of the government.

more active player on the world stage. Canada's riches and small population made it a middle power. In this role Canada acted as a mediator between the world powers, and also between the developing and the developed countries of the world. Its commitment to international affairs would lead to closer relationships with many countries and to participation in many multinational and bilateral organizations.

The Cold War

Canada played a key role in the forma-tion of the North Atlantic Treaty Or-ganization (NATO) in 1949. This Treaty linked North America with a number of Western European countries in a strong defensive alliance.

After the Soviet-backed North Kore-ans invaded South Korea in 1950, Canada increased its contribution to NATO. The West saw the invasion as a cold war ruse to draw NATO troops away from the defence of Europe. Canada rushed troops and 12 fighter squadrons to Europe. Canada also had some 22,000 Canadians fighting under the UN flag in Korea.

The cold war inevitably led to the integration of the American and Canadian airforces under the North American Air Defence Command (NORAD) in 1957. NORAD was designed to help protect North America from Soviet nuclear bomber attacks.

Réne Levesque

Quebec's majestic Parliament building.

Réne Levesque was undoubtably the most famous, loved and influential politician in the history of Quebec. The chain-smoking Levesque could electrify crowds with his hard-hitting emotional oratory.

Levesque began his career as a war correspondent during World War II. After the war, he joined and then later headed Radio Canada International. In 1956, Levesque moved from radio to television, hosting the popular television series "*Point de Mire*" (Point of View). This current affairs show made him one of Quebec's most influential television personalities.

In 1959, Levesque was elected to the Quebec Legislative (provincial) Assembly where he soon held a series of different cabinet posts.

Fighting for change in Quebec, Levesque was in the vanguard of the Quiet Revolution. He convinced his cabinet colleagues to nationalize the electrical utilities. Besides providing job opportunities for young French Canadians, this also gave Quebec greater control over its economy. Levesque also played a leading role in making Quebec politics less corrupt.

Levesque, one of the province's most popular cabinet ministers, sat as an independent in 1967 after his Liberal Party refused to accept his proposals for a sovereign Quebec.

In 1968, Levesque united the divided French separatists to form the Parti Quebecois (PQ) whose main platform was sovereignty-association. The PQ quickly gained popularity, and

The Suez crisis clearly illustrated Canada's role as a world mediator. After

President Nasser of Egypt nationalized the French and the English controlled

Levesque was elected Premier in 1976. During his first term in office, he introduced a number of popular reforms, including Bill 101 which confirmed French as the only official language in Quebec and removed English from all outdoor signs.

Levesque's dream of an independent Quebec lay in tatters after the "No" side won 60 percent of the vote in the 1980 referendum. Levesque himself was partially to blame. His passage of Bill 101 helped undermine the necessity for sovereignty-association since it had removed English from sight.

Quebec might not have wanted an independent Quebec but it still continued to want Levesque. He won an even larger majority in the 1981 election.

During the final constitution repatriation talks in 1981, Levesque had thought an agreement was all but impossible between the provinces and the Federal government. This suited him fine because he felt Quebec wasn't being offered enough. Unfortunately for Levesque, a small group of Federal and Provincial ministers reached a compromise at the last minute. The next morning, a surprised Levesque had trouble believing a compromise had been reached without his participation. The document was presented to Levesque as a *fait accompli*. The humiliated Levesque refused to sign the agreement and, mockingly, Levesque said the Canadian way of compromise was "to abandon Quebec at the moment of crisis."

During Levesque's second term in office, his government became unpopular when economic difficulties forced him to cut public expenditures. Levesque divided his party when he refused to fight the upcoming election over sovereignty-association. Although still leader, Levesque decided to step down in 1985. He died in 1987. If Quebec achieves independence, Réne Levesque will become one of its founding fathers. The Parti Quebecois continues to be a major force in Quebec politics today.

the Suez Canal in 1956, France and England got the Israelis to attack Egypt, so the French and English could rush in to "protect" the canal. The USSR and the Third World were enraged with this underhanded tactic. The United States was also incensed, as it had not been given any advance warning. With the USSR making threats to bomb Paris and London, the skilled Canadian diplomat Lester Pearson, diffused the situation. His proposal for sending a multinational peacekeeping force to the canal zone was adopted. In recognition of his efforts, the following year Pearson was awarded the Nobel Peace Prize.

The Cultural Revolution

The 1960s were a decade of turbulence. The cultural revolution spread from the United States into Canada. Rebelling against the establishment, Canadian youths wanted to change society for the better. Canadians became caught up in the American Civil Rights movement and protested the US involvement in the Vietnam war and the establishment of nuclear weapons on Canadian soil. The generational gap widened as rock stars like Jimi Hendrix and the Beatles became the heroes of the youth. The birth control pill coupled with the burgeoning growth of feminism gave power to Canadian women.

The Quiet Revolution

The Quiet Revolution was the term given

The heart of Quebec City.

to the rapid pace of economic, political and social reforms in Quebec during the first half of the 1960s. These reforms led to the political awakening of Quebec and demands for a greater French role in the province's English-speaking dominated economy. For some, this was not enough and separatist groups were formed to pull Quebec out of Canada.

The most notorious of these groups was known as the Front de Libération du Québec (FLQ), which started waging a terrorist campaign in 1963. The FLQ robbed banks and armories, and bombed mailboxes and even the Montreal Stock Exchange. The FLQ's wave of terrorist activities culminated in October 1970 with the kidnappings of the British Trade Commissioner, James Cross, and the Provincial Labor Minister, Pierre Laporte.

Like any terrorist group they had a list of demands they wanted in exchange for the release of the hostages, including free passage to Cuba. The Quebec government asked for federal help and the Canadian government imposed the War Measures Act, which gave the police sweeping powers of arrest and detention. Pierre Laporte was later found dead in a car trunk, and James Cross was freed when the kidnappers were given safe passage to Cuba.

The Royal Commission

In response to the growing unrest in

A government building in Montreal City.

Quebec, the Royal Commission on Bilingualism and Biculturalism was created in 1965. The commission studied the problems the French faced. A number of the Commissions' recommendations were eventually implemented by the Federal government.

Prime Minister Pierre Elliot Trudeau passed the Official Languages Act in 1969. It recognized English and French as the two official languages. And wherever there was a justifiable demand for it in terms of number, bilingual services would be provided for everyone across the country.

This angered both the English and the French. The English saw it as giving too much concessions to the French while the French saw it as not enough.

Parti Quebecois

In 1968, Réne Levesque, a former Quebec provincial cabinet minister, united two separatist groups and formed the Parti Quebecois (PQ). Their main platform was sovereignty association, meaning a sovereign Quebec within a Canadian economic union.

Support for the PQ swelled until, finally, they won the 1976 Quebec election. The PQ win and their promise of holding a referendum on sovereignty association sent shock waves through the rest of Canada.

Luckily, this option was defeated in the 1980 referendum and Canada remained intact.

The Royal Citadel Guards during their morning parade.

Repatriating the Constitution

Up until the 1980s, Canada could not amend its constitution without the consent of the British Parliament. Although approval was nothing more than a rubber stamp, it increasingly became seen as anachronistic. Previous attempts at repatriating the constitution had broken down over the division of powers between the Federal and Provincial governments. The idea of repatriation

worried about the Charter conflicting with their own rights to pass provincial laws. The second problem dealt with future constitutional amendments. When a compromise couldn't be reached, Trudeau threatened to get England to pass the constitution without the consent of the provinces.

A compromise was eventually obtained with every province except Quebec, and Canada got a new Constitution. Quebec refused to sign. They simply wanted more concessions. The exclusion of Quebec proved to be a costly error as it delved the country in more constitutional wrangling and soured relations between Quebec and the rest of Canada. Brian Mulroney, elected Prime Minister first in 1984, tried twice and failed both times to bring Quebec into the Constitutional fold.

Kim Campbell became Canada's first female Prime Minister when an unpopular Mulroney stepped down as leader of the Conservative party.

Campbell quickly alienated many voters in the runup to Federal election and led her party to a stunning defeat: they won only two seats in the House of Commons. Liberal leader Jean Chrétian became prime minister. The election of 1993 also saw the rise of two regional parties. The separatist Bloc Québecois emerged as the official opposition party followed closely by the Western-based Reform Party. The rise of these two parties could further fragment Canada along regional lines and, in the case of the Bloc, could fragment it literally.

cropped up again during the PQ sovereignty-association campaign where Federal Ministers promised Quebec more rights in a new constitution.

The repatriation process soon became bogged down over two main points. The provinces were not happy with Trudeau's Charter of Rights and Freedom protecting the individual. They

E c o n o m y

Canada's natural wealth has always played an important role in the Canadian economy. During the 20th century, this rich resource base and the growth of manufacturing created the world's seventh largest industrialized economy.

Canada experienced a painful recession during the early 1990s in which the recovery has been excruciatingly slow. Ominously, the recovery hasn't created a lot of new jobs for Canadians as it was expected to. The unemployment rate still persists in hovering around 11 percent.

The debt and the economy are the two biggest issues facing Canadians today. Both the federal and the provincial governments have been living beyond their means for years and are now saddled with enormous debts. About 25

A log-filled lake that serves as a warehouse for Canada's rich resource of timber.

The stock exchange at Toronto's Bay Street.

percent of all federal spending is used just to pay the interest charges on its debt. There isn't much room for tax increases since Canada is already one of the most heavily taxed countries in the world. Both the provincial and federal governments have been making painful, and often unpopular, spending cuts in order to reduce their deficits.

Trade

Canada is a major trading nation. Roughly a quarter of its goods are destined for export. Nearly 80 percent of its exports go to the United States. Canada and the United States share the largest trading relationship in the world.

The Heartland

Ontario and Quebec form the industrial heartland of Canada. In fact, Ontario is referred to as the engine of the Canadian economy. Concentrated in these two provinces are three quarters of Canada's manufacturing and 70 percent of its financial industry.

Toronto is Canada's business and financial capital and nearly 40 percent of Canada's corporate head offices are located here. Toronto's Bay Street is the equivalent of New York's Wall Street. Along with the Toronto Stock exchange, Canada's largest, banking insurance and other businesses are concentrated in the Bay Street area.

Soldering copper at Quebec – an area rich in mineral produce.

Vital Minerals

Mineral wealth is distributed throughout the country. The Appalachian region of Quebec is rich in asbestos, copper and zinc. The Canadian Shield is rich in metallic minerals such as nickel, gold, uranium and zinc. The prairies have oil, natural gas, potash and gypsum while British Columbia has abundant supplies of coal, lead and zinc.

Canada is one of the world's leading producers of non-fuel minerals. Nearly two thirds of these minerals are exported, accounting for 15 percent of all Canadian exports.

Canada's mineral production reads like a list of superlatives. The country is the world's largest producer of uranium and zinc concentrates; the second largest of nickel, asbestos, potash and elemental sulphur; the third largest of platinum group metals and aluminum, fourth of copper, coal, silver, cadmium, gypsum, molybdenum and titanium concentrates. The most valuable of the non-fuel minerals are gold, copper, zinc and nickel.

Oil and Natural Gas

Alberta, with its vast reserves, is the center of Canada's oil and natural gas industry. Canada exports large quantities of oil and natural gas to the United States while at the same time importing

The Decline of Montreal

The eye-catching sculpture at the Bank Nationale de Paris in Montreal.

Montreal was once the industrial, commercial and financial center of Canada as well as its largest city. A series of complex and interrelated factors knocked Montreal off its pedestal. But what is one city's loss is usually another's gain, and in this case - Toronto gained. By the 1970s, Toronto became Canada's largest city and the undisputed economic center of the country.

Montreal's position in Canada had already been in descendance when the political crises of the second half of this century affected Que-

bec's business community. The terrorist campaign waged by the FLQ during the 1960s highlighted the province's fragile political situation and alerted the Canadian and American business elite, that controlled Montreal, to the precariousness of their position.

The next jolt came with the election of the Parti Quebecois (PQ) in 1976. This party, whose avowed goal was to pull Quebec out of Canada, sent all businesses steadily streaming out of Quebec. By this time, Toronto had already

oil from other countries. This odd trading pattern has developed because it is cheaper for the Maritimes and eastern Quebec to import oil from other countries than to buy Canadian oil transported across the country. The northern

tar sands of Alberta contain one of the world's largest known reserves of oil. These sands contain a mixture of water, sand and bitumen. Bitumen, a tar-like oil, is refined to make synthetic crude oil. Unfortunately, most of these reserves

become the economic center of Canada, so for some companies, it made ample sense to leave Montreal anyway.

The business climate deteriorated when the Quebec government introduced Bill 101 in 1977, making French the only official language of business in the province. Bill 101 increased the difficulty of hiring English speakers from outside the province because it became almost impossible for them to send their children to an English-speaking public school.

Between 1976 and 1981, over 100 head offices and some 14,000 employees fled Montreal. This might not seem like much but these companies were engaged in finance, insurance and high tech manufacturing, the backbone of any modern city. Some companies just moved out certain divisions, such as those involved in finance and research.

These desertions underlined Montreal's continuing decline over the last century. Toronto in the 20th century grew rapidly for a variety of reasons. The city had a geographical advantage over Montreal during the development of the West. American investment, which fuelled Canada's economic growth during this century, preferred to set up shop in Toronto or Southern Ontario because there weren't any cultural or linguistic barriers. Furthermore Southern Ontario was right next door to Detroit enabling the auto manufacturers to set up shop in Ontario and evade restrictive tariffs.

Many other complex factors also helped Toronto to overtake Montreal during this century. Toronto became the centre of economic activity. Montreal still plays a vital role in the Canadian economy and has, despite the gamut of changes, never lost its charm – a quality that Toronto will never be able to take away from it.

will remain untapped until new and cheaper extraction techniques are found.

Low prices have stifled exploration of the vast amounts of untapped oil and natural gas in Canada. However, one massive project steaming ahead, mainly as a result of large government involvement and financing, is the Hibernia oil field off the coast of Newfoundland. Billions of dollars have been poured into this project in order to tap an estimated 615 million barrels of oil. Pumping is expected to begin in 1997.

Agriculture

Canada, a major agricultural nation, exports half of its agricultural products. These exports account for one tenth of its exports. Like other industrialized nations Canada has seen a sharp decline in the number of people engaged in agriculture, employing only 3.2 percent of the population.

Farming takes place throughout most of Canada. Nearly 70 percent of Prince Edward Island is given to potato farming. Fruit are grown in Nova Scotia and New Brunswick. The warm, fertile earth of the Niagara peninsula provides much of Canada's fruit and tobacco. In Quebec, dairy farming tops the list of agricultural produce.

Prairie Produce

The Prairies contain over 80 percent of Canada's farmland. Wheat, barley and canola are the main grains grown here. Saskatchewan produces over half of Canada's wheat. Most of Canada's cattle are raised on the plains, particularly in Alberta. The Okanagan Valley of British

Montreal's old port is still alive with tour activity.

Columbia produces most of Canada's apples along with grapes, apricots, cherries and plums.

Of all the agricultural products, Canada is best known for its wheat, yet the value of wheat production lags behind both cattle and dairy products.

Forestry

With its vast forests, it is no wonder that Canada is one of the world's biggest producers of forestry products. Canada is the world's largest producer of news-

forestry has been making news around the world. Clayoquot Sound, on the west coast of Vancouver Island, has become a rallying point for environmentalists. Clayoquot Sound has the largest remaining coastal temperate rainforest in the world. Over 800 protesters were arrested for trying to block the logging of the forest during the summer of 1993.

Fishing

European fishermen were the first to exploit Canada's natural resources. These maritime waters are still the richest in Canada, providing Canada with 75 percent of its fish. Fishing is the economic backbone for nearly half the villages and towns in the Maritimes. The most popular exports from the Atlantic region are crab, lobster, shrimp, halibut, scallops and cod.

The Atlantic cod fishermen have been hit hard over the last two years as cod stocks dropped to a precipitous level. Some areas have seen cod stocks dropping by 95 percent over a four year period. In 1992, the federal government imposed a moratorium on cod fishing in most areas, resulting in the layoff of almost 40,000 fisherman and fish plant workers. This was indeed bad news. New evidence suggests that cod stocks will not revive for many years to come.

Scientists believe cooler water conditions are the main reason for the decline. To a lesser extent, scientists blame overfishing by foreign vessels outside

print, the second largest of pulp and the third largest of sawn lumber.

Forest products make up 15 percent of Canada's exports and forestry employs, directly and indirectly, one out of seventeen Canadians. British Columbia is the largest wood producing province, followed closely by Quebec and Ontario. Recently, Canadian

The Trans-Canadian Railway.

Canadian waters.

British Columbia also has a thriving fishing industry. Salmon is far and away its most valuable fish.

The smallest of the fisheries are the inland fisheries, which are concentrated around the Great Lakes and the larger lakes and rivers of northwestern Ontario, the prairies and the Northwest Territories. Common commercial species include pickerel, perch, pike, lake trout, whitefish and smelt.

Fur

The fur industry upon which Canada was built is little more than a footnote in its present day economy. An old fur trader wouldn't even recognize the industry of today, most pelts are taken from animals raised on farms. Mink has replaced beaver as the fur most in demand in the western world.

Manufacturing

Now it might seem strange that Canada's largest manufacturing industry is the automobile industry. After all how many Canadian cars can you name? In reality, there aren't any exclusively Canadian car companies.

Most cars in Canada are built by subsidiaries of the Big Three: General Motors, Ford and Chrysler. Automobile manufacturing began in Canada in 1904, with the establishment of a Ford plant at Windsor. Soon the other auto makers branched into Canada to avoid Canadian import tariffs and to take advantage of preferential British tariffs for goods manufactured in Canada.

Further expansion of the Canadian automobile industry occurred after the signing of the Auto Pact in 1965. The agreement allowed the free trade of automobile and automobile parts between Canada and the United States as long as certain conditions were met.

The Canadian push for a Free Trade Agreement with the United States started in earnest in the mid-1980s. A number of protectionist bills were being introduced into the American congress and Canada was worried that it might lose access to its largest market. The debate in Canada quickly became acrimonious. There were worries about Canada's cultural, economic and even political sovereignty. The 1988 election was fought over the issue of Free Trade and when Brian Mulroney was re-elected with the help of the business community, the Free Trade Agreement came into effect on January 1, 1989. Certain sectors of the economy such as breweries were protected while other tariffs were to be phased out over a period of 10 years.

NAFTA

The North American Free Trade Agreement (NAFTA), joining the economies of the United States, Mexico and Canada, came into effect on January 1, 1994.

The vastness of Canada is simply mind boggling. When Canadians discuss distances in their country, they speak about thousands of kilometers. The country stretches 5,514 km at its greatest east-west distance and 4,634 km from North to South. Canada's 9,970,610 sq km of territory is bounded by the Arctic, Atlantic and Pacific Oceans.

Despite Canada's tremendous size, the United States is the only country bordering it. Canada shares two borders with the United States. One border is along southern Canada and the other is with Alaska in the northwest.

The majority of Canadians live within a narrow band hugging the American border to the South. Some 80 percent of the Canadian population lives within 160 km of this border. This isn't due to any Canadian desire to be within range of American television stations, but to a combination of geographic and climatic factors.

Canada's climate can generally

The iridescent beauty of rushing waters at Yoho National Park.

Geography & Climate

45

be summed up in one word: cold. More than half the country is dominated by arctic and subarctic conditions. Winters in the Arctic may last a good 10 months or more.

The most favorable climate in Canada is found within a narrow region on the coast of British Columbia. This fact is not lost on Canadians living in other parts of the country.

Canadian newscasts seem to derive sadistic pleasure from showing people jogging in shorts along the Pacific Ocean while the rest of the country is digging itself out from another major snowfall.

This wet temperate climate has mild wet winters, where temperatures rarely fall below freezing. The moderating influence of the Pacific keeps the summers warm.

Southern portions of Quebec and Ontario and most of the Maritimes have a cool temperate climate with warm summers and cold winters. Temperature extremes increase moving inland away from the Atlantic Ocean.

The southern portions of the prairie regions have a semi-arid climate. This area usually receives less than 500 mm of precipitation each year. Winters are rather cold and quite long while the summers are warm.

Canada, being so vast, has six main geographical regions, each having their own physiographical characteristics. While being relatively homogeneous physically there are still variations to be found within each region giving each one a distinctive identity.

The Canadian Shield

The Precambrian or the Canadian Shield, as it is commonly called since most of it lies within Canada, covers almost half the country and underlies much of the rest. This oldest region in North America hugs Hudson Bay like a horseshoe and stretches all the way from Labrador, covering most of Quebec, Ontario and the northern reaches, all of the three prairie provinces up into the Northwest Territories.

Although it is hard to imagine it today, this land was once dominated by towering mountains that rivalled the Himalayas. These mountains were formed in a series of mountain building cycles beginning some 3.8 billion years ago. Both volcanic processes and repeated folding and faulting uplifted the land. The forces of erosion over millions of years has worn down these once mighty mountains to their roots. The present landscape is quite rugged with elevations generally under 600 m. The Shield is rich in minerals and dotted with an almost infinite number of lakes, ponds and streams.

The Appalachians

The Canadian Appalachians form the northern tip of the Appalachian mountain chain which runs all the way down the eastern United States into Alabama. In Canada this region spans the Gaspé

The incomparable Niagara Falls.

peninsula and most of the Maritimes.

The Appalachians began forming some 600 million years ago with the collision of the North American and European plates. Erosion and differential uplift have resulted in a number of low rounded mountain ranges, lowlands and plains.

The range has shrunk considerably with the highest mountain being Mount Jacques Cartier in the Gaspé peninsula which rises to only 1,268 m.

The Interior Plains

The Plains cover most of Saskatchewan and Alberta and as well as parts of the Northwest Territories, British Columbia as well as Manitoba.

Eroded material from the Canadian Shield was deposited in a shallow surrounding sea. Over time thousands of meters of eroded sediment accumulated, giving rise to the Plains.

The Plains are not just one large piece of even terrain as they are usually misconceived to be. There are scattered uplands interspersed throughout the Plains. In addition, two escarpments, the Missouri and the Manitoba escarpment, divide the Plains into three sections. The Plains rise in elevation towards the Cordillera. Starting at 330 m in the east, the Plains rise to 1,300 m near the foothills of the Rockies.

Large areas of glacial deposits have made the Plains an extremely large and

Grand Banks

The Grand Banks were considered the richest fishing grounds in the world with cod so bountiful that when John Cabot publicized the area in 1498, English, French, Spanish, and Portuguese ships began making the long, arduous journey over the Atlantic every summer in small open boats.

The Grand Banks are actually several separate banks lying in a wide area off the southeast coast of Newfoundland. These banks form a great underwater shelf of shallow waters – the depth is generally less than 100 m – that are also sources of haddock, redfish, halibut, mackerel and herring.

Many fishermen never made it home, drowning in the storms that could suddenly rise up or falling victim to the fogs shrouding the banks. The water mainly comes from the southward-flowing cold Labrador Current with some eastward-flowing warm Gulf Stream waters.

Warm air masses moving from the Gulf Stream over the colder Labrador Current produces thick fog, particularly in the spring when the air-sea temperature differences are greater. Huge icebergs obscured by the thick fogs add another threat: the Titanic went down just 150 km to the south in 1912.

Despite the dangers, ships continued to come. The French, Portuguese and Spanish had large enough supplies of salt to remain on board ship during their fishing trip. The English, however, lacked quantities of salt, requiring them to go ashore to dry and lightly salt the cod for transporting it back to Europe, thus establishing the first settlements in Newfoundland.

In the 1950s huge Japanese and Soviet vessels joined the Europeans, Americans and Canadians fishing these banks. In 1977, when Canada extended its jurisdiction to 320 km offshore, which includes most of the Grand Banks, foreign fishing was greatly reduced.

Still, some Canadian fishermen blame foreign fleets for overfishing cod and flounder on the international zone of the Grand Banks, reducing the stocks to the extent that the Canadian government in 1994 banned all cod and flounder fishing except around the southwestern coast of Nova Scotia. And even that quota has been cut slightly to more than 25 percent of the 1985 quota levels. With these drastic measures, it's hoped cod stocks will increase by the turn of the century.

Overfishing by high technology, super-efficient fishing vessels have contributed to the decline of fish, but continuing cold water, poor reproduction and the unexplained mortality of young fish have also played a role.

In the meantime, work on the Hibernia Oil Fields is the goal of thousands of unemployed fishing and cannery people. The oil fields, located on the northeast Grand Banks, is an $8.5 billion project, the largest and most expensive development ever undertaken in Canada. The construction of the shore-based facilities at Bull Arm, Trinity Bay, and the concrete-gravity production platform, which will be towed to Hibernia and extended from the seabed to five m above sea level is expected to take a few years to complete. Production for this enormous project is only scheduled to start around 1997.

fertile region.

The St. Lawrence Lowlands

Covering southern Ontario and southeastern Quebec the fertile St Lawrence Lowlands covers less than two percent of Canada but contains 60 percent of the Canadian population. The lowlands are split into two parts by a protrusion of the Canadian Shield. Gently rolling hills and flat plains predominate. This area, like the Plains, was formed from eroded material from the Shield, and it also contains numerous glacial deposits.

Two of the most striking landforms within this area are the Niagara Falls

The Canadian Rockies with its timeless, spellbinding beauty.

Visual harmony in Peyto's turquoise-colored lake.

and the seven Monteregian Hills which start east of Montreal and continue to the Appalachians. The falls were formed around 10,000 years ago when the erosive action of the ice sheets exposed the Niagara escarpment and forced Lake Erie to drain into Lake Ontario.

The Rockies are so well known that the majority of Canadians probably assume they are the only mountains on the West Coast. However, in reality, the Cordillera is composed of numerous mountains ranges. These ranges are oriented in a north-south direction

by two mountain systems.

The Coast Mountains on the West Coast are separated by the Fraser River from the northern end of the Cascades which run down through the Western United States and eventually give way to the Sierra Nevada. Beautiful winding fjords cut deep into the Coast mountains. North of the Coast Mountains are the St. Elias Mountains in the Yukon. Here, the highest mountain in Canada, Mount Logan, stands at 5,951 m. Many of the St. Elias Mountains are covered by permanent icecaps.

Interior Plateau

The interior plateau, made up of gently rolling uplands, is surrounded by mountains on three sides. Its rugged plateaus are cut by deep spectacular canyons such as that of the Fraser River. Glaciers and rivers have made some of these areas rich in silt and clay deposits.

The eastern system is split in two by the Rocky Mountain trench. The trench, the longest valley in North America, extends from the Yukon to Montana, a distance of 1,500 km.

The Columbia Mountains, west of the trench, are almost as high as the Rockies to the east and make for rugged climbing. The Columbia mountains consist of the Cariboo, Selkirk, Purcell and the Monashee Mountains. These mountain chains run parallel to each other and are separated by narrow and precipitous valleys. Their sharp peaks

separated by parallel valleys. The Cordillera at its widest, near the U.S. border, is about 1,000 km.

Most of British Columbia, the Yukon, which is a small part of both the Northwest Territories and Alberta fall within the Western Cordillera. This extensive region is composed of three major parts, an interior plateau flanked

Rockies

The rugged and jagged Rockies.

The Rocky Mountains run from New Mexico to just south of the Yukon border in British Columbia. The mountains reach their highest altitude in Colorado; however, the 1,200 km stretch of the Canadian Rockies is the most scenic, with spacious valleys and rugged exposed rock faces.

About 50 million years ago, the western part of Alberta was uplifted and folded and faulted to form the Rocky Mountains with peaks averaging 2,130 to 3,747 m. The highest is **Mount Robson**, at 3,954 m, which is located in Mount Robson Provincial Park, 72 km northwest of Jasper. Although the last ice age was about 10,000 years ago, there are still glaciers and icefields on the mountains that remain active.

Walking on icefields can be dangerous since they are not solid ice masses, but deeply split by crevasses which can be as deep as 1.5 km and 90 m wide. Signs at the Columbia Icefields advise against venturing out on your own, but people disregard the notice, including one family whose son died after falling into a crevasse close to the edge of the icefields. On the Alberta side of the Rockies, foothills form a gentle link between mountains and prairie landscape. In British Columbia, the Rockies descend into one of the longest valleys in the world, the **Rocky Mountain Trench** that separates the Rockies from older mountain ranges.

The glaciers created four ranges within the mountains: the **Western Ranges**, the **Main Ranges**, the **Front Ranges** and the **Foothills**. The Canadian Rockies depicted in song, movies, photographs and paintings are the Main Ranges, made up of limestone, sandstone and shale. These contain the oldest rock and form the rise 2,000 - 3,000 m above sea level daunting many travellers.

Niagara Falls. The highlight of the Rockies is Mount Robson which has the highest point.

Rockies

The Rockies have many peaks over 3,000 m. The Rockies are one of the country's two best known and most visited geographic features; the other being the

Arctic Tundra

The tundra encompasses nearly a third of Canada covering most of the Northwest Territories and Northern Quebec.

The Great Lakes

The five Great Lakes comprise the largest body of fresh water in the world. Their total surface area is about 246,000 sq km which is slightly larger than the United Kingdom. Canada shares Lakes Ontario, Huron, Erie and Superior with the United States. Lake Michigan is wholly within U.S. territory.

The lakes drain into the Atlantic by way of the St. Lawrence River and together make up the world's largest inland water transportation system. From the Atlantic it is possible to move some 3,800 km inland.

Lake Agassiz

The formation of the Great Lakes began during the last ice age. Repeated advances and retreats of ice sheets deeply eroded this area. Glacial lakes started forming when the ice sheets began melting 14,000 years ago.

These lakes reached immense proportions as the receding glaciers prevented their drainage. The largest glacial Lake in North America was Lake Agassiz, forming some 11,500 years ago.

Being 1,500 km long and 1,100 km wide, it covered much of Manitoba, northwest Ontario and parts of Saskatchewan, North Dakota and Minnesota. Lake Agassiz drained only 7,700 years ago. This is a comparatively short while in history.

Continental Divide – the geographic point where all waters flow either west to the Pacific Ocean or east to the Atlantic Ocean.
The rocks span from the Precambrian to the Cretaceous time period. At the Burgess Shale fossil beds in **Yoho National Park**, more than 120 marine animal species of preserved fossils dating back 530 million years to the Cambrian period are exhibited.

In each of the four mountain ranges is a national park: Banff, Jasper, Kootenay and Yoho, forming the largest body of mountain parkland in the world. Over four million visitors a year go to Banff, over one million to Jasper. The other two national parks, on the British Columbia side, are less developed for tourism and receive fewer visitors.

Some unusual geological features in the Rockies are the *hoodoos*, pillars of glacial silt topped by precariously balanced rocks, which look like toad-stools. They can be found at Yoho and Banff. Melting glaciers color **Lake Louise** and **Emerald Lake** a bluish-green. The waters feeding these lakes contain silt which reflect the green rays of the spectrum.

Indians who settled in the Rockies about 12,000 years ago stained themselves, their tee-pees and their clothing with the bright brownish-orange mud from the Paint Pots in Kootenay National Park. This bright color comes from the iron tinting these cold springs. Faulting also created the natural mineral springs at the park's Radium Hot Springs, where two outdoor pools average about 35°C.

The mainland Arctic tundra is really part of the Canadian shield so the topography is similar. The Arctic islands rise in elevation from west to east. The western islands are quite flat while the eastern islands such as Baffin Island are mountainous, having an average elevation of between 1,800 m and 2,100 m. Much of the eastern islands are covered by permanent ice caps.

Canada is a country blessed with an abundance of forests. Almost half the country is blanketed by forests, which represent 10 percent of the world's total.

Since the distribution of flora is determined primarily by the climate alone, Canada's vegetative zones closely mirrors its climatic ones. The flora of Canada contains many hardy, thriving species – after all, arctic and subarctic conditions prevail over half of the country.

It is amazing that anything can even grow in the Arctic, but during the brief summer the arctic springs to life. Some 900 species of small flowering plants add color to the otherwise desolate tundra. The landscape is dominated mainly by mosses, sedges, grasses and lichens.

Summers are too cold and brief for even the hardiest of tree species to survive. Shrubs such as dwarf birch and scrub willow dot the tundra.

Stretching across the subarctic, the boreal forest is the largest vegetative zone in Canada. Here, a handful of sturdy coniferous trees dominate:

The branch horned wapiti or elk is a common sight in Southern Canada.

Flora & Fauna

Black and White Spruce, Jack pine and the larches. These species are well suited to the inhospitable northern climate and its poor soil conditions. Except for the larches, these trees are all evergreens. Evergreens, unlike deciduous trees, don't shed their foliage all at once. They allow them to photosynthesize food all the year round.

Poor drainage and a cold climate have resulted in extensive peatlands or muskeg, as it is called in Canada, scattered throughout the boreal forest.

The more temperate climates of the Southern boreal forest zone have mixed forests. Both coniferous and deciduous trees grow in this zone.

A favorable climate allows the large deciduous forests of the United States to extend into southwestern Ontario creating Canada's smallest vegetation zone. More than half of all tree species found in Canada are present in this zone. Maples, oaks and beeches are some of the more typical hardwood trees.

Sadly most of these forests have already been cleared in the interest of agriculture and urbanization, leaving only a few behind.

Grasslands

Grasses, the natural vegetation of the semi-arid climate in the southern prairies, have been supplanted by a more valuable species of grass – wheat. Violets, daisies, goldenrod and crocuses brighten the grasslands.

Artic summer flowers refresh the landscape with its bright hues.

Further to the north, aspen parkland marks the transition zone between the grasslands and the boreal forest.

The Western Cordillera with its varying climate and topography is the most diverse of the vegetative zones. On the higher mountains, vegetation changes according to latitude much the same way as it happens to the rest of Canada's vegetation. At the top lies the alpine tundra, then this zone gives way to grassland, coniferous forest and to mixed forest at its base.

Abundant rain on the west coast has produced lush temperate rainforests. The largest and oldest trees, the Douglas fir, can soar over 90 m and span 5 m in diameter. Some of these trees are over 1,000 years old.

Butchart Gardens comes to life in the vivid colors of spring.

Fauna

Canada's large size together with its varying climate, topography, vegetation and vast areas of water provide many different habitats for Canada's rich and diverse fauna.

Buffalo

The largest land animal in North America is the buffalo or the bison. The buffalo were just one of the numerous animal species driven to the brink of extinction through over exploitation.

During the early 19th century, over 40 million of these majestic creatures roamed the plains in huge herds. Within less than a hundred years, settlers and professional buffalo hunters had reduced the herd to below 1,000. Fortunately, conservationist measures and the establishment of national parks have brought the buffalo back from the edge of extinction.

The largest free-roaming buffalo herd can be found in Wood Buffalo National Park, which spans the Alberta-Yukon border.

Muskox

Inhabiting the northern extremities of Canada is the muskox, which looks like a shaggy ox. Its long wool is one of the

A groundhog pops up to greet spring.

Various species of deer as well as the elk can be found at Jasper Park.

finest in the world.

Deer

There are five species of deer in Canada. They are the caribou, moose, white-tailed deer, mule deer and the elk. The mule deer, found mainly in the cordillera and the white tailed deer which inhabit nearly all regions of southern Canada, are the most common.

Besides being found in scattered locations the caribou or reindeer, as they are called in Europe and Asia, can also be found across northern Canada. Some 300,000 - 500,000 caribou graze in the Arctic during the summer.

After the buffalo, the moose is the second largest animal in North America. Moose are common throughout the boreal forest.

Bears

There are three different species of bear in Canada. The supple black bear is found in most of the forested areas across the country.

The most ferocious, the dish-shaped face grizzly bear, lives in the Western Cordillera and the western Arctic. The polar is the largest of the bears.

Their fur ranges from white to yellow and their dietary staple are seals. Polar bears live on pack ice and along the coast of Hudson Bay and the Arctic

The Fur Trade

The settlement and gradual discovery of large parts of Canada was prompted by the popularity of the beaver hat. It wasn't a hat made out of fur like the coonskin hat, but a stylish felt hat made from the soft inner fur of the beaver. These wide-brimmed high-topped hats became a status symbol in Europe during the latter half of the 16th century.

The first Europeans to dip their toes into this lucrative market were the fishermen working off the Maritime coast in the 16th century. These seafarers realized they could earn some extra income on the side by trading European goods for the Indians' furs.

French merchants formed fur trading companies in the second half of the 16th century to satisfy the demand for beaver pelts. The French government got into the act later when it decided to hand out fur trading monopolies to companies which promised to bring over settlers and missionaries. This policy was a dismal failure. The successive fur trading companies were much more interested in their bottom line and Quebec remained, twenty years after its settlement, little more than a fur trading post. By 1627, Quebec had only 65 inhabitants.

The French government took matters into its own hands and shipped over thousands of settlers who were to become the foundation of an agricultural community. Unfortunately for the Crown, many of these settlers disappeared into the woods to engage in the more lucrative fur trade.

In the early stages of the fur trade, the Indians would bring down their furs to trading posts along the St. Lawrence River. In exchange for the furs the Indians could obtain a whole slew of European goods, including knives, mirrors, axes, kettles, needles, cloth, blankets, beads, liquor and firearms.

As each successive area became depleted of fur bearing animals, the French started going deeper and deeper into the bush.

Building fur trading posts, besides helping to establish France's territorial claims, helped cement bonds between the French and the Indians. The Indians became invaluable allies of the French in their wars against the English.

The fur trade was the main reason for the expansion of New France. By the late 17th century, fur traders had claimed all the land in the Mississippi basin down to Louisiana in the name of their King. When the Hudson Bay Company started competing in the North, the French rushed to cut off the supply of furs going to them and expanded France's frontiers to the Saskatchewan River.

After the conquest of New France, British merchants took over the fur trade in Montreal. Like the French before them, the British opened up the colony further, reaching both the Arctic and Pacific Oceans.

The fur trade, which played such a large role in the development of Canada, became less important during the 19th century as the population grew and the economy diversified.

Ocean. Polar bears can endure the most extreme of cold weather as they have a shaggy, thick coat of fur to protect them.

Grey Wolves

Once found all across Canada, the grey wolf has been pushed back into the boreal forest and the Arctic where they normally live in packs of between 3 - 20 wolves. Coordinated hunting allows them to bring down large game animals.

Foxes

The red fox has the greatest range of any Canadian carnivore and inhabits just about every part of Canada. The arctic fox, as the name implies, inhabits the Arctic regions.

The Beaver

The national emblem of Canada is the beaver, a fitting choice because beaver fur subsidized the first permanent settlement at Quebec and became the backbone of the economy. Meanwhile, fur traders expanded the colony's boundaries in search of richer sources of beaver pelts.

The beaver has two coats of fur. The outer coat consists of long coarse guard hairs while the inner coat has dense, soft fur. By the end of the 16th century, this inner fur was in great demand by European hatters.

Beaver hats were extremely fashionable. The fur was ideal for making durable, pliant, and waterproof hat felt. Heavy demand and high prices caused the fur trade in New France to grow in importance.

Beaver Fur Trade

Fur traders traded with the Indians for two kinds of beaver pelts: coat beaver and parchment beaver. Coat beaver were basically secondhand coats. Beaver pelts were scraped and rubbed with animal marrow, then worn by the Indians. After several months of wear, the long guard hairs would fall out. Hatters could then process the fur.

Parchment beaver was less valuable. After a beaver was skinned, the pelt was left to dry in the sun and then shipped to Russia. Until the late 1700s, the Russians were the only ones who knew how to remove the guard hairs.

The era of beaver hats came to an end with the popularity of the silk hat in the 1830s. However, this didn't stop beaver trapping because their fur was still popular to wear.

Beavers are found in most forested areas of Canada. North America's largest rodents normally weigh 15-35 kg. While beavers are clumsy on land they can be graceful in water, staying underwater for up to fifteen minutes. Their webbed hind feet and flat black tail are used for propulsion whilst swimming.

Beavers have two large incisors on both the bottom and top. With their powerful jaws, beavers can actually cut down trees over one meter in diameter.

The beaver, like man, has a great impact on

A beaver dam at Quebec.

the environment. Beavers build dams across streams which can flood large areas. Made of logs, branches, rocks and mud, dams can be several meters high. The beaver builds dams to create large pools of water. Deep water protects the lodge and makes it easier to obtain food and building materials. Beavers are also safer from predators in the water.

The lodges, which are made of the same materials as the dams, have underwater entrances. The beavers live in an enclosed area of the lodge above water level.

The beaver symbolizes industriousness, diligence, reliability and honesty. What more could a nation ask for in a symbol?

Of course, this also promotes commercialization of the beaver. Besides being used for commercial purposes, the beaver also adorns coats of arms for many cities, military units and other organizations. Many books on Canada are adorned with pictures of the beaver.

A white-tailed deer strikes an enquiring pose.

The biggest Canadian cat is the cougar (also known as the puma, mountain lion and panther). Weighing up to 100 kg, these solitary hunters stalk mainly deer. Cougars are found across Canada in mountainous terrain and in dense forests.

The bobcat and the lynx are the two other Canadian cats. Both look like large domesticated cats. The lynx is found in most parts of Canada while the bobcat roams throughout the south.

Mountain climbers

Mountain goats, Dall's sheep and the Bighorn sheep are found mainly in the Western Cordillera. All three are great climbers, but the mountain goat is the most agile and adept.

Sea life

More than 20 different species of whales live in Canadian waters. The high Arctic is the only region where these mammals are not found. Whaling in Canadian waters was banned in 1972, though the Inuit are allowed to hunt whales for personal needs. Two of the most impressive whales are the Blue and the Sperm whale, which are found off both the Atlantic and Pacific coasts. The Blue whale is the largest creature to ever inhabit the planet. The Sperm whale is renowned for its fierce battles with giant

Birding in Canada – by Morten Strange

Wherever you travel in Canada nature is there all around you and makes its presence known. Most Canadians grow up with a strong admiration and respect for the outdoors and the natural world, and visitors are usually struck by the grand and spectacular character of the Canadian countryside. Canada amazes from the stunning fjords and mountains along the west coast across the vast expanses of prairie and forests in the interior to the picturesque lakes and wild coastlines of the east, not to mention the wilderness of the north and the high arctic where few people ever go. Birds are everywhere in this landscape, different species adapt to different conditions, some are plentiful and tame, others are scarce and shy. Watching out for them can be a lot of fun.

A king eider etches its profile.

A goose sits on its newly built nest.

Vancouver and the Rockies

With the growing importance of the Asia-Pacific region, the city of Vancouver, B.C. has become a major gateway into Canada. Vancouver is also the stepping stone to some wonderful scenery and great birding sites nearby. Common birds in the city area include House Finch, American Robin, Red-winged Blackbird and near flowering bushes, the tiny Rufous Hummingbird. Check out Stanley Park north of the city center for close views of Rufous-sided Towhee and several species of wrens and warblers. There is waterfowl to look at in Beaver Lake and Lost Lagoon, some are introduced exotics, others authentic residents or visitors from the northern breeding grounds. Take a close look and then consult your field guide for identification and status.

More freshwater birds can be found at the large Burnaby Lake, like several merganser species plus American Coot and Pied-billed Grebes which breed at the lake during spring. Depending on where you are in the city try to stop over at maybe Lighthouse Park to the north or Sea and Iona islands for some rural countryside and good birdlife.

For the most massive concentrations of waterfowl however, proceed south and out towards the coast to the Reifel migratory bird sanctuary where huge flocks of ducks, 'geese and swans congregate in winter. Personnel from the Canadian Wildlife Service help them with supplementary feedings. Coastal shorebirds feed on the surrounding mudflats and birds of prey like Osprey, Red-tailed Hawk and even the occasional Bald Eagle can be seen flying overhead. Campbell River Park lies further inland near the American border and offers a pleasant woodland habitat and some good arboreal birds including many owls and raptors.

If you cross the Strait of Georgia to Vancouver Island there are rich opportunities to see coastal and pelagic birds from the ferry such as gulls, shearwaters, loons and cormorants. On the large island even the provincial capital, Victoria has some good birding areas around Beacon Hill Park and nearby Clover Point. A bit further out of town the Goldstream Park is a popular outdoor stopover; thrushes, warblers and other arboreal birds are numerous. If you are there in the spring (March or April) drive up to Nanoose Bay and see the spawning of the herrings near the beach, this phenomenon attracts thousands of sea birds looking for an easy meal.

The piercing glare of the hawk owl.

Penguins on the rocks at Stanley Park.

Inland from Vancouver the Rocky Mountains tower steeply. Places like the national parks of Mount Revelstoke, Glacier, Yoho, Brannf (with Lake Louise) and Kootenay which you pass going east along the Highway 1 are world renowned and for good reasons, you simply have to see this scenery to believe it. The area just around the highway can be a bit touristy and it is crowded during peak season but just take a short walk into the mountains and you are surrounded by nothing but wilderness. The density of birds is not remarkable but you will find some birds here that you will never see at other places in Canada like Golden-crowned and Brewer's Sparrow, MacGillivray's and Townsend Warbler, Varied Thrush, Townsend's Solitaire and Mountain Chickadee.

The Interior and the East

Driving further east on the Trans Canada Highway you enter the interior provinces and a vast landscape of prairies, farms, pine forests and further east, more deciduous forests. The prairie lakes break up the terrain and provide some great birding opportunities, especially in spring and fall when countless ducks, geese, shorebirds, gulls and terns rest and feed here. Two such locations are the famous Delta Marsh National Park and nearby Oak Hammock Marsh north of Winnipeg in Manitoba.

The summers here are hot, the winters are cold but clear and calm. Some birds stay back during the winter season and move around the countryside, often entering close to farm houses and gardens. Watching a Downy Woodpecker, a Bohemian Waxwing or a Pine Crossbeak feeding in the deep, powdery snow on a sunny winter day in the Canadian interior is a special experience, sometimes the birds are so tame you can almost touch them.

Further east in Quebec, New Brunswick, Nova Scotia and Newfoundland the Atlantic coastline offers yet another habitat, equally spectacular, except this area is much less hospitable. The weather is cold, windy and wet, up in Labrador even the pine trees are few and far between.

But the sea offshore is rich and packed with fish so sea birds are plentiful. On the most easterly and exposed rock islands of the Newfoundland coast thousands of Atlantic pelagic birds like Razorbill, Kittiwake, Gannet and several species of petrels and sherwaters congregate each summer to breed close together on the steep cliffs facing the sea or inside burrows on the grassy slopes above. Funk Island in particular is special, this was the major North American breeding location for the penguin-like Great Auk which was flightless, overexploited and finally exterminated in the early 18th Century.

The High Arctic

Most of Canada is totally uninhabited by

humans, you tend to forget that if you spend all your time rushing about in the modern cities of Vancouver or Toronto. Few people go to the north but nobody ever regret it if they do! Some places in the north are opening up to tourism, most notably the town of Churchill, Manitoba on the shore of the Hudson Bay. Since this is an area right at the northern limit of the so-called Spruce Belt scattered tree habitat and tree-less tundra meet here so Churchill is particularly good for birds, mixing arctic and sub-arctic species, it is an easy access location with road and air connection and hotel facilities.

Polar Bear watching has become popular around Churchill in recent years but don't forget the birds. Scores of arctic specialties breed here and are easy to find such as Sabine's Gull, Snow Goose, Semipalmated Sandpiper and many other shorebirds, Greater Scaup, King Eider and Parasitic Skua (or Jaeger as this family is commonly called in America).

Even then there are some birds that do not breed so far south! To find species like Yellow-billed Loon, Brant, Sanderling, Grey Plover (Black-bellied Plover in America), Red Knot, Buff-breasted Sandpiper, Thayer's Gull, Pomarine Skua and others you have to go north. In the North-West Territories there are visitor facilities at Bathurst Inlet and at nearby Cambridge Bay on Victoria Island. To see Ivory Gull at nest, however, you have to go on up further than that to the north coast of Ellesmere Island – the last stop before the North Pole!

More Information

A good book on the birds you come across makes birding so much more enjoyable, and luckily Canadian birdlife is well covered in literature. First of all you need to familiarize yourself with the birds you see and differentiate the various species, for this several so-called field guides covering all of North American birds are available. The concept was pioneered by Roger Tory Peterson and his books from 1934 and 1941 respectively: "*A Field Guide to Eastern Birds*" and "*A Field Guide to Western Birds*" have been revised several times and are still used by many American and Canadian birders. The newer "*Field Guide to the Birds of North America*" by the National Geographic Society revised in 1987 is however preferred by a lot of people today as it covers all species from Ellesmere Island to the Mexican border in one handy volume.

For more in depth information "*The Birds Of Canada*", 1986 by W. E. Godfrey is the major handbook covering all 500 Canadian birds in detail. The "*Wild Birds of Canada*", 1990 by T. Fitzharris is a more popular photographic introduction to Canadian birdlife.

For information on where to go to find the best birding sites, several local regions in Canada are well presented in separate titles. Of them, the three major ones are: "*A Birder's Guide to Vancouver Island*", 1989 by K. Tailor, "*A Birdfinding Guide to the Toronto Region*", 1988 by C.E. Goodwin and "*Birding in Atlantic Canada*", 1992 by R. Burrows.

"*There the Birds Are*", 1990 by J.O. Jones is however especially useful as it covers not only the whole of Canada but also all 50 American states in great detail. This title has also been recommended by Roger Tory Peterson himself and is useful to keen birdwatchers.

squid at depths of 2 km or more. At 20 m in length, these squid are roughly the same length as the Sperm whale.

The black and white Killer whale are sometimes seen entering estuaries and inlets along both coasts.

Past media attention has made the

Harp seal the most famous of the Canadian seals. During the early 1980s, world attention was drawn to the seal hunt where hunters clubbed baby harp seals to death. The killing of these white cuddly seal pups touched an emotional cord throughout the world and celebri-

A cuddly, white baby harp seal in its icy habitat.

ties such as Brigitte Bardot came to Canada to dramatize the seals' plight and bring an end to the hunt. In 1983, Europe banned the importation of certain seal products, forcing many natives out of work.

There are more than 3,000,000 harp seals in the Arctic and the Maritimes, and hunters still kill about 60,000 seals a year. The pine martin, mink, beaver and muskrat are all valued for their furs. These furry animals are found almost everywhere except in the Arctic.

The prairies have over 8 million ponds and potholes. These watering spots are the breeding grounds for more than half of North America's duck, geese, swan and pelican population. One is always greeted by a cacophony of noises.

Bird Sanctuaries

One of the oldest bird sanctuaries in North America was established by the conservationist Jack Miner in 1908. This site, which became a provincial crown reserve in 1917, is located south of Windsor in Southwestern Ontario. Miner lectured extensively throughout North America on his bird sanctuary, which was the model for some 25 bird sanctuaries in the United States.

During the migration seasons in late March and late October to early November, thousands of ducks, geese and swans can be seen feeding in this 120 hectare reserve. They make a colorful sight.

Who is a Canadian? Defining Canadians as a group is a little tricky. Even Canadians find it difficult, which helps explain why Canada has the occasional identity crisis. Factors such as language, ethnicity, high immigration and regionalism have contributed to make Canada, in ex-Prime Minister Joe Clark's words, "a community of communities."

67

■ ■ ■ ■ ■ ■

The sunny smile of Canada.

The largest group in Canada has British origins and they make up 28 percent of the population. The second largest group of Canadians have French origins and they compose 23 percent of the population.

The fastest growing segment of the population are Canadians whose roots are in neither of the colonizing countries. This group encompasses 31 percent of the population. The noticeable trend in this group is that it is less European in origin.

In 1961, 85 percent of all immigrants came from the United States or Europe. In 1992, roughly two-thirds of Canada's immigrants

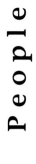

Canadians from different ethnic groups reflect the multicultural society.

came from Africa and Asia while immigrants from the United States and Europe have dropped to less than 20 percent. Canada's restrictive non-white immigration policy was abandoned in 1967, allowing more immigration from the developing world.

Multiculturalism

Until 1971, Canada was defined as a bicultural nation based on its two founding races. This definition left a sizable and growing segment of the population without any official recognition and acceptance whatsoever, making some feel like second class citizens. A policy of multiculturalism was adopted by the Federal government in 1971 to remedy this situation.

Canadian society was built on British laws, institutions and traditions. However, these have been modified for the large French minority. Quebec has French Civil Law, for example, while the rest of the country's laws are based upon British Common Law.

Immigrants and their children have embraced parts of Canadian culture while at the same time retaining some of their old traditions. High levels of immigration have made Canadian society one of the most cosmopolitan in the world. Canada's cultural diversity is mirrored by Toronto's population, of whom a staggering 40 percent were born outside Canada.

In 1992, Canada accepted some 220,000 immigrants, giving Canada one of the highest immigration rates in the world on a per capita basis. About 16 percent of Canadians were born in a different country.

Today, many feel that Canada is accepting too many immigrants, especially during these economically troubled times with the national unemployment rate hovering around 11 percent. Many Canadians fear that newer immigrants with cultures so alien from their own will never be able to integrate fully into Canadian society.

Looking on the bright side, if history is any guide, fears will decrease when the economy picks up and the newer ethnic groups start moving into the mainstream of society.

Fugitives and immigrants

While many immigrants have been drawn to Canada by its economic opportunities, others have come here out of political or social necessity.

The Loyalists had no burning desire to make Canada their home, but loyalty to the Crown and possible American retribution sent large numbers streaming quickly into Canada after the American Revolution.

Religious and political harassment during the 19th century brought, among many, the Mennonites, Doukhobors, Hutterites and Jews to Canada.

Others didn't have a choice, they were forced to come to Canada. The British, trying to reduce the drain on their treasury, sent off boat loads of its destitutes during the 19th Century.

East Indians from Uganda, Vietnamese boat people, Iranians and Lebanese are just some of the refugees that Canada has accepted in the last two decades.

Native People

As European immigration surged during the 19th century, the government shunted the Indians aside. In exchange for giving up their land the Indians were given money, placed on reserves and given a new life.

They came under the control of the Federal government whose paternalistic policies were to protect them from unscrupulous whites and to bring about their assimilation.

Today, there are over half a million legally recognized Indians in Canada and less than $^2/_3$ still live on reservations. Indians have been making great strides in the last three decades and given more control over their lives. The

The French and English: A Perennial Problem

The younger generation of French and English live side by side in perfect harmony.

French Canadians have always fought an uphill struggle to preserve their own identity in an English dominated Canada. In the process, strains have been placed on national unity.

In the early 1960s, English was the language of business within Quebec, yet the English only composed 13 percent of the population. The French had little control of their economy and usually ended up with the lowest paying jobs.

To placate the French, the Official Languages Act was passed in 1969 to promote their language. However, successive Quebec governments had their own ideas. A series of language bills established French as the only official language of government and business. French became the only visible language in Quebec. Business signs and billboards were not allowed in any language except French.

In 1981, Quebec alienated itself from the rest of Canada when it refused to sign the new Canadian constitution. The exclusion of Quebec was ironic because the main impetus for changing the constitution was to satisfy. Although Quebec hadn't signed the constitution, it was still bound by it and made good use of the constitution's "non-withstanding clause." Quebec exercised this clause to override certain parts of the language laws declared unconstitu-

Assembly of First Nations, which represents most Indians, has become a strong voice in Canada.

The two most important issues facing Canadians today deal with land claims and self-government.

Many Indians never surrendered their lands because they were in remote

tional by the Supreme Court. This, of course, did not go down well with the rest of Canada who felt Quebec was suppressing the English language while English Canada was having bilingualism "shoved down their throats."

In the 1980s and 1990s the Canadian government's attempts to bring Quebec back into the Constitutional fold became bogged down in constitutional talks.

The first attempt was the Meech Lake Accord in 1987: Quebec would be recognized as a distinct society and be given additional powers. The accord was vehemently opposed by numerous groups. Some disagreed with granting Quebec any special status, it should be treated just like any other province. The Accord died in 1990, after the provinces failed to ratify it by the set deadline.

The failed Accord infuriated Quebec and Lucien Bouchard, with a handful of disgruntled Liberal and Conservative Members of Parliament (MPs) formed the Bloc Quebecois. Their platform: the formation of an independent Quebec. Another constitutional deal fell through in 1992 after it was rejected in a nation-wide referendum by a majority of Quebecers and Canadians alike.

In 1993, the separatist Bloc Quebecois became the largest opposition party in the Federal Parliament. The Parti Quebecois (PQ), the separatist provincial party, has promised to hold a referendum on independence by the end of 1995 – if they win the Quebec provincial election in 1994.

Most Canadians are sick and tired of the prolonged constitutional haggling. Some would be happy seeing Quebec going its separate way and leaving Canada.

As ominous as recent developments appear, independence is still only a possibility. Quebec has succeeded in protecting and promoting its culture, making independence less necessary.

locations never threatened by white settlement. These lands are concentrated mainly in the North and in parts of British Columbia.

The Métis

Being part European and part Indian, the Métis have never received the same recognition as other native groups. The Métis lost their lands when European settlers expanded across the Prairies during the 19th century. In response to their claims for lost lands, the Alberta government in 1989 entitled the Métis to 500,000 ha in Northern Alberta.

The Inuit

These people are no longer called Eskimos in Canada. The word Eskimo was a derogatory Indian term meaning "eater of raw meat." Today, they are called Inuit, which in their language, Inuktitut, means "people.".

The Inuit have been more successful with their land claims. The territory of Nunavut will become Canada's third Northern territory on April 1, 1999. It will include most of the Arctic islands and the eastern half of the Northwest Territories, making it larger than any other province or territory.

Nunavut will be a self-governing and Inuit-speaking territory since 80 percent of its 22,000 residents are Inuit. The Inuit themselves will receive title to nearly 20 percent of the land, and the valuable mineral rights to a third. At last, the Inuit seem to have a sense of security and they have a place to call their very own home.

A French Canadian sports her own style for the winter.

The French Canadians

England inherited some 65,000 French Canadians with the defeat of New France. French traditions and many of its institutions were allowed to continue, and today Quebec has one of the strongest identity of any Canadian ethnic group. French language is used as the first language in Quebec and some of its shops depict French names. There have always been tensions between the English and the French (see box), but it wasn't until the 1960s that there were widespread calls for separation. The constitutional crises of the 1980s and 1990s have brought renewed calls for an independent Quebec.

The British

After the arrival of the Loyalists, England encouraged and, sometimes, provided economic assistance for its emigrants. By Confederation, the English along with the Scots dominated Canadian society numerically, politically and economically. British influence can be seen everywhere in Canada today.

The Irish

Repeated potato crop failures in Ireland during the late 1840s brought famine to Ireland, and over 90,000 of its impoverished to Canada. The Irish moved to the

A German Canadian has his fill.

ment was established around Kitchener, which was called Berlin up until World War I. During the war, they were harassed and some had their property confiscated. German Canadians were, however, treated more leniently during World War II.

Because of a ban on immigration from Germany, the only Germans who came following the war were from Eastern Europe. After the immigration ban was lifted in the 1950s, hundreds of thousands of Germans fled their war-ravaged country and came to Canada.

larger population centers where they established their own neighborhoods, and most preferred low paying laboring jobs rather than farming. The Irish were the first large European group of immigrants to face discrimination: the Protestant British were not very tolerant of Irish Catholicism.

The Germans

Germans have been settling in Canada since the age of New France. They were welcomed for their Protestant work ethic and their conservatism. At Confederation, the Germans were the largest group of Canadians who were neither French nor English. One large German settle-

Scandinavians

Scandinavians generally formed tight knit farming communities on the Prairies. One community was Gimli, which was settled by Icelanders in 1875. Gimli, which means Paradise, was a bit of a misnomer. Within the first couple of years, Gimli was hit by floods and a smallpox epidemic which nearly caused the settlement to collapse. To this day, Gimli hosts the annual Icelandic festival of Manitoba.

Ukrainians

Between 1891 and 1914, some 170,000 Ukrainians came to Canada. They were drawn by the Canadian Government's offer of low-priced farmland on the Prairies. The government had first been reluctant to have Central and Southern

The Cry of the Natives

Two young Indians, full of hope for a better future.

One of the saddest legacies of the European colonization of Canada was the treatment of the natives.

When the Europeans first arrived in Canada, the Indians were treated fairly well. They were valuable allies in the colonial wars and the backbone of the fur trade. But as the importance of the fur trade declined, agriculture and other pursuits became more important and the once useful Indians were pushed off their lands to make way for settlers.

The Indians lost most of their lands through a series of treaties that placed them on reserves. In exchange for giving up the titles to their lands, they were given financial compensation and other inducements that were sometimes not forthcoming. Unfortunately, the Indians often didn't really understand exactly what they were signing away.

The Plains Indians were a particularly tragic case. Hit hard by the annihilation of buffalo by European and Métis hunters, these Indians soon became destitute. With their main source of food and clothing gone, the Plains Indians were in no position to turn down promises of government assistance in exchange for entering into various treaties. Many took up farming but despite government help, they had trouble growing enough food. Thousands of these Indians died of starvation during the late 19th century. Disease and sickness, fostered by overcrowding and poor sanitary conditions, led to more deaths on the reserves. By the time of Confederation in 1867, the Indian population had been halved. This trend was not reversed until early in the 1900s.

At Confederation, the Canadian government assumed direct responsibility for the In-

European settlers, but there just wasn't enough immigration from the "preferred" countries.

The Chinese

During the gold rush in the Fraser Valley in the 1860s, some 7,000 Chinese came to Canada. In the 1880s, some 15,000 Chinese helped build the lines for the Canadian Pacific Railway (CPR). The CPR exploited the Chinese, paying them lower wages than whites. About 600 were killed in accidents or racial incidents. By 1900, the Chinese and Japanese comprised 11 percent of British Columbia's population. Whites viewed the increasing numbers of Chinese as a threat to their way of life, both

dian population. In effect, they became wards of the state. Government policies were geared to assimilating the Indian population. It was hoped that the natives would eventually give up their Indian status and move into the general population. In compensation, the Indians would be given the rights of full citizens: they would be allowed to vote, own land and buy liquor. The Native People only received the right to vote in Federal elections in 1960.

The Federal government also tried to assimilate the Indians by destroying their culture. Missionary boarding schools were set up far from the reserves, to minimize exposure to the Indian culture. The students were made to feel ashamed of their ancestry: they were forbidden from speaking their native language. And the government banned, with varying success, traditional Indian ceremonies, such as the Sun Dance and the Potlatch.

More than half of all legally recognized Indians live on reserves today. Most of these are isolated without any economic resources, which has led many Indians to rely on welfare payments from the government. Besides poor living conditions, reservations are characterized by higher rates of alcoholism, violence, crime, poverty, infant mortality and suicide.

The First Nations – as Indians now call themselves – have banded together into organizations to fight for their rights. This politicization is giving them a more powerful voice in dealing with the government.

culturally and economically. Anti-Asian riots inevitably broke out in British Columbia and there was widespread outrage. This led to the imposition of a $500 head tax on Chinese immigrants in 1903. Legislation that was passed in 1923 effectively shut the door to Chinese immigration. Changes in the immigration laws during the 1940s and 1960s brought large numbers of Chinese

to Canada.

Fears over the British handover of Hong Kong to China in 1997 have scared tens of thousands of Chinese into emigrating to Canada since the 1980s. So many have lately settled in Vancouver that it is sometimes jokingly referred to as 'Hongcouver'.

The Italians

The Italians have been coming to Canada since the 1860s, and, until recently, this was primarily due to Italy's poor economy. The largest numbers of Italians came to Canada following World War II. Between 1946 and 1965, almost 400,000 Italians came to Canada, primarily to Montreal and Toronto. Construction would come to a halt if Italians left the country.

A Typical Canadian

Canadians are predominantly European in origin and most speak only English. Even though Canada is officially bilingual, most Canadians are not. Today, only 16 percent of the population is considered bilingual.

Ask Canadians for a description of themselves and they tend to talk about how they differ from Americans. A Canadian might describe himself/herself and the country as more caring than in America, citing universal medicare and better social assistance as two exam-

The streets of Chinatown, distinctly Oriental.

ples. The *Economist* magazine calls a Canadian "An American with health care and no gun."

Generally, Canadians can be characterized as quiet, non-aggressive and polite people. Step onto a Canadian's toe and chances are, the Canadian will say, "Sorry."

Canadians also have the habit of saying "eh," used most often at the end of a question. For example you might hear on your travels in Canada "It's a nice day, eh?"

How United are Canadians?

Canada is such a large and ethnically diverse country that divisions are guaranteed. The centralization of power, industry and population in Quebec and Ontario further exacerbates matters.

There are also divisions between provinces. Provinces find it easier to sell certain products in the United States than in the other provinces, due to provincial trade barriers.

Provincial squabbles erupt over the awarding of large federal contracts. A lot of bad feelings were created in the West when the federal government awarded a contract worth $1.4 billion to Quebec in 1986. The contract to service CF-18 fighter planes was given to Quebec despite the fact that a Western firm had submitted a lower bid.

Although the country is dominated by a primarily Waspish elite there isn't really a visible "upper" and "lower" class

The face of tomorrow's Canada.

in the British sense. People are divided more by their personal wealth or profession instead of class.

Canadian Patriotism

Despite regional tensions, the majority of Canadians are very patriotic. They have a country which is both rich and enormous and plays a role in world affairs. Canadians are proud of their diversity and their tolerance and literally wear their patriotism as a badge of honor. Canadian flags are seen on shirts, caps and backpacks all over the world. Of course, this insures they are not mistaken for Americans – a distinction Canadians are quick to make.

Religion

Despite its diversity, Canada really is a Christian country. While only one quarter of the population attend weekly religious services, more than three quarters of the population profess adherence to one of the Christian faiths.

Canadians generally keep their personal faiths separate from their public life, feeling that this is a personal matter. This is reflected by its absence from the public milieu. Politicians, advertisers and the media take precautions from mentioning anything bordering on the religious.

Plumed and painted Indians preserve their rich traditions in their vibrant ritual dances.

The face of religion in this country is undergoing a slow transformation. Increased immigration from countries outside Europe have led to a rise, though still small, in the number of Canadians with a non-Christian faith. Islam, Hinduism, Buddhism and Sikhism have all been growing steadily in Canadian society.

Missionaries bring Christianity to the Natives

The missionaries came on the heels of the French fur traders,

Stanley Park, a preserve of fantastically carved Indian totem poles.

ready to devote their lives to life in a harsh virgin land converting the "heathen" Indians to Christians. Of course the Indians had their own religions which made up an important part of their culture, but the missionaries could only express horror at their-un-

Christian-ways.

Although Indian religions varied, they did have some common themes. The rocks, the clouds, the beaver and everything else in nature were living and had a soul. The world was control-led by powerful spirits for whom rever-

dure their presence for fear of being cut out of the fur trade.

Most Indians were hostile to the presence of the missionaries who were basically trying to supplant the Indian culture with Christianity. Despite dogged determination and faith, these missionaries made few true converts.

Roman Catholicism

Nearly half of all Canadians consider themselves Roman Catholic. Quebec, with its large French population, is overwhelmingly Catholic in terms of religion. The Roman Catholic Church has been undergoing an ethnic transformation since the days of New France as large numbers of Catholic – Irish, Italians, Portuguese, Ukrainian, Filipino, as well as Central and South Americans have come to Canada.

United Church

The United Church, with the largest membership of any Protestant Church in Canada is uniquely Canadian in nature. The United Church was formed in 1925 from the union of the Methodist, Congregationalist and most of the Presbyterian Churches.

They united to create a larger and stronger church that could better serve the widely scattered and diverse congregations. People from all over Canada proudly claim to belong to it.

ence had to be shown in order to have a successful hunt or enough rain.

The Jesuits, who first came to New France in 1625, were more zealous than the earlier Recollects. The missionaries picked up the native languages and moved into the bush to live with the Indians. Missionary work concentrated mainly on the Huron who had to en-

Pristine white, steepled churches reflect the
large following of Christians in today's Canada.

Today, the United Church is the most liberal of the mainline churches. It has alienated some of its conservative followers with its pro-choice stance on abortion and the ordination of homosexuals. Its liberal policies have won it many new members.

Anglican Church

The third largest church in Canada grew rapidly after the American revolution caused a large number of Loyalists to migrate to Canada.

The Catholic Church in Quebec

The Roman Catholic Church dominated the lives of the French Canadians until the 1960s. Before then, an outsider might think the church was the real government of Quebec. It ran the French schools, universities and hospitals, looked after the destitutes and kept the birth, death and marriage records. Through a system of parish churches it kept a tight grip on French Canadian society.

All this was soon to change, however, as Quebec became more urbanized. The church did everything in its power to staunch the flow of French Canadians from the rural areas to the cities, where secularizing influences would lead them away from the Church, resulting in a lessening of church power.

As the movement of people to the cities increased, the church began devising new ways to retain its influence in these "hedonistic" environments. Catholic trade unions were formed, not so much as to fight for better working conditions or higher pay, but to keep the individual attached to the church and out of the hands of the secular unions.

The church's power over French Canadians was actually harming them and helping them remain poor. The French schools and universities focused on teaching the classics instead of teaching business or technical skills. This put French Canadians at a distinct disadvantage when it came to competing with English Canadians in the modern world.

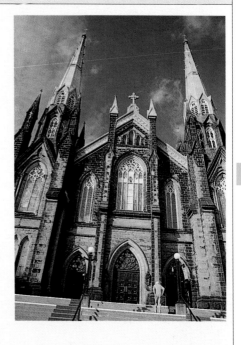

A Catholic church in Quebec City.

Despite demands for reform, the church still wielded considerable power up until the 1960s. The modernizing reforms of the Quiet Revolution stripped the church of most of its powers.

Most of the Loyalists fleeing American prosecution were Anglican. Later British immigration made it the largest of the Protestant Churches. Unlike the Anglican Church in England it never became the established church of Canada. Besides lacking the resources, the Roman Catholic Church and other Protestant Churches were too strong to be brushed aside and they still command a large following today.

The Jews

The first Jews came mainly from the United States. They were relatively affluent Jews who became involved in various businesses in Montreal. Later Jewish arrivals, who started coming to Canada in the latter half of the 19th century, were mainly fleeing turmoil and persecution in Eastern Europe.

Roman Catholics' worship of the Madonna in St Anne's Church.

Large scale Jewish immigration led to increased discrimination. From Montreal to Winnipeg, Jews were banned from the elite clubs, living in certain neighborhoods and frequenting particular beaches and holiday resorts. This racist atmosphere and public pressure forced the government to restrict Jewish immigration following World War I. One of the saddest chapters in Canadian history was the government shutting its door in the face of desperate Jews fleeing Nazi persecution. Racist immigration policies were finally dropped after the war, but it was too late.

The Mennonites

The Mennonites were a Protestant pacifist group which was often persecuted in Europe for their religious beliefs. They were considered heretics because they believed in the separation of State and church. What seemed to cause the most controversy, however, was their belief in only baptising consenting adults, instead of automatically after birth.

The first Mennonites came from the United States after the American revolution. They hadn't been made welcome by the Americans because of their pacifist beliefs. This group was soon followed by Amish Mennonites and they eventually formed their own communities in Southern Ontario.

From the 1870s until World War I, thousands of Mennonites emigrated from Russia, Prussia and the United States. Many were lured to the Prairies because of government offers of free land, guarantees of educational and cultural autonomy as well as exemption from military service.

World War I showed how fragile these promises were. When war casualties mounted, the Mennonites along with other pacifist groups such as the Hutterites and the Doukhobors, were scorned by other Canadians. Manitoba forced the closing of all private Mennonite schools and, in 1919, the Federal government barred all three groups from entering the country.

Today, there are over 200,000 Mennonites in Canada. There are many sects within the Mennonite community. The Old Order Mennonites eschew most modern conveniences and live pretty much the way they did in the last century. The men can still be seen driving their horse and buggy down rural roads in the Kichener-Waterloo area. The men dress in black from head to foot. The women wear plain large bonnets and long skirts. Electrical lines and machinery are absent from their farms.

The Sikhs

Sikhs first came to Canada around the turn of the century and settled mainly in British Columbia. White discrimination eventually closed their immigration door in 1908.

In the 1950s, Sikh immigration resumed and temples were soon established in most major cities across Canada. Some cities have more than one temple because of the divisions in their religious, social or political opinions. Through close ties with their homeland in the Punjab and cultural and religious instruction, the Sikhs have managed to retain a larger part of their culture and religion than many other immigrant groups.

Recently their religious traditions have stirred debate across the country. The controversy started when a Royal Canadian Legion Hall in British Colum-

A Canadian Hindu devotee in traditional Indian dress.

bia refused to permit the entry of Sikh war veterans because they were wearing turbans. Legion Halls forbid the wearing of hats out of respect for the Queen and the war dead. Sikh organizations along with groups of Canadians protested that the turban was part of their religious attire and was not a hat. This is not so much a dispute about religion, but about how much Canadian society has to change for its immigrants.

Hindus

Hindu immigration picked up speed after the relaxation in 1967 of the immigration laws. The majority of Hindus live in Ontario where they make up just over one percent of the population. Hindus come from all over the world, not just India, and in cities with a large enough Hindu population, such as Toronto, there are different temples for the African Indians, West Indians and the Indians who migrated directly from India.

Islam

Canadian Muslims are quite diverse, coming from over 60 different countries, speak different languages and have different cultures. The first wave, who came to Canada after World War II, were mainly very highly educated professionals. Lately many Muslim immigrants to Canada have been

Beadwork complements the traditional garb of an Indian woman.

refugees, fleeing political turmoil in Iran, Afghanistan and Lebanon.

Buddhists

Since Buddhism was first brought to Canada by the Japanese in the late 1800s, tens of thousands more Buddhists have made their way from Southeast and South Asia. The plethora of different societies that have formed reflect their various philosophies, ethnic backgrounds and rich culture.

C

anadians are sociable people who enjoy celebrations, so it's not surprising that there are more festivals in Canada than days in the year. Festivals celebrate, commemorate or re-enact events or seasons and have done so since early days.

Indid Rites

Indian Rites

Long before Europeans came to Canada, the First Nations people had their own celebrations, some of which continue to this day. The West Coast Indian tradition, the *potlatch*, was a feast over several days in which hundreds of guests were fed and showered with gifts. It was held for numerous reasons, including the raising of a new totem pole. The more gifts and the more food handed out, the higher the status of the donor chief. Victorian sensibilities in 1884 pressured the Canadian government to ban *potlatches*, con

Festivals &
Celebrations

■ ■ ■ ■ ■

A young Indian attends potlatch.

Magnificent ice sculpture at the Quebec Winter Carnival.

sidering it an immoral squandering of time and money. However, in 1955, the ban was overturned.

The government also banned the Indian Sun Dance (see box) and *pow wows* and both went underground until 1955. Held throughout the West, *pow wows* bring together native people of all tribes for this thanksgiving and celebration ceremony.

At Western Canada's largest indoor *pow wow* held in the Spring by the University of Regina's Saskatchewan Indian Federated College, the ceremony starts with prayers to the creator progressing to the grand entry of participants where dancers in traditional bead-decorated outfits of hides, furs and feathers move in a clockwise pattern typify-ing the movements of the sun.

In Ontario, the Six Nations Native Pageant re-enacts Indian history and culture in the Forest Theatre on their reserve near Brantford over a three-week period in August.

Religious Festivities

Europeans brought some of their religious observations with them, such as the 17th century St. Jean Baptise Festival. In Montreal, this June 24th holiday is celebrated with a huge parade. In the past, separatists hijacked the occasion to air their demands for independence from Canada.

The Quebec Winter Carnival in

Merrymaking during the Klondike Days.

Quebec City began in 1894 as a chance for Roman Catholics to have a last fling before the penitent days of *Lent* started. (See box).

Early Settlers

Many festivals celebrate the city's heritage, such as the Calgary Exhibition and Stampede, and Edmonton's Klondike Days. Edmonton's largest and grandest summer event takes place over 10 days at the end of July.

The 1890's theme is reflected in the period costumes worn by participants in the kick-off parade and in the entertainment. *Cancan* dancers kick up their heels at the Klondike Dance Hall on the grounds of Edmonton Northlands, which becomes a fairground with rides, craft exhibits, and western music concerts. A Klondike Village has old-time stores, a casino, and, of course, a gold mine for gold panning.

Out on the long cattle drives, cowboys use to spin stories. Today, poets, singers and musicians, from age six to 80, use western imagery to tell similar tales in rhyme at the Cowboy Poetry Gathering and Western Art Show in Maple Creek, Saskatchewan.

Participants in the art show include saddlemakers, horsehair braiders, and silversmiths. It's held over a weekend in late September and invites numerous participants from amongst Canadians and even some tourists.

257

Indians at their annual ceremony.

The highpoint of some Plains Indian religious ceremonies was the Sun Dance, which included a ritual of self-torture. The Plains Indians were the buffalo hunters of the prairies who ardently believed the sun was the manifestation of the Great Spirit.

Preparations for this annual ceremony resembled that of a war party. Scouts would search for a tree worthy of being the sacred dance pole.

The leader would address the tree, saying it should be proud to be selected. As men stood by, four young maidens chosen for their virtue, chopped the tree. The men caught the tree before it fell to the ground, then solemnly bore it to the ceremonial site. The tree was treated as a sacred object during the ceremony. When the procession came in sight, mounted warriors raced to be the first to touch the sacred spot where the tree would stand and would proudly claim victory.

Test of Endurance

Poles covered with leaves and branches made up the sacred sun dance circle. They attached ropes to the sacred tree and ceremoniously placed it in the center of the circle. Men and boys as young as 15 would anchor the other end of the rope around their pectoral muscles. The men danced forwards and backwards, thrusting the pole, until their skin was stretched to the breaking point. Finally, with a great effort of will power, they broke free.

This test of endurance was only a small part of the three-day ceremonies which included elaborate feasts of buffalo, particularly the savoury humps and tongues, and conjuring displays by the shamans.

The ceremony brought families and related winter bands together in harmony at the height of summer to give thanks to the *Great Spirit,* although one large sun dance was held for political aims. *Big Bear,* the half Cree, half *Ojibwa* leader of the biggest band of Cree in 1884, convened a sun dance on the reserve of the *Plains Cree Chief Poundmaker.*

More than 2,000 people participated in this dance aimed at selecting a single representative who would speak for and unite all of them together in obtaining a single large reserve on the North Saskatchewan River.

The government, determined that such a large assembly would never again be held, passed an amendment to the Indian Act disallowing any Indian from being on another reserve without official approval. They followed that law in 1895 by banning the endurance rituals of the sun dance, then in 1914 they prohibited all dances in aboriginal dress without official approval.

The Indians ignored the bans and the sun dances went on secretly. When missionaries discovered these underground practices, they pressured the government into enforcing the ban. The RCMP raided communities and confiscated ritual objects. Although the ban was overturned in 1955 when the Religious Freedom Act was introduced, many of the ritual objects had, unfortunately, disappeared.

The carnival parade reflects the fun-loving side of the Canadians.

Maple Syrup Festivals

The end of the long, cold winter and the awakening of nature prompts many festivals. When the days become warmer, temperatures rise above 0°C in daytime, and nights remain below freezing, the sap flow is stimulated and boring holes in sugar maples produces syrup that over 30 Ontario communities celebrate with a Maple Syrup Festival. The best-known is in Elmira which has a pancake flipping contest, tour of maple farms, quilt shows and, naturally, taste-testing of maple syrup snow cones.

Spring is greeted with the Annual Blossom Festival during May in Niagara Falls with a parade among the events and in British Columbia's fruit belt with blossom time sailing regatta in Kelowna. The Annapolis Valley Apple Blossom Festival heralds the arrival of the apple blossoms at the end of May with parades and concerts in Kentville. Ukrainians in Saskatchewan greet spring with a cabaret and cultural displays at Saskatoon's *Vesna* Festival.

The Tulip Festival announces spring in Ottawa with a gaily decorated boat flotilla along the Rideau Canal that passes some of the more than million tulips that have been graciously sent over the years by Queen Juliana of the Netherlands. It marks an annual thank you gift to the state of Ottawa where her daughter was born in safety during World War II.

Brilliant fireworks light up the night on Canada Day.

National Pride

On Canada Day, July 1st, the whole country celebrates the country's birth as a nation with festivities ranging from boat races to airshows. As the capital of Canada, Ottawa hosts the biggest celebrations with concerts, dancing, and other activities on Parliament Hill and elsewhere in the city that start in the morning and finish with fireworks lighting the sky at night.

Country festivals

Many festivals in rural communities pay homage to food. Corn Festivals. Apple Festivals. Beans. Strawberries. Blueberries. Salmon. Luscious Peaches in Penticton, B.C. Shrimp in Matane, Quebec. Brussel sprouts in Rogersville, New Brunswick. Squid in Bide Arm, Newfoundland and oysters in Prince Edward Island. The end of the lobster season is celebrated in Picton, Nova Scotia.

As befits a country with its roots in farming, many rural communities hold agriculture fairs, a combination of farm equipment displays and livestock competitions, sometimes accompanied by contests for best pies and quilts. This heritage is kept alive even in large cities, such as Vancouver's Pacific National Exhibition. Canada's explosion of festivals in the warmer months focuses on everything from art to logging. *Squamish*

Pretty participants of the Festival of the Arts.

Days Logger's Show in Squamish, B.C. has tree climbing, tree felling and chair carving in August. At the Canadian *North Yellowknife Midnight Classic* in June, residents, tourists and celebrities tee off for golf at midnight.

Theatre Festivals

Another feature of Canadian summers are the cultural festivals. Among the most popular theatre events are *The Shaw Festival* in Niagara-on-the-Lake, the *Shakespearean Festival* in Stratford, Ontario, and the *Fringe Theatre Festival*. Alternative theatre is held outside and indoors in Strathcona which is the old section of Edmonton.

A friendly rivalry exists between Montreal's *Film Festival* and Toronto's *Festival of Festivals*. The two cities also compete with jazz festivals attracting international musicians. Music, opera, and dance are spotlighted during Banff's *Festival of the Arts*. The B.C. *Festival of the Arts* adds films and workshops to the mix. The *Winnipeg Folk Festival* offers at least about 200 concerts along with a craft fair.

Multicultural Heritage

Canada's diverse ethnic population has sprouted many festivals. Toronto attracts more than a million people from across Canada and the United States to "jump up" to *calypso* during Caribana, a duplicate of Trinidad's famous *Mardi Gras Carnival*. The highlight is a parade that can take at least four hours to pass. Whites, Blacks, Indians – everyone is dressed in bright, fanciful costumes that can take a year to make.

Over 40 pavilions highlight the dances, music and crafts of groups ranging from Irish to Latin American at Winnipeg's *Folklorama*.

Highland dances and trilling bagpipes awaken the Scottish heritage in many locations. The Antigonish Highland Games in Nova Scotia are the continent's oldest continuously scheduled highland games. Exciting dragon boat races in Vancouver, Regina and Toronto highlight the Asian heritage. Mennonites celebrate with the Manitoba Sunflowers Festival in Altona, Manitoba. The *"Blessing of the Fleet"* takes place at the Acadian Festival in Caraquet, New Brunswick and Kitchener/Waterloo celebrates Oktober-fest.

Winter Festivals

It may be freezing outside, but rather than succumb to "cabin fever," Canadians go out to play. In Whitehorse, the Yukon Sourdough Rendezvous features dogsled and snowshoe races and, the food first eaten in the north by prospec-

tors, sourdough pancake breakfasts.

Winterlude in Ottawa centers around the world's longest skating rink, the 5 km Rideau Canal which is drained in the fall to make a good surface for barrel jumping and races by bartenders with full trays.

Traditional Métis activities – fiddling and jiggling contests – and snow sculptures and an 18th-century dress ball recalls the fur trade era at Winnipeg's *Festival du Voyageur*.

Calendar of Activities

Pacific National Exhibition, Vancouver - 17 days, August

Fringe Theatre Festival, Edmonton - 10 days mid-August

Banff Festival of the Arts, Banff - May to August

Winnipeg Folk Festival, Winnipeg - 2 weeks, July

Folklorama, Winnipeg - 2 weeks, August

Jazz Festival, Toronto - 10 days, June

Caribana, Toronto - 10 days, July

Festival of Festivals, Toronto - 10 days, Sept.

Canadian National Exhibition, Toronto - 20 days, August

Tulip Festival, Ottawa - 1 week, May

Loyalist Days Festivities

Colorfully clad Ukrainian dancers during a Loyalist Day Festival.

The Loyalists, Americans who chose to remain under the British Empire and left the United States at the time of the American Revolution, settled in much of Eastern Canada.

The largest celebrations take place at Saint John's, New Brunswick, called the "Loyalist City" because about 15,000 people arrived there in 1783. Each year, their arrival is re-enacted during the lavish week-long *Loyalist Days* in mid-July. During this celebration, the city is transformed back to 1783 with strolling *Loyalist* soldiers and citizens dressed in colorful period costumes against a background of musical concerts.

The First Nations people also participate by erecting teepees in an aboriginal encampment and presenting native drum performances. His-torical lectures on the era and other events in New Brunswick's past are given, and those who want to get totally in the mood can buy tricorn hats.

Shelburne, Nova Scotia, where *Loyalists* from the Eastern Seaboard first landed, marks its historical ties with a Loyalist Garden Party in July at Ross Thomson House, a combination house and store built around 1784. Guests dressed in appropriate costumes enjoy entertainment and demonstrations.

Prescott, Ontario, an area mainly settled by *Loyalists* from New York State, pays tribute with Canada's largest annual military pageant. The *Loyalist Day* activities take place during the third weekend of July at Fort Wellington, built to guard the St. Lawrence River when the United States declared war on England in 1812. Troops in period uniform, regiments of Canada, the United States, and France, display the military tactics used in the War of 1812 by staging large-scale mock battles. There are also demonstra-tions of the crafts and trades of the time.

Winterlude, Ottawa - 10 days, February

Jazz Festival, Montreal - 11 days, July

World Film Festival, Montreal - 10 days, August

Shrimp Festival, Matane, Que. - 12 days, June

Bide Arm Squid Festival, Bide Arm, Nfld - 2 days, August

Acadian Festival, Caraquet, N.B. - 10 days, August

Pictou Lobster Carnival, Nova Scotia - 2 days, July

Antigonish Highland Games, Nova Scotia - 2 days, July

Tyne Valley Oyster Festival, P.E.I. - 2 days, August

The Yukon Sourdough Rendezvous, Whitehorse - 10 days, February

Canadian North Yellowknife Midnight Classic, N.W.T. - 2 days, June

Arts & Crafts

Canadians are genuinely interested in the arts. Surveys have repeatedly shown that participation in arts events exceeds that of sports. Yet, until this century foreign culture dominated artistic activities.

Amateur theatre groups have always been popular, but in the past they concentrated on classical or contemporary British plays. The elaborate theatres erected before the turn of the century predominantly presented productions by touring companies, usually from the United States or Britain.

The seascape inspires a painter to capture it in watercolors.

The transition from a principally amateur to a principally professional theatre began with the founding of the Stratford Festival in 1953. Now internationally recognized, the festival in Stratford, Ontario, presents Shakespearean productions as well as contemporary drama and musicals on its three stages: the Avon Theatre, the Third Stage, and the main Festival Theatre, a tent-shaped building reminiscent of the festival's first performance

A modern sculpture on Ile St. Helene.

hall. The season runs from early May to mid-November.

Plays by George Bernard Shaw are the specialty at Niagara-on-the-Lake, a short distance from Stratford. Its historic atmosphere adds an additional inducement to the *Shaw Festival*, which also presents contemporary works and musicals at its three stages, the Royal George Theatre, the Festival Theatre and the old Court House Theatre. The season also operates from May to late Fall.

The thirst for bigger theatres in Toronto resulted in two additions in 1993 to an already thriving theatre city. The no-expense spared North York Performing Arts Centre and the lavish Princess of Wales Theatre were built for hugely successful megamusicals such as *Miss Saigon* and *Showboat*.

Most Canadian works, however, are mounted in smaller theatres. There are dramas written by such playwrights as David French, Judith Thompson, First Nations playwright Tomson Highway and Michel Tremblay, a highly successful Quebec playwright whose works are translated for English-speaking audiences.

"*Anne of Green Gables*," ranks among the longest performing productions, playing for 27 summers as part of the Charlottetown Festival in Prince Edward Island. Other well established stages in Canada include the Citadel Theatre in Edmonton and the Vancouver Playhouse Theatre.

There are more than a dozen fringe

Musicians rehearse assiduously at Place des Arts.

festivals, producing hundreds of new and old small plays, throughout Canada, including Cowichan, in Toronto, British Columbia and in Edmonton which has the largest.

In Canada's warm summers, theatres follow their audiences and move outdoors. In Vancouver's Stanley Park, *Theatre Under The Stars* mounts Broadway musicals. Dozens of summer theatre festivals stage mainly light fare in popular resort areas such as Blythe and Peterborough in Ontario.

Music

Place des Arts is home to the Montreal Symphony Orchestra, a classical orchestra trained in the French and Viennese repertoires, and led in the 1960s by the then-unknown Zubin Mehta and now by Charles Dutoit.

Financial problems have plagued many Canadian orchestras, including the Vancouver Symphony Orchestra and Ottawa's National Arts Centre Orchestra, founded by one of the few internationally recognized Canadian-born conductors, Mario Bernardi. The Toronto Symphony Orchestra, which plays in Roy Thomson Hall, replaced its conductor with the young, flamboyant Jukka-Pekka Saraste while the Winnipeg Symphony Orchestra regained audiences with its New Music Festival.

Innovative music included *Pressing Time*, a symphony written by local jazz

Highland music trills from
Scottish bagpipes.

guitarist Greg Lowe.

Composer R. Murray Schafer has written both theatre pieces and lyrical compositions while Harry Somers is known for his composition of what is sometimes classified as Canada's most memorable opera, *Louis Riel* – the Métis hero in the 1800s.

Operatic societies are more traditional in Canada than full-fledged opera companies. In fact, the country's professional Canadian Opera Company has been trying unsuccessfully for years to have an opera house built in Toronto. Yet, Canada has produced singers with the tremendous calibre of Maureen Forester and Jon Vickers.

Choral societies flourish in all sizes in communities throughout Canada.

Most small cities claim to possess at least one choral group, whilst it is the practice in larger cities as in Canada's oldest surviving mixed-voice choir, the Toronto Mendelssohn Choir, to collaborate with a local orchestra.

Toronto, Vancouver, Victoria, Saskatoon and other cities hold jazz concerts, however, it was the Festival International de Jazz de Montreal that *Musician magazine* rated in 1993 as "the most important jazz event on this continent, perhaps in the world." For 11 days in early July, top musicians, showcasing the depth and range of jazz, perform in various musical halls and even outdoors on streets cordoned off from traffic.

Canadian musicians who have performed at Montreal's jazz festival include the highly celebrated Oscar Peterson as well as the up and coming Holly Cole Trio and Chelsea Bridge.

In clubs and on radio and television, you're more likely, however, to hear the best-known popular singers. Recording artistes like Bryan Adams and Joni Mitchell are favorites. Among the newer groups are Blue Rodeo, Mae Moore and Celine Dion, now recording in English as well as French.

The throat singers of the Northwest Territory rate a category of their own. Usually performed by two female Inuit, they produce a wide range of sounds from deep in the throat and thorax.

Canada's English ancestry reveals itself in numerous fiddling competitions, like the *Down East Old Time Fiddling Contest* in Lower Sackville, Nova Scotia, and folk festivals. Newfoundland alone has over 2,000 indigenous folk songs. Toronto's *Mariposa Folk Festival* is one of the best-known folk festivals. Winnipeg hosts a huge festival featuring such Canadian singers as Gordon Lightfoot, Buffy Sainte-Marie and Ian Tyson.

Country music star K.D. Lang's anti-beef campaign displeased cattle ranchers in her home province of Alberta, but she's a big draw at the many country music festivals. Over 40,000 people descend each year on Craven, Saskatchewan for the *Big Valley Jamboree*. Country and western bars offering linedancing are popping up everywhere observed by some to be a mix of '70s disco music from *Urban Cowboy*.

A French painter adds the finishing touch.

Dance

An important cultural export for Canada is ballet and modern dance companies. Canada's oldest surviving company is the Royal Winnipeg Ballet which, like Toronto's National Ballet of Canada, runs its own school for aspiring dancers. Les Grands Ballets Canadiens is Montreal's foremost troupe and Vancouver has Ballet B.C. Toronto's major contemporary company is the Toronto Dance Theatre while Calgary has Decidedly Jazz, Canada's only performing jazz dance company.

Art

Similar to theatre, Canadian art did not really come into its own until this century. In Quebec, James Wilson Morrice laid the groundwork for Canadian modernism, but it was the *Group of Seven* who gave Canada a national form of painting. Other artists and critics

Toronto's Tiny Museums

One of the clerks in period costume posing with a horse on the site.

Toronto has the huge traditional museums, but it also houses some little museums appealing to people with special interests.

Stamp collectors enjoy Toronto's First Post Office. Located in a three-story red brick building, the home and office of Toronto's first postmaster, this postal museum opened in 1983, 100 years after the house was built. It continues to be used as a post office and the clerks still dress in period clothing and hand-cancel all letters, franking them with the original "York-Toronto 1833" or "City of Toronto, UC" (Upper Canada – the original name for Ontario).

On reproductions of early 19th-century notepaper, you can write letters – with quill pens, naturally – and then fold them for mailing without envelopes. The clerks seal them with wax and a ribbon. In the gift shop, you can purchase 19th-century writing materials, such as personal seals, post cards, and quill pens.

Health care over the centuries is the focus of the Museum of the History of Medicine. The highlight of the more than 12,000 artifacts is an Egyptian mummy, a teenage Egyptian boy who

died over 3,000 years ago. In 1974, forensic scientists removed him from his glass case and, using the newest diagnostic techniques, performed an autopsy. A tissue examination revealed he had died from a disease still affecting people in that region – *schistosomiasis*.

The collection covers Canadian achievements in medicine, such as the Franks anti-gravity flying suit which was designed to stop World War II pilots from blacking out, as well as historical medical devices, including a pottery of a duck from 1500 BC.

Step back into the past at a number of historic homes, which have been refurnished to the proper period. Campbell House, the colonial mansion of the Chief Justice of Upper Canada; Colborne Lodge, a Regency-style house supposedly haunted by the ghost of the architect's wife who died in an upstairs bedroom; and Casa Loma, a Scottish-style baronial castle filled with the greatest luxuries and inventions of 1911. Todmorden Mills, attractively situated in one of Toronto's ravines, at the site of a 19th-century mill has two restored pre-Confederation homes, a renovated brewery and a railway museum in the Old Don Station.

disparaged their work, dismissing it because it did not conform to what was fashionable in Paris in the early 1900s.

Their truthful pictures of Canada's raw wilderness were considered no more

than posters, scenes of Canadian cities were preferred, not A. Y. Jackson's bold-coloured art-nouveau composition, *The Red Maple*, nor Frank Carmichael's lyrical feeling *Jackfish Village*. Like most of

NITASSINAN ~ NOTRE TERRE

Canadian art portrayed through stark, abstract images.

the group, Arthur Lismer travelled through the Rockies, the Maritimes and Ontario to find his inspiration.

A huge number of the Group's works can be seen in a timber and fieldstone building, originally a private home, in Kleinburg outside of Toronto.

The McMichael Canadian Collection display of some 5,000 works includes work by Franz Johnson, Frederick Varley and the vibrantly colored landscapes of Tom Thomson whose shack is on the grounds of the gallery. Perhaps the most famous picture, one hung in Ottawa's National Gallery of Art, is Thomson's *Jack Pine*. In 1917, he unfortunately drowned on one of his regular trips to his favourite spot, Algonquin Park.

Lawren Harris, a member of the *Group of Seven* whose landscapes became increasingly abstract over the years, was a major influence on Canada's celebrated female artist, Emily Carr.

Her vigorous post-impressionist style depicted the vanishing villages, houses and totem poles of British Columbia Indians.

In Quebec, Alfred Pellan returned from Paris under the influence of Picasso while Jean-Paul Riopelle was one of a group under Paul-Emile Borduas that was responsible in the 1940s for the emergence of modern thinking in art in Canada. Among the best-known practitioners of modern art were Jack Bush and Harold Town.

Tales and mythological characters

Notre-Dame-du-Portage.

Ranking behind in popularity are prints which in Cape Dorset are often stylized stonecut prints depicting traditional lifestyle or figures from the spirit world.

In the south, sculpture began in the 17th century with ornamentation for Roman Catholic chapels. Religious sculptures were supplanted by pieces depicting the "noble savages" while the world wars greatly stimulated sculpture with its demand for war memorials. Michael Snow's cookie-cutter walking woman, made of thick stainless steel, exemplifies the more adventurous sculpture of the 1960s. One sculptor of the Canadian scene is Joe Fafard whose cows graze outside the MacKenzie Art Gallery in Regina.

Northwest Coast Indian art was revived by Bill Reid, known for his magnificent huge *Haida* sculptures including the $1.5 million black bronze canoe *The Spirit of Haida Gwaii*, in Canada's Embassy in Washington, a second casting is in Vancouver's airport.

symbolized the contemporary First Nations artists who were influenced by Norval Morriseau, an Ojibwa from Northern Ontario. Others consider themselves artists first, then Indian, such as Alex Janvier, a *Chipewyan* from Northern Alberta. His abstract explosions of color and representational works tell the political history of his people.

Sculpture

Sculpture in Canada dates back to elegant ivory carvings made by the Inuit in the Northwest Territories. Contemporary Inuit art emerged in the 1950s, with soapstone carvings of animals and hunters being their most distinctive work.

Crafts

Every province and territory has a major craft organization and craft shows are regular events in cities where the range of works runs from pottery to gold and silver jewelry. Newfoundland is one province where people have revived the traditional crafts of birch-broom making, thrummed knitting and tea-dolls. These are made by First Nations people in Labrador.

Nova Scotian art.

Quilting bees – women getting together to make a quilt – were a regular part of social life in the 19th century. Quilt making has also been resuscitated, although today most women make them individually and the quilts are more for decorative purposes than utilitarian bedspreads. The designs are truly unique ranging from simple to intricate patterns.

Museums

Canada's national museums are housed in Ottawa, but you can find museums in nearly every city and many small communities, often displaying household items and other artifacts from its early

days. The Canadian Museum of Caricature rates a mention of its own because humor museums are rare.

This tiny museum in Ottawa displays mainly political cartoons by Len Norris and the Montreal Gazette's Aislin among others, all of whom have their own distinctive style. The wit is sharp and humorous which appeals to Canadians of all ages.

Literary Pursuits

"Many a man in love with a dimple makes the mistake of marrying the whole girl," wrote Stephen Leacock, whose humorist and appealing view of the world made him one of the few authors

Indian totem wood carving is a craft that is passed from generation to generation.

lionized enough by Canadians to turn his home near Orillia, Ontario, into a historic site, the site of the 10-day *Leacock Festival of Humor* with stories, theatre and literary competitions.

Political satire was common in Loyalist communities, but what has survived from the early 1800s is autobiographical writing, such as the stories of hardship written by Susanna Moodie to warn the English middle class against immigrating to Canada.

Some of the most notable fiction in modern-day Canada is in short-story form: Margaret Atwood, Margaret Laurence, and Morley Callaghan were a few able to make the transition to novels. More recent authors are Carol Shields, Douglas Coupland and, for

A vivid array of Indian artifacts can be found in Newfoundland.

Hand loom demonstration.

mysteries, Howard Engel.

Few books have hit the public eye like Mordecai Richler's 1992 *Oh Canada! Oh Quebec!*: requiem for a divided country. His ridicule of Quebec's language law and account of the anti-semitism that tinged the province's history incensed French Canadians.

Canada's diversity is reflected in its novels. There are tales of traditional First Nations experiences by Markoosie, for instance, and stories about immigrating to Canada by Austin Clarke and John Metcalfe.

Gabrielle Roy and Marie-Claire Blais are among the best known French Canadian authors today. The French and English differ distinctly in their attitudes towards culture.

An Indian craft shop nestling in the foothills.

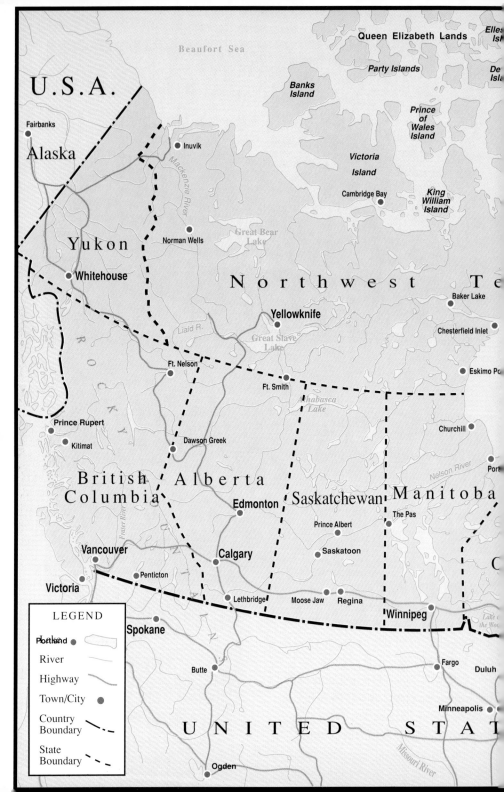

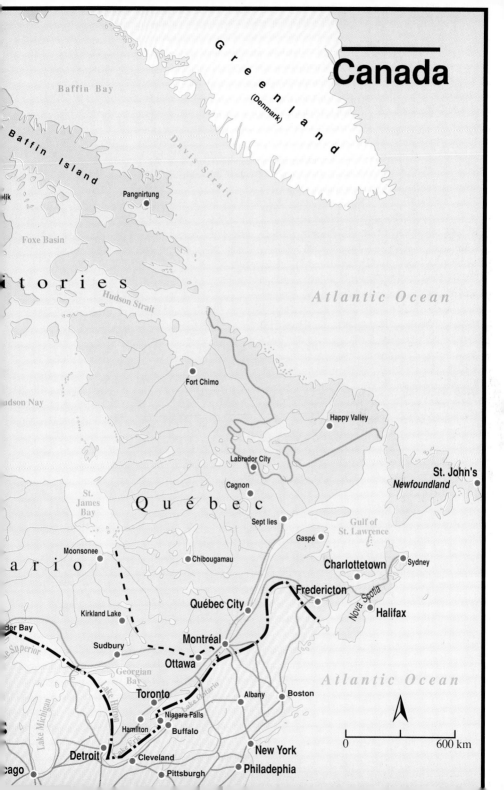

Toronto

The British bought the land, which we know as Toronto today, from the Mississauga Indians. It made an ideal military base because it was situated between two rivers, the Don and the Humber, and its natural harbor on Lake Ontario was sheltered by sandy islands.

The first Governor, John Graves Simcoe, laid out the city in straight lines with the main street, Yonge Street, leading from the harbor up to the gentle rolling fertile hills into the hinterland.

City view across Lake Ontario.

113

Overview of the City

At first glance, Toronto may look like any big American city south of the border, but this stimulating, energetic city is the envy of American city planners, a city the science fiction writer Ray Bradbury called, "the most perfect city in the Western Hemisphere." Canada's economic and cultural center is a city of glittering office towers overlooking heritage

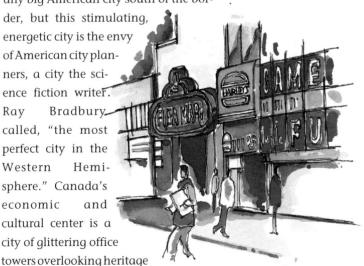

The Chateau Laurier and war memorial, a throwback to the past.

buildings where people from around the world live, work and play on safe and clean streets. An American movie company shooting a film that required duplicating a New York street had to haul in garbage to give it the right look. After a one-hour lunch break, they returned to find all the garbage had been picked up.

Yonge Street remains the central street. Running north and south, it divides the city into east and west sectors. **Downtown** is usually the stretch between Spadina Avenue in the west and Jarvis Street in the East and from Eglington in the south to the water. The actual city of Toronto is comparatively small. Rather, the sprawl to its east, west and south is made up of suburbs large enough to be cities, such as Scarborough and Mississauga. To get around, you can take the subway, bus, or streetcars. Much of downtown can be covered by foot, although it would be exhausting to try and do it all in one day.

From the CN Tower to Lake Ontario

Start your visit with a panoramic view of the city from the **CN Tower**, the thin needle piercing Toronto's skyline. The tallest freestanding structure in the world, built as a radio and television transmission tower, has four observation levels as well as a skyhigh revolving restaurant and nightclub. From the

Toronto's modern skyline.

highest level, 447 m, you might spot Lake Simcoe in the north and the mist from Niagara Falls in the southeast.

That rounded white dome at the base is the **Skydome**, where you can eat in a restaurant or book a hotel room overlooking a *Blue Jays'* game (the base-

ball team that won the World Series in 1992 and 1993) or a concert. This massive stadium boasts the world's first retractable roof.

Going west takes you back to the era of Governor Simcoe. **Fort York** was rebuilt after American troops torched the fort built by Simcoe, an act that prompted the British to retaliate immediately by attacking and burning Washington, including part of the White House, in 1814.

If you want to learn more about the War of 1812 and Toronto's days as a fur trading post, head south, underneath the Gardiner expressway, the overhead highway running east and west. Enter through the stone gates of the vast Exhibition Place, home of the annual exhibition with a midway and technological exhibits and the Marine Museum of Upper Canada. This gray limestone building was originally the barracks built in 1841 as part of Fort York.

Waterfront Toronto

Jutting out into Lake Ontario, across Lakeshore Boulevard are the futuristic domes of **Ontario Place**. It is a marvellous entertainment complex set on man-made islands suspended over the water on 32 m concrete columns. Among the canals and lagoons is an IMAX theatre, creative activities for children, an outdoor theatre and the World War II destroyer, the *Haida*.

To the east lies **Harborfront**. Until about 10 years ago, this was a dismal area of docks and warehouses. Redevelopment has turned this long, narrow strip into a trendy mix of condominiums and restored buildings for cultural events and exhibits as well as expensive specialty shops.

Thrills & spills while whitewater rafting.

Toronto Islands

A unique aspect of Toronto and a welcome relief in the humid summer months are the picturesque four tree-lined islands – Center, Ward's, Algonquin, and Hanlan Point – right at Toronto's downtown doorstep. Take the ferry from the foot of Yonge Street at Harborfront for an 8-minute ride to a world where cars are banned.

Center Island has a turn-of-the-century amusement park and a small farm with piglets, cows, sheep, hens and other animals.

The islands were originally part of the dramatic Scarborough Bluffs until erosion and violent waves split them

The old City Hall of Toronto.

apart. You can rent a bike or walk through the connected islands interspersed with ponds, lagoons, picnic areas and, on two islands, cottages inhabited by permanent residents. Gibraltar Lighthouse on Ward's Island was once on the water's edge. Sandy beaches which are ideal for swimming, encircle each island.

Architectural Highlights

Many of Toronto's skyscrapers belong to banks. The financial area is clustered around King and Bay Street. **Bay Street** is Canada's equivalent to Wall Street.

These financial pinnacles, among the city's most dramatic examples of

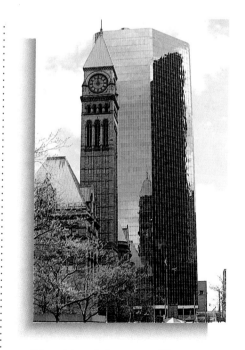

The old and the new in Toronto.

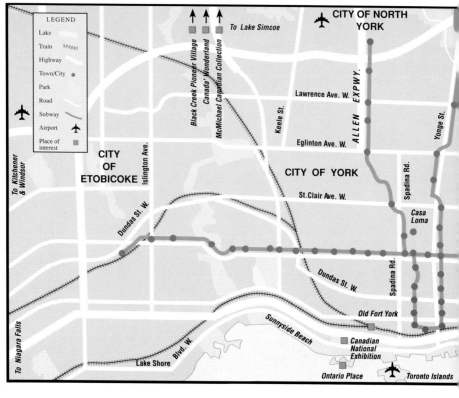

LEGEND
Lake
Train
Highway
Town/City
Park
Road
Subway
Airport
Place of interest

To Lake Simcoe

CITY OF NORTH YORK

Black Creek Pioneer Village
Canada' Wonderland
McMichael Canadian Collection

Lawrence Ave. W.

Keele St.

ALLEN EXPWY.

Eglinton Ave. W.

Yonge St.

CITY OF ETOBICOKE

Islington Ave.

CITY OF YORK

Spadina Rd.

St. Clair Ave. W.

Casa Loma

Dundas St. W.

Dundas St. W.

Spadina Rd.

Old Fort York

To Kitchener & Windsor

To Niagara Falls

Sunnyside Beach

Canadian National Exhibition

Lake Shore Blvd. W.

Ontario Place

Toronto Islands

modern architecture, are faced with black glass, white marble, stainless steel, and even gold. The glistening **Royal Bank Plaza** reflects the coating of 70,874 grams of real gold. Inside are opulent lobbies, often a mixture of bronze, marble and aesthetically pleasing artwork. Underground is a vast network of interconnected passageways with restaurants and shops which provide protection against the winds created by these high buildings.

Intermingled with these skyhigh money temples are many charming turn-of-the-century buildings, including the castle-like **Old City Hall** which is a stark contrast to the modernist crescent-shape towers of the new **City Hall** across

the street. Hailed as a masterpiece when completed in 1965, this much-photographed symbol of Toronto consists of two towers anchored by a two-story rotunda. An international competition selected the Finnish architect, Viljo Revell, to design the building. In front, **Nathan Phillips Square**, is a gathering spot for musicians and other street theatre performers as well as for concerts scheduled in the summer. In the winter, the small pool becomes an artificial skating rink.

Museums

Behind the new City Hall is **Chinatown**

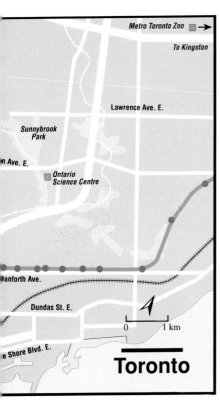

Toronto

Crowded and clustered Chinatown.

where nondescript two-story buildings are eclipsed by colorfully lit restaurants, crowded shops and sidewalks filled with a variety of food stalls. A few steps west from City Hall is the elegant wrought-iron fence circling Osgoode Hall, the mansion currently housing the Law Society of Ontario.

The stately 1892 **Legislation Building** at the northend dominates the sedate office buildings which line the boulevard at University Avenue. The pink-tinted sandstone home of the **Ontario Parliament** and the grassy oval in the middle

of the road make up Queen's Park. The park is a favorite place for civil servants from surrounding government buildings to have a quick picnic lunch.

Museum alley to the northwest includes the elegant mansion housing the **Gardiner Museum of Ceramic Art**, the **McLaughlin Planetarium** and overshadowing the others in its exhibits is the renowned **Royal Ontario Museum** (ROM).

An $80 million 15-year renovation is opening up more space for this imposing stone-faced museum to show some of its vast treasures. Its collection of Chinese art and archaeology is con-

Yonge Street

Eaton Hall's spacious and busy shopping arcade.

Yonge Street, the longest street in the world, is like a kaleidoscope, changing as you move through a landscape of strip clubs to shops catering to Toronto's elite. The city's principal north-south street was laid out by Governor John Simcoe back around 1800. At that time, Yonge Street was the road that led settlers into the wilderness just a short distance from downtown Toronto.

During the mid-1800s, it was the battleground for an armed revolt led by fiery newspaper owner William Lyon Mackenzie against the establishment. The ruling elite tried to stop the scathing denunciations he printed in "*The Colonial Advocate.*" Elected to Ontario's legislature twice and expelled twice, the embittered Mackenzie finally gathered his supporters and marched down Yonge in 1837 while the military was away suppressing a rebellion in Montreal. Citizens unsuccessfully tried to stop them. When troops arrived, the rebellion collapsed and Mackenzie escaped to the United States. He died at his home, Mackenzie House, which is now a historical site on Bond Street, two blocks from Yonge Street.

Yonge Street begins where the ferries take off for the Toronto Islands in the revitalized Harborfront. Via the Gardiner Express, Yonge bypasses Union Station, the elegant monument to classical revival that's been impressing train travellers since 1907. The equally handsome **Royal York Hotel** lies opposite, while on the northwest, inside the exuberant rococo facade of the 1885 **Bank of Montreal** resides the **Hockey Hall of Fame and Museum**.

The temples that banks lavished their money on in the early 1900s can be seen just a few steps north. The downtown shopping core starts at sidered one of the finest outside of China. The 90-year-old institute is unusual in that it spans the fields of art, archaeology and science in its delightful walk-through Bat Cave, a reconstruction of the St. Clair limestone cave in Jamaica, complete with models of bats and other inhabitants emitting squeals and appropriate sounds.

The **Ontario Science Center**, the principal science museum, 7 km away in the suburbs, was designed by Raymond Moriyama, a top Canadian architect. The series of buildings seemingly cascade down the ravine it sits on. This is truly a unique sight and has caused much wonderment amongst visitors. This non-traditional museum offers continual demonstrations and exhibits that ask you to "Please Touch."

the **Bay**, a huge 1895 department store. A skywalk three floors high connects the Bay to **Eaton's Center**, a beautiful glass-covered mall with three levels of boutiques and restaurants designed by the same architect responsible for Ontario Place. Unfortunately for the smaller retailers on Yonge Street, the mall has become a popular tourist attraction. Many left and in their place, a mishmash of bargain stores, fast-food restaurants, and record stores, including the huge **Sam the Record Man** where you can preview CDs in a brass-railed coffee bar.

A booth outside Eaton's Center sells half-price same day tickets to some lavishly refurbished live theatres on Yonge: Pantages, a 1920 vaudeville theatre and, stacked upon one another, two other *vaudeville* houses, the Elgin and Winter Garden Theatres. Near the ritzy **Bloor** and **Yorkville** shopping areas, a red brick wall hides an architectural gem designed by Raymond Moriyama. A pool and waterfall greets you in the foyer of the spacious Metropolitan Toronto Library.

Yonge Street dips and rises over hills as it crosses through some of Toronto's wealthiest areas, parks and a huge variety of stores. North of the 401, the main east-west highway circling the city, is **Gibson House**, which immerses visitors in the rural life of these supporters of William Lyon Mackenzie. Yonge Street continues, for a total of 1,886.3 km, becoming Highway 11, crossing Northern Ontario into the United States and ending in North Dakota.

These surprisingly eloquent touches have caused the Science Center to be a much visited site.

Universities

North of the ROM is the chic shopping street of **Bloor Street** and just behind is **Yorkville**. A hippie hang-out in the 1960s, the Victorian-style stone houses have been transformed into expensive boutiques, antique stores, and outdoor cafes. Today's younger generation of teenagers prefer the much lower key atmosphere around the Ontario College of Art on Queen Street West.

The other older buildings by Queen's Park belong to the **University of Toronto**. Unlike the young modern face of Ryerson University on the east side of Yonge Street, this highly ranked school, where insulin was discovered, presents an ivy-covered facade reflecting the architectural styles in fashion since its creation in 1827 under a charter signed by King George IV.

The Gothic style student center, **Hart House** was contributed by the Massey family which is well known for its celebrated brothers Vincent and Raymond Massey – the former, Canada's first Canadian-born Governor General and the latter, an actor.

A short walk away, an oasis of calm on a bustling Chinatown street, is Toronto's most important art gallery. The **Art Gallery of Ontario** is known for its extensive Canadian art and for having the largest public collection of Henry Moore sculptures.

Its recent $28 million renovation added exhibition space and a modern new face. Time has stood still for **The Grange**, behind the gallery. The brick Georgian facade of this 1817 house belonged to the Boultons, part of the ruling Family Compact.

This small elite group of wealthy

Harvest for Halloween time.

men with strong ties to Great Britain practically ran Upper Canada, as Ontario was then known, until the mid-1800s. For a view of an even richer lifestyle the 98-room baronial castle, **Casa Loma**, should be visited.

Torontonians are proud of their "world class city," as they insist on referring to it. Outside the city, the name "Hogtown," still clings to it, although there is admission that Toronto has changed for the better since the days when an elite of predominantly dour Scottish and English men dominated the mainly British inhabitants. They had imposed their own rigid morality and had caused a sort of 'puritan' outlook. In "Toronto the Good," movie theatres were closed on Sundays, the Lord's Day. Shopping was also sinful on this day and Eaton's, one of Canada's main department stores, covered their windows on Sunday.

Ethnic Diversity

Toronto has metamorphosed into a vibrant, cosmopolitan city, thanks mainly to the relaxation of Canada's immigration laws in 1967. With more than 80 ethnic groups, speaking over 100 different languages, it's understandable why the United Nations called Toronto the world's most ethnically diverse city.

Toronto is home to North America's largest Portuguese community, Canada's largest Chinese community,

Quaint and exclusive boutiques occupy the older buildings along the sidewalk at Yorkville.

over 500,000 Italians, and thousands of Greeks, Filipinos, Vietnamese, South Americans, and West Indians. So many from some islands live in Toronto that they exceed the number back home. The city celebrates its multicultural make-up each June with Caravan – 50 international pavilions spring up all over town with dancing, parades and music from oom-pah-pah to the sitar.

These new Canadians have brought their distinctive cultures to neighborhoods that blend with each other. Part of the charm of Toronto is wandering through these colorful areas, soaking in the atmosphere of myriad cultures in one city.

On St. Clair Avenue West between Dufferin and Lansdowne, Italian fami-lies sip espresso in Little Italy's cafes set among Italian designer clothes stores. A few blocks east, *pasta* meets *rasta* with stores selling goat meat and roti, Trinidad's spicy curried meat sandwich.

Along Bloor West, German and Ukrainian shops sell food from their homeland, not far away from the heart of the Polish community.

On the Danforth, dripping sweet baklava fills Greek pastry shops situated between outdoor cafes spilling onto the sidewalks. The rhythm changes below the Danforth on Gerrard Street East where the gold thread on saris glitters from racks outside shops next to curry restaurants. There are so many Chinese that you can find mini-Chinatowns throughout the city.

Ontario

The heart of Canada, its most populated and wealthiest province, is Ontario a name derived from an *Iroquois* Indian word meaning shining waters. Nearly everywhere you look, there's water – ranging from rivers that are tributaries of the **St. Lawrence** to the **Great Lakes**. About 90 percent of the population live on the narrow strip of land along the scenic waterways bordering Southern Ontario with the United States.

This huge province is split into Northern and Southern Ontario. The vast northern wilderness yields abundant mineral and forest resources, but limited opportunities drive many younger people to Southern Ontario. This prosperous area is diversified in its economy, from manufacturing to agriculture, and population. A high percentage of Canada's immigrants come

125

The annual skating on the frozen canal, a delight for everyone at Ontario's Winterlude Festival.

Visitors in waterproof suits experiencing the falls at Niagara.

to Ontario, adding a rich multicultural fabric to a province in which Loyalists who fled the United States after independence had settled in.

The Niagara Region

Loyalists settled at **Niagara-on-the-lake**, one of North America's best-preserved 19th century cities. The town is a delight to meander through, to see the neoclassical and Georgian homes and original stores along its main street. The development craze, tearing down old buildings to replace with new, bypassed this port and ship building center when the **Welland canal** was constructed. What sparked tourism, creating pros-

perity, was The Shaw Festival, which offers plays by George Bernard Shaw and others.

Near the main Festival theatre on high ground commanding the entrance to the **Niagara River** is **Fort George**, captured by the Americans in the War of 1812, then recaptured by the British. The town's proximity to the United States was the reason it lost its title as Capital city to Toronto in 1796.

The Niagara Parkway connects Niagara-on-the-Lake to **Niagara Falls** and **Fort Erie**, a 55-km drive that Winston Churchill called the most beautiful Sunday afternoon drive in the world. On the 26-km drive to Niagara Falls are several vineyards, some selling ice wine. This is wine harvested during the first

winter frost when the grapes are completely frozen.

Niagara Falls remains one of nature's most impressive sights. The city is packed with activities and numerous opportunities to get close to the falls.

Ontario's Southern Tip

Point Pelee National Park, a highly rated bird watching spot, lies under two migration flyways. While strolling on the boardwalk over the marshes, keep your eye out for monarch butterflies which flit around the jungle-like forest in the park. The scenic Highway 50 along Lake Erie travels west by passing

Fort Malden in Amherstberg, a rallying point for troops before the British attacked Detroit in the War of 1812.

Detroit and Windsor are linked by a high bridge and tunnel under the river. The only conflict today is for tourist dollars: Windsor has the edge now as the Ontario government has awarded it the province's first casino, to be opened in 1994.

An Indian museum and archaeological dig is an unlikely attraction in a city named London. Yet, archaeologists have unearthed a rich supply of artifacts dating back to 9,000 B.C. The most fascinating exhibit at **Ska-nah-doht Indian Village**, however, is the high palisade enclosing a reconstructed

Niagara Falls

Spray and mist shroud the vivid beauty of the Niagara Falls.

After Jerome Bonaparte, Napoleon's brother, supposedly travelled by stagecoach from New Orleans to spend his honeymoon in Niagara Falls, thousands followed. It was popular in the early 1800s to emulate royalty, and the area became known as the "Honeymoon Capital of the World."

The spellbinding sight of these spectacular waterfalls, the dramatic drop of the water, the roar as the waters crash down the falls, continues to attract honeymooners, helped by hotels offering heart-shaped beds and tubs. These honeymoon packages are replete with champagne, sightseeing tours and gifts. The city does its part, welcoming brides and grooms with an official honeymoon certificate, free passes to some attractions and discount restaurant coupons.

Most attractions are on the Canadian side of the falls. Actually, Niagara Falls consists of three falls. The two visible on the American side look flat compared to the **Horseshoe Falls** in Canada where more than 90 percent of the water, at a rate of approximately 60,000 cubic meters per second, rushes down it.

Colored lights sparkling over the falls every night add a romantic touch, especially during the **Festival of Lights** from about the end of November to the end of February, when over 6 km of colored lights transform the entire area into a Christmas wonderland.

At the seven-storied **IMAX Theatre**, the film "*Niagara: Miracles, Myths and Magic,*" transports you on a breathtaking ride over the falls and makes you cheer for the miracle of the

longhouse that housed 48 people. **Fanshawe Pioneer Village** revives life of the later inhabitants of this area while within the tree-shaded city, **Eldon House**, shows how the more affluent had lived in the 19th century.

On the banks of the river **Avon** in the dignified little city of Stratford, Shakespeare's plays have been presented since 1953 to critical acclaim, from early May to mid-November. The main stage of the **Stratford Festival** is the tent-like Festival Theatre, where theatre-goers picnic while watching the swans glide gracefully past on the Avon.

Lee Shore

The **Lee Shore** starts in Sarnia along Lake Huron and curves up to the **Bruce Peninsula**, a 260-km stretch of sandy

ONTARIO

128

A snow sculpture of two frozen snowmen paddling bravely.

seven-year-old boy who survived the plunge in only a life jacket.

For over 100 years, Niagara Falls has entranced visitors, including Abraham Lincoln and General U.S. Grant. Their signatures line the guest book of the **Niagara Falls Museum**. Founded in 1827, the museum houses everything from Egyptian mummies to a daredevil exhibit featuring a wax dummy of 43-year-old Annie Taylor, the first person – and the only woman – to go over the falls in a barrel, in 1901. She was one of the few who survived.

The fascination of the Falls has drawn daredevils to ride inside a rubber ball, strapped inside inner tubes. One of the most famous daredevils was Charles Blondin who set off firecrackers during the mid 1800s on one of his numerous walks on a tightrope across the falls.

You can see the falls at much safer angles; from below on the *Maid of the Mist* boat rides, down tunnels that bring you close to the face of the falls, or up the towers. Skylon Tower, 244 m above the falls, is praised for its delicious meals served in the revolving restaurant.

About 4 km downstream, an elevator at the **Great Gorge Trip** takes you onto a boardwalk by the turbulent waters squeezing through a gorge. The **Spanish Aero Car** swings from cables crossing the gorge above the foaming **Whirlpool Rapids**.

Up the hill, past the flower beds and the great expanse of lawn around the Falls, the atmosphere is more like a carnival, a fun sideshow of souvenir shops, restaurants and museums for nearly any subject you could name.

beaches and pleasant towns. Some claim the 5-km white sandy beach at **Ipperwash** to be the best in the province. Massive sand dunes distinguish **Pinery Provincial Park** from the other parks along the lake.

Grand expanses of maples shade the little resort town of **Bayfield**. On its outskirts, a Dutch farmer has followed the traditions of his family and built a 29-m high operational windmill he uses to saw logs.

Bruce Peninsula

The drive continues through little villages with turn-of-the-century homes and popular trout fishing areas before ascending the **Bruce Peninsula**. **Tobermory** is a pretty little town poised between **Lake Huron** and **Georgian**

Walking tall with ice skates & stilts.

Bay. A popular spot for divers coming to explore the 21 shipwrecks is the clear waters of **Fathom Five National Marine Park**. Glass-bottom boats tour the wrecked sites as well as **Flowerpot Island** with its caves and namesake, two water-eroded pink and gray rock pillars.

The marine park is part of the **Bruce Peninsula National Park**, home to rare orchids that grow in its diverse habitat of cedar swamps, woodlands and rocky barrens. On Lake Huron, the land slides gently into water unlike the more dramatic shores of Georgian Bay where the **Niagara Escarpment**, a rugged wall of limestone winding across the province from Niagara Falls to Tobermory, has been carved by the bay's waters into weird rock formations and overhanging limestone cliffs. It is a sight that has inspired many of Canada's top artists, including Tom Thomson. Some of his work can be seen at the **Tom Thomson Art Gallery** in Owen Sound, which incidentally is his birthplace.

Georgian Bay

The shore turns into sandy beaches as you travel along Georgian Bay to **Collingwood**, known for its **Blue Mountain** pottery and skiing. The mountains on the other side of the road are the highest section of the Niagara Escarpment. In the summer, you can slide by sled or take a water ride down Blue Mountain.

Dog-sledding – a popular past-time.

Young Canadians pitch in eagerly for maple syrup at Morrisburg's farming community.

Midland became famous after Iroquois Indians massacred hundreds of their rivals, converted Huron Indians, and eight Jesuits, including the founder of the mission, Jean de Brébeuf, in 1649. The Jesuits abandoned the mission and Sainte-Marie only reopened among the Hurons in 1968 after archaeologists uncovered the stockade's walls, buildings and thousands of French and Huron artifacts. Guides dressed as farmers, blackrobes, and natives duplicate life inside the reconstructed fortress of weathered buildings and wigwams.

In 1993, the Ursuline nuns in Quebec finally returned their half of Father Brebéuf's skull to the Jesuits and the intact skull was placed in **Martyrs' Shrine**, a charming twin-steepled stone church with a sandalwood roof shaped like a canoe. On its green sloping lawn, where Pope John Paul II preached in 1984, are some exquisite bronze statues depicting the Stations of the Cross.

The Huron Indian Village in Midland offers a glimpse of 16th-century native life in a village of bark-covered frame houses.

Mennonite Country

Persecuted for their religion, Mennonites came to Canada, settling around the predominantly German towns of **Kitchener-Waterloo**. Strict Mennonites continue to dress in 16th-century clothes and travel via horse-drawn buggies. A

Ottawa Lumber Days

Winterlude in present day Ottawa.

Queen Victoria's decision to name **Bytown** the capital of Canada shocked the elite of Toronto and Montreal because Ottawa, as it was renamed, was known as the roughest frontier town in the country. Thugs roamed the dirt streets, committing assault, robbery, arson and murder without much worry of apprehension. The small police force was voluntary while British officers at the garrison considered such crimes a civilian matter.

As the headquarters of the Ottawa Valley lumber industry, producing more lumber than any other region of North America, Ottawa was used to the rowdiness of men coming in from long winters in the bush. But nothing prepared them for the Shiners who took control of the city in the 1830s.

The Shiners were Irish immigrants who had arrived in Ottawa after digging out the Rideau Canal. While lumber barons lived in stone villas, like the one now housing Canada's Governor-General, the Irish Catholics lived in shacks and mosquito-infested damp caves along the canal. When a cholera epidemic occurred, they were the hardest hit. The only jobs these mainly uneducated men could find were menial. The lumber barons favored the experienced French Canadians. In retaliation, the Shiners started attacking Frenchmen.

The number of assaults on the French increased until they found it impossible to even cross the bridge from Hull into Quebec. To protect their honour, they often called upon

Joseph Montferrand, a nearly two-meter tall Montrealer with phenomenal strength that has inspired songs and stories about "Big Joe Mufferaw." On one memorable occasion, a gang of Shiners attacked him on a bridge. Using a man as a flail, Montferrand knocked over several Shiners and threw them off the bridge. The Shiners fled.

The violence escalated until eventually the leading citizens created a paid police force. By the mid-1840s, improved living conditions and law enforcement ended some of the violence, only to rise again when a depression united the French and Irish against the men who controlled the city. It peaked with a riot resulting in injuries and one death that was quelled by armed troops in 1849.

Loggers lived in a shanty, from the French word *chantier*, a shed. The new **Logging Museum** at **Algonquin Park**, north of Ottawa, has a one-of-a-kind exhibit showing the history of logging, including a typical shanty of the 1830s. About 52 men crammed together in its one-room log building, lined with bunks. It was a long, boring life for men trapped in these remote, primitive outposts during the winter. Much of the work was done in winter since it was easier to move logs in the snow.

Logging was dangerous work, often causing serious injuries and death. Children as young as 11 years old worked at least 10 hours a day, six days a week, alongside adults among the dangerous saws in the mills and on the rivers. Frequent log jams required them to hop onto the logs and try to break up the jam. If that didn't work, they planted dynamite.

model of an original Russian mennonite village is part of the Kitchener pioneer settlement, **Doon Heritage Crossroads**, but their spiritual capital is the charming **St. Jacobs**. Among the 18th-century stores featuring local crafts is a Mennonite museum, the **Meeting Place**.

Another haven for artists and craftspeople is **Elora**, attractively situated around the **Grand River**. A massive 1870 stone mill, now converted to an upscale inn and restaurant, sits beside a natural waterfall that accelerates the flow into the narrow gorge just downstream from the mill. A path in the **Elora Gorge Conservation Area** follows the gorge's turbulent ribbon of water as it flows over the limestone walls. Toronto is a busy, active city with enough to see and do to keep you busy for at least a week. If you prefer not to go into the city, the **Trans-Canada**, highway 401 will lead you close to **Black Creek Pioneer Village** and the **Metro Toronto Zoo** – attractions with a much more relaxed atmosphere than in the city.

Elora allures with its nature retreats.

Thousand Islands

Kingston's 19th-century limestone buildings and graceful houses, including **Bellevue House**, the Italian villa of Canada's first Prime Minister, Sir John A. Macdonald have a calming, soothing effect although on a bluff overlooking the city stands the massive **Fort Henry**. Strategically located on the St. Lawrence River, the stone fort is the site of a dramatic 1867 retreat ceremony three nights a week during the summer.

A short distance away is **Gananoque**, the central town for reaching the **Thousand Islands**. Actually, there are around 1,700 islands, some just large enough for a cabin. So many trees still grow on the islands that, from the Skydeck on the bridge crossing to the United States, the land appears a blur of green mass, broken only by roads of water. American millionaires turned it into a retreat for the rich in the 1800s, though George Boldt, owner of New York's Waldorf Astoria hotel was the only one who went to the extent of building a full-size replica of a German castle. Construction on the $2.5 million **Boldt Castle** stopped in 1904 when his

The Museum of Civilization, a building designed
by Douglas Cardinal in contemporary style.

wife died. Boldt returned home, but the partly furnished castle is open for visitors on boat tours.

The Thousand Island Parkway goes east through scenic views of the islands and the St. Lawrence River. Upper Canada Village at **Morrisburg** ranks among one of Canada's top restoration projects. More than 40 restored and recreated buildings typify the pastoral farming community set up by Loyalists who crossed the St. Lawrence after the War of Independence.

Many of their ancestors work at this living museum, demonstrating cheese-making, flour milling, and whisk broom making – products which are sold in the general store. The home based products are good value for money.

The Nation's Capital

Queen Victoria selected **Ottawa** as the capital of Canada because it was far from the American border. This is a small charming city with miles of parks bordering the **Rideau Canal** as well as the two other waterways flowing through downtown.

The **Ottawa River** is the border between Ontario and Quebec. About 40 percent of residents are French-speaking and many people speak two languages, since the government requires most employees to be bilingual. While the government is the dominant employer, enough high-tech companies are based in the suburb of **Kanata** for the area to be known as Canada's Silicon Valley North.

A strong British influence is evident in the pomp of the Changing of the Guard ceremony held each summer morning on the grassy lawn in front of the Parliament Buildings. The Gothic-style stone buildings, resembling its London counterpart, sit on a cliff overlooking the Ottawa River.

The Hull River

Across the river is **Hull**, framed by the ski hills of **Gatineau Park**, a forest of walking trails intersected by lakes for swimming in the summer. On Hull's river banks is the new **Museum of Civilization**, Canada's history museum. This architectural masterpiece by Métis architect, Douglas Cardinal, has a curved sensuous shape which mimics the natural shape of the Canadian landscape.

1980's Architecture

A burst of building in the late 1980s also produced Ottawa's new **National Gallery** designed by Moshe Safdie, the architect for Habitat, the innovative apartment complex built for Montreal's Expo'67. The Gallery's soaring glittering glass towers echo the shape of the

Library of Parliament which is visible in the distance. Inside is a treasure-house of paintings and sculptures by Canadian and foreign artists. Be sure to wind your way to the reconstructed old **Rideau Convent Chapel** with its fan-vaulted ceilings and delicate cast-iron columns and woodcarvings.

A World War II tank guards the entrance to the **War Museum**, adjacent to the National Gallery and next door to the castle-like **Royal Canadian Mint**. Nearby is **Byward Market** where a constant stream of people come to buy from the food stalls and shops or resort to some of its trendy restaurants and clubs.

The largest stone castle, complete with turrets, is the **Museum of Nature**. Buffalo, gems and other exhibits offer a journey into Canada's natural resources.

An unusual attraction for the downtown of a city is the **Experimental Farm**. This is a working farm where families come to play games on the lawns, picnic by the waterside and take a horse-drawn wagon ride around the outdoor gardens, greenhouse and animal barns. There is a general countryside atmosphere of complete abandon and relaxation.

Canada's largest province is also its most unique: a huge French-speaking enclave with an atmosphere distinct from anywhere else in North America. French Canadians rarely move out of their province, staying because of their pride in their culture and their love of the land. Magnificent cities and beautiful scenery, reflect the dominating role played by the Roman Catholic Church until the 1960s. Wherever one looks there are innumerable church steeples nestled primarily around the central nerve system of the province, the mighty St. Lawrence River.

The air of French and English in Montreal's architecture.

137

Montreal

This chic, economic and cultural center of Quebec is Canada's second largest city as well as the second largest French speaking city in the world, after Paris. Montreal grew up between the St. Lawrence River

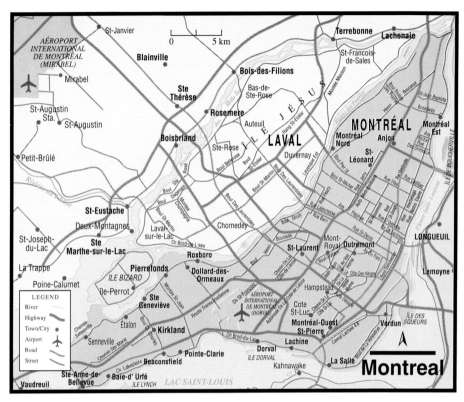

and Mount Royal, the 232 m mountain crowned with a cross with lights visible for miles at night. Below, this island city pulsates with a strong French character, but it is also a city of neighborhoods, frequently made up of different types of ethnic groups.

When people talk about going downtown, they usually mean **Ste. Catherine**, the main shopping street. For more elegant shops, walk north up **McGill College**, a wide broad avenue redesigned in the 1980s, to allow a view of Mount Royal. The avenue ends at the stone gates fronting the campus of the English speaking **McGill University** on **Sherbrooke**. The street, appropriately enough, housed the wealthy Scottish and English who controlled about 70 percent of Canada's wealth in the 1800s.

The remaining 19th-century mansions have been converted to charming European-style hotels, expensive boutiques, art galleries, restaurants and antique stores. This elegant tree-lined street is also where you'll find two newly expanded museums, the **McCord Museum of Canadian History** and the **Montreal Museum of Fine Art**, Canada's oldest art museum.

Montreal lost its economic dominance when demands for separation of Quebec from Canada sparked violence in the 1960s. Companies and English-speaking residents gradually flocked out of the province, mainly moving to

A picture postcard view of Montreal's old terraced houses.

Scintillating Chinatown.

Toronto. The recent recession has also hurt Montreal badly, although the cafes and restaurants in the row of old stone houses lining Bishop, Crescent and de la Montagne and in the predominantly French quarters of St. Denis and Laurier Avenue in Outremont are as lively as ever with lots of visitors.

European-type squares add to Montreal's foreign flavor, as do the massive churches, such as the elaborate Italian Renaissance basilica, **Saint Joseph's Oratory** on **Mont-Royal**. At Dorchester Square, the center of the city in the 1960s, statues of saints stand solemnly above the facade of **Mary Queen of the World Cathedral**, a scaled-down replica of St. Peter's in Rome.

In the past, most English and French

Visitors and shoppers along St. Louis Street.

shopped and lived in separate parts of the city. The museums, clubs and major stores were in the downtown core and the English rarely ventured east past Aylmer Street into the French area of Ste-Catherine. The city has made a concerted effort to develop the French section, installing the **Musée d'art contemporain de Montreal**, Canada's only contemporary art museum near **Place des Arts**, Montreal's top center for the performing arts.

You could drive to the east or take the metro to the tranquil **Botanical Gardens** and **Olympic Park**, the site of many of the **1976 Summer Olympic Games**. (see box)

In 1967, Montreal also basked in the world's eye when it hosted the very successful **Expo'67** on the two small islands of Notre Dame and St. Helen's. The **La Ronde** amusement park is a popular venue with 32 rides and the Old Fort, where soldiers dressed in 18th-century uniforms re-enact the military manoeuvres of the past in the summer. For a more in-depth look at Canada's history, go inside the fort to the **David M. Stewart Museum**. On the smaller **Notre Dame Island**, there is the brand new Casino, Quebec's first legal gambling den, which has proven to be wildly popular, and the new **Dinasaurium**, a dinosaur theme park.

A "must-see" are the wonderfully restored 17th to 19th century buildings of Vieux Montréal, or Old Montreal. Tourists and Montrealers alike come to wander through its narrow cobblestone streets, to admire the architecture, shop in the craft shops, eat in cafes and some of the city's best restaurants.

At Place d'Armes, near where the Iroquois battled the settlers who arrived in 1642, is a statue of the colonists' leader, **Paul de Chomedey de Maisonneuve**, a man determined to christianize the natives. The statue of Maisonneuve faces Notre-Dame Basilica, renowned for its stunning stained glass windows which were imported from Limoges, France.

St. Paul is the old city's most fashionable street and **Place Jacques Cartier** is the main square with a large flower market, handicraft center and a rendezvous for street performers all

Madeleine Island's sea-washed and chiselled rocks.

Christ church's medieval facade is reflected on glass and steel.

gathered around the **Nelson Monument**. This is actually a column topped by a statue of Lord Nelson. Erected in 1809 to honor the English victory at Trafalgar, the statue is a bone of contention to many Quebec separatists.

Within view is the ornate **Montreal City Hall** (Hôtel de Ville). From its balcony over the main door, **Charles de Gaulle** stopped here long enough, while on a visit to Expo'67, to make his famous *"Vive le Quebec libre"* speech.

The other end of the square, the **Old Port**, entertains tourists and locals alike with a replica of a 1693 frigate and a flea market. This is also where you can take cruises on a paddle-wheel boat, an amphibious vehicle, and a jet-boat to shoot the Lachine Rapids.

The Laurentians

The Laurentians.

The Laurentians are the major outdoor recreational area for Montrealers. It is a land of forested mountains, rivers, and French-Canadian hamlets with silver-spire churches and steep-roofed houses located around some of the innumerable lakes. Throughout are charming inns and large luxury resorts, many noted for their gourmet meals.

This year round playground is best known for its winter sports, with more than 20 ski areas and a lively après-ski scene that goes on until the wee hours of the morning. The Vancouver real estate company that turned Whistler, B.C. into a major ski resort is spending $414 million to renovate Mont Tremblant, at 650 m, the highest vertical peak in Eastern Canada. The 55-year-old resort has long been known for its skiing, but has deteriorated over the years. The transformation, to be completed by 1996, includes increasing the number of runs and lifts as well as building an 18 hole golf course.

Cross-country ski trails flow through **Mont Tremblant Park**, a 1,490-sq-km protected wilderness, formerly home to the Algonquin Indians. With 405 lakes, seven rivers, and waterfalls, this beautiful park is also a summer delight to campers, cyclists, hikers, fishing enthusiasts and tourists.

With 20 ski runs on its mountain, Gray Rocks resort has only about half the number at Mont Tremblant, but this attractive and oldest resort in the Laurentians is an active competitor, especially in the summer as it has its own large golf course, tennis school, and activities centered around its lake.

At the eastern end of the harbor, past the old **Bonsecours Market Building** is the tiny "Sailors' Church," *Notre-Dame-de-Bon-Secours Chapel*. Dedicated in 1672, its observatory offers a good view of Old Montreal.

Eastern Townships

Southeast of Montreal and extending to the U.S. border are the Eastern Townships or **Estrie**, the French name given to the area in 1981. A pastoral region of sleepy hamlets, 19th-century villages, farms, forests and mountains, part of the Appalachian chain, the area is a winter skiing playground as well as a center for summer resort activities. There is an English theatre and art galleries at trendy North Hatley. The zoo at Granby should prove a tempting prospect for

The Alonquin Indians formerly occupied Mont Tremblant Park.

Name an outdoor activity and you'll find it in the Laurentians, from dog sledding at the resort complex, **Hotel l'Estérel**, to sailing on the lake at **Saint-Sauveur-des-Monts**, the gateway to the Laurentians. At nearby **Morin Heights**, there's snowboarding, riding a skateboard down its hills which, in the summer, are navigated by mountain bikers.

Set in a little valley, this tiny predominantly English community is home to many artists, where the cuisine at the rustic **La Sapiniére Hotel** attracts gourmets.

Sitting on the slope of a mountain overlooking a lake, Sainte-Adéle was the birthplace of Claude-Henri Grignon whose novel became the popular French television program, *Les belles*

histoires des Pays d'en-Haut. In a reclusive wooded area outside the town, a miniature train runs through **Seraphin Village**, the recreation of his novel's rural setting in the **Upper Laurentians** *(Pays-d'en-Haut)* during the 1880s.

Near *Sainte-Agathe-des-Monts* is Village du Mont-Castor, a charming new turn-of-the-century Québécois village with over 100 privately-owned homes made the old-fashioned way: full-length wood logs set one upon the other.

Spring in the Laurentians brings the tapping of maple trees and the opening of sugar shacks where you can fill up with all sorts of maple syrup treats. Spring is also when the rivers reach their highest level, ideal conditions for canoeing. The loveliest season, however, is fall when any outing sets before you a feast for the eyes, a panorama of bright colored leaves of contrasting colors.

the free-spirited. Mount Orford near Magog has a summer music festival. This is an attractive resort town sitting beside Lake Memphremagog where the local vineyard, Le Cep d'Argent, is open to the public.

Saint-Benoît-du-Lac

Through the trees, you might spy the unmistakable steeple of Saint-Benoît-du-Lac, where Benedictine monks make cheese and apple cider, and welcome visitors to their services accompanied by Gregorian chant.

Now predominantly francophonic, the Eastern Townships were first settled by Loyalists who left the United States after Independence. Their legacy can be seen in the predominantly Loyalist architecture of the charming villages of

Leisurely fishing on the St Lawrence River.

Cowansville and Compton.

wood-sculpting museum.

Handicraft Center

The Gaspé

Those realistic small wooden statues of Quebec farmers and other figures sold in Quebec craft shops usually come from **Saint-Jean-Port-Joli**, a village along the St. Lawrence River. Quebec's greatest concentration of wood sculptors and craftspeople reside in this community enroute to the Gaspé. You can visit studios and galleries and a

Jutting out of the St. Lawrence River, the north shore of the Gaspé becomes increasingly dramatic the further east you travel.

The sea clashes against steep cliffs while snuggled into rocky coves at the mouth of each river are tiny fishing villages steeped in

Olympic Park

A baseball game at the Olympic Park.

The 1976 Summer Olympic Games hosted by Montreal left a legacy of excellent sports facilities, futuristic architecture and debt.

Located among the wide tree-lined streets of Montreal's east end, the Olympic Park contains the Olympic Stadium, the Aquatic Center with six swimming pools, the Maurice Richard Arena, the Velodrome, a cafeteria and across the street, the Olympic Village. This accomodation for 9,000 athletes and escorts has been turned into private apartments.

The landmark building is Olympic Stadium, a giant mollusc-shaped building now attached to a slanted tower and home to Montreal's baseball team, the Expos. It has also become the venue for rock concerts and anything else that can fill its 70,000 seats.

Designed by the French architect Roger Taillibert, the innovative stadium was built almost entirely of precast concrete with 38 self-supporting concrete ribs, eliminating the need for interior columns. The roof is made of a nylon-type fabric supported by 26 cables which descend from the tower. The tower's main function is to hold and stabilise the 65-tonne roof when it is retracted.

The roof has been a major problem. In fact, the roof and tower were not finished until 1989, 13 years after the games ended. And three years later, in 1991, a panel of engineering experts recommended scrapping the roof because more than 17 major tears had been reported. The

stadium management have asked the Quebec government for $57.2 million to replace the retractable roof with a permanent cover.

The stadium's image as an accident waiting to happen has become a running joke in Canada, a very expensive joke. In 1991, a 55-tonne concrete beam collapsed, causing the closure of the stadium for 77 days. In 1994, a brick wall collapsed and experts recommended strengthening 20 similar walls, further increasing the $2.4 billion already spent. The stadium has become a very expensive joke played at the expense of Montreal taxpayers.

For a spectacular view, take the two-minute cable car ride up the 169 m tower, the tallest inclined tower in the world. Spread out below you is the city of Montreal, the Laurentians in the Northwest, the St. Lawrence river and the Montérégiennes hills in the southeast at a distance of 80 km. The tower also has hands-on exhibits about the complex.

A tour train travels throughout the complex, including all the attractions and changes made since the 1976 Games held at the Velodrome in its route. Built for cycling events, the vast building became the **Biodome** in 1992. In this living environmental museum, you wander along a 500 m nature path through four ecosystems – a tropical forest, a boreal forest, marine life of the St. Lawrence and the polar world. In addition to botanical specimens from far flung regions and a natural science interpretation center, there are river otters, a two-toed Sloth and other animals and birds appropriate to the settings. After your visit, hop on the free shuttle service from the Biodome's doors for a ride to the **Botanical Gardens** across the street.

A speedboat traverses the St Lawrence River.

the history of their French, Scottish, Acadian, Irish and Loyalist founders.

Percé, a town tucked between vertical mountains and coastal hunks of rock by the sea is the main destination of visitors to Gaspé, who want to see **Bonaventure Island** and the 100-m Percé Rock with its 20-m natural hole.

At low tide, you can reach the giant rock on foot. Bonaventure Island is a sanctuary for thousands of gannets, puffins, and cormorants. These provide a wonderful source of visual delight in terms of color and multitude.

Sports Haven

Anticosti Island between the Gaspé Peninsula and Quebec's north shore in the mouth of the St. Lawrence is only 222 km long, yet this miniature wilderness encompasses a 4-km long canyon, waterfalls and caves.

There are rivers for salmon fishing and animals for hunting, thanks to a French chocolate factory owner who introduced many animals to the island in the late 1800s, including white-tailed deer. Their population now numbers about 120,000. These places hold a special promise for holiday-makers because of their seclusion.

Tadoussac

The little community of **Tadoussac**

The charming and cobbled facade of Chevalier House.

clings to the top of a cliff at the junction of the Saguenay and the St. Lawrence Rivers where you can take cruises through the stunningly beautiful Saguenay River fjord with its 300-m cliffs lining the river.

Originally a fur trading post, Tadoussac was the site of the first mission to convert the Indians. The Jesuits built the "Indian" chapel, officially known as the Old Chapel. When the original chapel burned, it was rebuilt in 1747 and now houses some interesting old religious objects.

Montmorency Falls

A few kilometers east of Quebec City,

Montmorency Falls impresses with its 83-m waterfall, which is higher than the Niagara. In the winter, its spray freezes to form a giant sugar loaf.

A new cable car ride unfolds the magnificent panorama as you ascend to the top where the **Manoir Montgomery**, a 1780 mansion occupied by Prince Edward, the father of Queen Victoria, now serves as a hotel.

Quebec City

The heart of Quebec is its capital city. This is a romantic mixture of historic buildings, cobblestone streets, a turreted castle, and surrounding it all, thick stone walls. North America's only fortified

The Chateau Frontenac's old world charm lures many a traveler to Quebec.

city has an European feeling intensified by the cosy candle-lit restaurants where food is taken seriously in the true spirit of French gourmets.

Period Buildings

Outside the city walls are the Renaissance-style parliament buildings – the government is the city's major employer. The newer portion of Quebec City sprawls for miles while the old city is divided into an upper and lower portion. On the top of the cliff overlooking the St. Lawrence River, the narrow, winding streets reveal beautifully preserved 18th and 19th century stone houses with copper roofs. Many of these have been converted to restaurants and shops, and massive religious buildings, now predominantly museums inside the austere facades. The classical exterior of **Notre Dame Basilica** hides an ornate interior decorated with gifts from Louis XIV and other dignitaries.

The main attraction, however, is the setting, the atmosphere of another era. The best way to capture this feeling is by walking or taking a *caleche* (horse and buggy) ride.

Chateau Frontenac Hotel

Don't worry about getting lost since you'll rarely be out of sight of the green copper-covered towers and turrets of the

The much visited Champlain Monument.

100-year-old **Chateau Frontenac Hotel**. It rises to one side of the main square at Place des Armes extending to the rear of **Dufferin Terrace**, a wooden boardwalk along the cliff's edge overlooking Lower Town.

Steep staircases lead down to Lower Town or you can ride the funicular to this first French settlement in North America. Jammed into its confined streets are 17th and 18th century mansions and narrow houses of a quaint little port city. On **Petit Champlain** many stores feature local arts and crafts.

Distinctive Homes

The distinctive homes of wealthy merchants are characterized by their steep roofs, dormer windows, and innumerable chimneys that encircle **Place Royale**, named when the bust of Louis XIV was placed here in 1686. This is also where Samuel de Champlain built his fortified residence until war with the British forced the villagers to move to the top of the cliff for protection. The cliff walls and other defenses were considered to be adequate protection by the French.

The British built the star-shaped citadel, the largest fortified group of buildings in North America that are still being occupied by the military. The only action was in 1775, when the British repulsed American troops wanting to annex Quebec. The star-shaped citadel is a tourist attraction today.

New Brunswick is the forgotten province of the Maritimes. The majority of tourists use New Brunswick as a thoroughfare to gain access to the better-known provinces of Prince Edward Island and Nova Scotia, much to the delight of many residents.

The province remains their secret, an unspoiled land of dramatic coastlines, picturesque nooks, majestic rivers, alluring parks and historic cities.

New Brunswick is Canada's only bilingual province, a tribute to the French and English who found sanctuary here. Many of their descendants continue to make their living from its two main resources, the land and the sea. Even the cities have a rural atmosphere; a laid back feeling enabling time for a chat with strangers.

Fredericton's Honor Guards stand tall in their resplendent uniforms.

New Brunswick

151

Saint John

Saint John sprawls over bluffs and valleys and water. This is where the Saint John River empties into Fundy

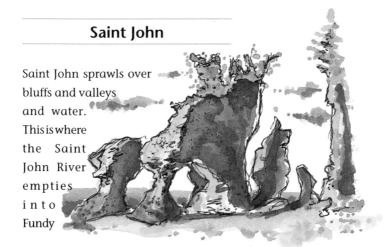

St John's well-stocked market place.

Bay, causing fog to often obscure the city and cool the temperature while other places swelter in the summer heat.

Samuel de Champlain claimed this area for the French King in 1604. The British took over the small fur trading post, but it was the large influx of Loyalists fleeing the United States after its independence that spurred the growth of Saint John, now New Brunswick's largest city with a population of at least about 100,000.

The Loyalists transplanted their own Georgian-style architecture, as seen in the 1810 Loyalist House with its symmetrical design, distinctive small-paned windows, and steep, hip roof.

In the past, Saint John paid little attention to this heritage, and tourists whizzed through only for the time-saving ferry ride across the unique Bay of Fundy to Nova Scotia. Saint John only very recently awoke to the benefits of tourism and in the 1980s inaugurated a renewal program to enhance its weatherbeaten downtown.

Near where the Loyalists landed in 1783, a row of 19th-century warehouses became part of **Market Square**, a complex of shops, boutiques, restaurants and a link to city hall with its observation gallery on the top floor. Another preservation project enhanced its residential 19th-century brownstones.

One tradition kept alive over the years are the summer concerts given since 1908 at the Edwardian bandstand in King Square. Nearby is the Old Loyal-

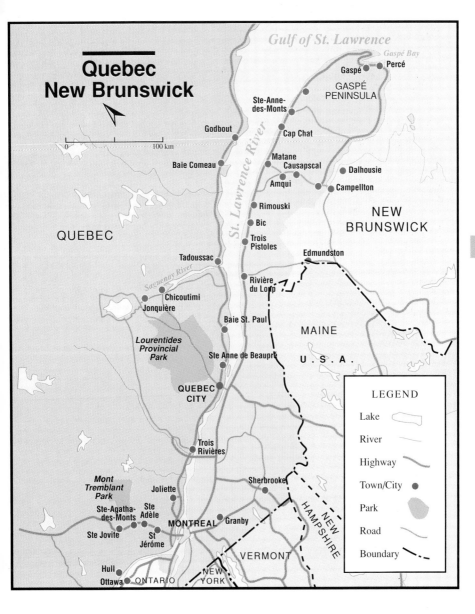

**Quebec
New Brunswick**

Gulf of St. Lawrence

Gaspé Bay

Gaspé • • Percé

GASPÉ
PENINSULA

Ste-Anne-
des-Monts

Godbout • Cap Chat

Baie Comeau

Matane
Causapscal

Amqui

Dalhousie

Campellton

Rimouski

NEW
BRUNSWICK

Bic

Trois
Pistoles

Edmundston

Tadoussac

Rivière
du Loup

Chicoutimi
Jonquière

Baie St. Paul

MAINE

Lourentides
Provincial
Park

Ste Anne de Beaupré

U.S.A.

QUEBEC
CITY

QUEBEC

St. Lawrence River

Saguenay River

LEGEND

Lake

River

Highway

Town/City •

Park

Road

Boundary

Trois
Rivières

Mont
Tremblant
Park

Joliette

Sherbrooke

Ste-Agatha-
des-Monts

Ste
Adèle

MONTREAL Granby

NEW
HAMPSHIRE

Ste Jovite

St
Jérôme

Hull

VERMONT

Ottawa • ONTARIO

NEW
YORK

ist Burial Grounds, established in 1784.

The Old City Market has been the place to buy meat, vegetables and other goods since 1876. Here you can purchase two New Brunswick specialties, lobster and dulse, seaweed made into a snack. Then head to **Moosehead Brew-eries** for a free tour and swig of beer from Canada's oldest independently owned brewery.

The **Carleton Martello Tower** was a circular stone defence fortification used as a fire command post during World War II that Saint John built as a protec-

New Brunswick's irresistible specialty – lobster.

tive measure against attacks from the United States. The neoclassical New Brunswick Museum, Canada's first museum, built in 1840, traces the Anglo-French wars over this territory and exhibits native bead and quilt work.

Bay of Fundy

Nearly overwhelming all the other Saint John attractions are the **Reversing Falls**. The Bay of Fundy has the world's highest tides, falling and rising to a height of 15 m a day in Saint John. At low tide, the tidal waters in the Bay drop to 4.4 m below river water levels. This causes the full force of the 724-km long St. John River to crash through a narrow gorge into the harbour. When the tide rises, the force actually causes the river to reverse its direction and flow upstream. Falls View Park, overlooking the gorge, gives an excellent view of the action. The 12-hour tidal cycle changes daily and a copy of the tide tables is available from the nearby tourist office, which also screens an interpretative film in its rooftop theatre.

A drive along the Fundy coast reveals a shoreline of sandy beaches, snug harbours, salty marshes and jagged cliffs sculpted by the sheer force of the water. The Bay of Fundy is like a giant funnel with one hundred billion tons of seawater advancing and receding every 12 hours. Eastward from Saint John are red cliffs, fishing villages, the historic former ship-

The arresting flowerpot rocks rising from the waters at the Rocks Provincial Park.

building town of St. Martins and Fundy National Park.

Deep valleys, streams and meadows of wildflowers cut through the park's wooded hills. Trout fishing is allowed in this naturally beautiful park, but deer and other wildlife are protected. There are secluded beaches for swimmers outside the park or inside at a heated salt-water pool, where there are also tennis courts and a golf course. The smell of the sea draws you to the park's 17 km stretch of wave-pounded cliffs. The low tide exposes tidal pools alive with exposed barnacles, sea anemones and other marine life while at high tide, the water rises to 10 m.

Outside the park gates, at the quaint fishing village of Alma, the Bay narrows, forcing the water to bunch up and produce tides over 13 m high. Further northeast, the **Rocks Provincial Park** has giant red flowerpot-shaped formations of compressed rock chiselled by glacier erosion and tides. These rocks, as a result, have the most unusual shapes. You can explore the caves and tunnels at the base of these amazing sculptures that often reach several storeys high at low tide when it's possible to walk on the ocean floor. **Moncton**, about 40 minutes away, is known for its tidal bore.

The higher waters in the bay cause the water in the placid **Petitcodiac River** to roll back upstream in one wave. Within an hour, the water level of the river rises to about 7.5 m. Another natu-

Loyalists

A present day Loyalist entertains during Loyalist Days.

Americans flocked to Canada in the late 1700s, the largest mass migration of the time. There were refugees who had fled established homes for the wilderness of Canada and most didn't have any choice.

During the American Revolution of 1775-83, some fought on the British side, others believed prosperity could best be achieved by staying within the British Empire. Many tried to remain neutral, but their fellow citizens insisted on wholehearted support of the Revolution, otherwise they were singled out for painful harassment.

They were tarred and feathered and run out of town. Some were beaten, others jailed, many had their property confiscated. They were branded traitors, although they preferred the term, Loyalists.

Some 100,000 Americans left the Thirteen Colonies. Some returned to England, others went to the Caribbean, and about half went to Canada. They came from every level of society from Maine to Georgia. Some were rich merchants, others were poor farmers from the backwoods of the Carolinas.

Many of the leaders were Anglican churchmen. About 2,000 were Six Nation Iroquois who had fought with the British under their Mohawk chief, Joseph Brant. They settled at Brantford, Ontario, a river valley that Brant had picked out on his way to fight the Americans at Fort Detroit.

About 10,000 people from frontier communities in New England, New York, and Pennsylvania travelled to the Eastern Townships and crossed the St. Lawrence River into Ontario. So many came that the British created the new colony of Upper Canada, now Ontario.

The approximately 35,000 people, mainly from the Eastern Seaboard cities, who sailed into Shelburne, Nova Scotia, included more than 3,000 blacks. About 1,500 were members

---

ral phenomenon in this Acadian-settled city is **Magnetic Hill**. You drive downhill and stop at a signpost at the foot of the hill. If you were to leave gears in neutral and release the brakes, the car seems to roll back uphill. This is an optical illusion produced by the surrounding hillside sloping away from the road.

The French Connection

Cajuns, the early settlers from Louisiana were originally the Acadians that the French colonists had rounded up and that the British had deported from the Maritimes in 1755. **Acadia** was the original name for the territory

of the all-black regiment, the Black Pioneers. Others were runaway slaves, many were freed blacks. Regardless of their status, they faced a harsh life in Nova Scotia, being forced to live in bleak and isolated communities. The discrimination finally persuaded almost 1,200 blacks in 1792 to sail to the new nation of **Sierra Leone**. They founded its capital city, **Freeport**, where they and their descendents have played a leading role in this African nation.

About 15,000 Loyalists relocated to the Saint John River Valley in 1783, overwhelming the approximately 1,500 residents and forcing the British to create the new colony of New Brunswick. A few wealthy Loyalists in Saint John and the capital, Fredericton, could afford a life of leisure, but most faced the backbreaking task of taming a desolate wilderness. The government gave the Loyalists free land and some provisions, but first they had to clear the heavily forested land, pull stumps and build a home before they could farm.

King's Landing in Prince William, New Brunswick and Upper Canada Village in Morrisburg, Ontario have some typical houses lived in by these pioneers.

The growing intolerance towards minorities in the United States many years after the war persuaded many other Americans to immigrate to Canada. To distinguish these "late" Loyalists from those who had arrived during the American Revolution or shortly after it ended, the British proclaimed that the "early" Loyalists and their children could use the designation, United Empire Loyalist.

comprising Nova Scotia and New Brunswick, an area fought over by the English and French that had ended with the battle at **Fort Beausejour**. About 300 Acadians took refuge in the French fort, but undermanned, it fell to the British in 1755. Some Acadians escaped, fleeing north. This historic site lies 8 km east of the prim university town of **Sackville**

that lies by the Nova Scotia border.

After the Peace of Paris in 1763, the Acadians returned to find their rich farmlands taken over by Protestant settlers. They settled elsewhere, many along the northeast coast of New Brunswick around the **Bay of Chaleurs** and the Gulf of St. Lawrence.

Their descendants, intensely proud of their heritage and traditions, have retained their French language (about one third of the province is French-speaking) and recreated the early days with an 18th-century settlement. The Acadian flag, the French red, white and blue tricolor with a star on top, flies over the **Acadian Historical Village**, a preserve of homes, church, tavern, farms and other buildings.

Capital City

In 1692, the capital of Acadia was **Fredericton**. The community prospered in trading fur with the local Micmac Indians. After the British swept through the Saint John river valley, burning French homes and expelling Acadians, English colonists moved in. Located on the banks of the Saint John River, safely inland from any American sea attacks, this gracious small city became the capital of New Brunswick in 1785.

Stately elm trees form canopies over the historic buildings of this government and university city. Dramatic commentary by period-costumed guides awakens the past through free walking

Houses with curved towers are typical of Fredericton.

tours of such historic sites as the Guard House and the Soldiers Barracks, built by the British Army to house 200 soldiers and families in 1827. Scarlet uniforms and the sound of bagpipes liven up the central Officers' Square during the Changing of the Guard ceremonies in the summer.

Lord Beaverbrook, who built a publishing empire based on London's *Daily Express* newspaper, left various legacies to his native province. Among them is the top-ranked **Beaverbrook Art Gallery** with British paintings and a large Cornelius Kreighoff collection. Kreighoff painted scenes of Canadian life in the 1800s.

King's Landing, 37 km west, recalls the Loyalist heritage with the help of some 100 costumed staff who weave, cut wood, plant and perform other typical chores from the 1800s. Many of the historic buildings were relocated to this 121-ha ground to avoid the flooding caused by the Mactaquac hydro project. The daily programs geared for children offer them the opportunity to live at the site for five days, as a child of the 1800s.

The pretty **Saint John River**, often described as the Rhine of North America, flows through gently sloping farmland. As you head north, the tranquil river passes under the longest covered bridge in the world – there are more than 70 in the province – at Hartland, but changes dramatically at **Grand Falls**, plunging down the falls and rushing through a deep, narrow gorge.

The river enters Canada through **Maine** at Edmundston, part of the mythical Republic of **Madawaska**, named for the river that flows into the Saint John River here. Tired of the squabbles about the location of the Canadian-U.S. border, the independent-minded residents declared themselves a Republic. They created their own language, "brayon", and, over city hall, fly their own flag which consists of a bald eagle and six red stars. A buck-toothed porcupine, the Madawaska mascot, carved out of a white pine log by Albert Deaveau, is one of the many sculptures he has installed around Edmundston.

This mainly French-speaking town, settled by Acadians, is the center of the pulp and paper industry. It was the timber cutting rights of the Upper Saint

The well-tended parks of Fredericton provide leisurely walks for everyone.

ers, both cross-country and alpine to the 304-m Sugarloaf Mountain. Whales and seals play around Grand Manan Island, the largest of the three islands in the Bay of Fundy, close to the Maine coast. The variety of birds attracted John J. Audubon, who sketched many of them.

Wealthy Visitors

Some Americans make a pilgrimage to one island that can be reached by land from Maine or by ferry from New Brunswick. **Campobello Island** was the summer home for President Franklin D. Roosevelt and where, after swimming in the chilly Bay of Fundy, he developed the first symptoms of polio. **Roosevelt Cottage** is a 34-room "cottage," part of the family compound, which contains furnishings, toys and other Roosevelt family belongings. Mansions of other wealthy families who spent their summers in New Brunswick ring the delightful resort town of St. Andrew's.

About half the buildings in the original town are over 100 years old. Some Loyalists brought their homes by barge when they fled the United States. This high Anglican haven is so Scottish that bellhops wear kilts at **The Algonquin**. With its tudor-style architecture, wide verandah and flower-sprinkled lawn, Canada's oldest hotel resembles Shakespeare's Globe Theatre. **The Huntsman Marine Laboratory-Aquarium** gives a peek at the crabs, sea urchins and other marine life found in the bay here.

John River Valley that were the source of the disputes about the border. Forests, covering about 85 percent of the province, form a thick wilderness that looks totally impenetrable. This is the province's greatest natural resource, supporting lumbering, hunting, fishing, pulp and paper.

Recreational Activities

The Miramichi River in central New Brunswick is famous for its Atlantic salmon where only fly-fishing is allowed. **Campbellton** on the **Bay of Chaleurs** celebrates its catch with a Salmon Festival in July. In the winter, nearby **Sugarloaf Provincial Park** attracts ski-

Nova Scotia quietly entrances visitors with its human-scale landscape of picturesque fishing villages, inland forests, glacial lakes and gentle mountains. Cut off by the sea from Canada except for a narrow isthmus attaching it to New Brunswick, the province's isolation has helped preserve a slower way of life and many of the varied traditions of its French-Acadian, Loyalist and Scottish settlers.

So many can trace their roots back to the Scottish immigrants who came to New Scotland enabling Scottish traditions to live on in the sound of bagpipes and whirl of kilts at numerous highland games each summer.

The people have a wry, self-depreciating wit and a generous spirit. In the summer, both the Mayors of Halifax and Springhill invite visitors to a complimentary traditional high tea,

The lighthouse at Peggy's Cove.

Nova Scotia

161

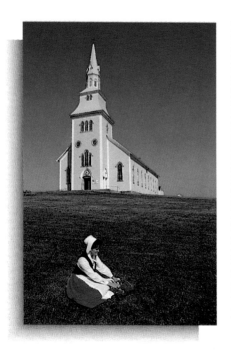

An old countryside church.

usually on weekdays between 3:30 p.m. and 4:30 p.m.

Halifax

Halifax is a small city steeped in history and attractive old buildings owing to its location on the world's second largest natural harbor (after Sydney, Australia). Across the harbor is Dartmouth, its neighboring city which you can reach by inexpensive ferry or toll bridges.

Known as the "Warden of the North" for its historic military defenses, Halifax grew up around the fortress still dominating the central core. The star-shaped Citadel, occupied by British troops until 1906 sits on top of the grass-covered Citadel hill.

The unique coastal defence network also includes the round thick-walled **Prince of Wales Tower**, the remnants of Fort McNab on an island at the outer extremity of Halifax Harbor and **York Redoubt**, the 200-year-old fortification on a high bluff overlooking the entrance to Halifax Harbor. During World War II, it was the command post for the defence of Halifax.

Many of these military defenses were constructed when the Duke of Kent was military governor. A stickler for punctuality, Prince Edward also gave the city its landmark **Town Clock**. The wedding-cake-shaped clock situated on the slope from the Citadel ensured his soldiers were on time. Though a strict disciplinarian on military matters, Prince Edward kept a mistress on his estate at **Hemlock Ravine Park**. Only the round white music rotunda remains. The Prince obviously favored this shape, designing the Byzantine-style **St. George's Round Church**, the only church designed by a member of the Royal Family. Called back to England to do his duty – he fathered Queen Victoria. Prince Edward left Julie de St. Laurent and Halifax.

The clock tower faces the **Grand Parade**, the old militia drill grounds, now a favorite spot for street musicians. At one end is **St. Paul's Anglican Church**, Canada's oldest Protestant church erected in 1750, the year after British Governor **Edward Cornwallis** and 2,500 settlers arrived in Halifax to

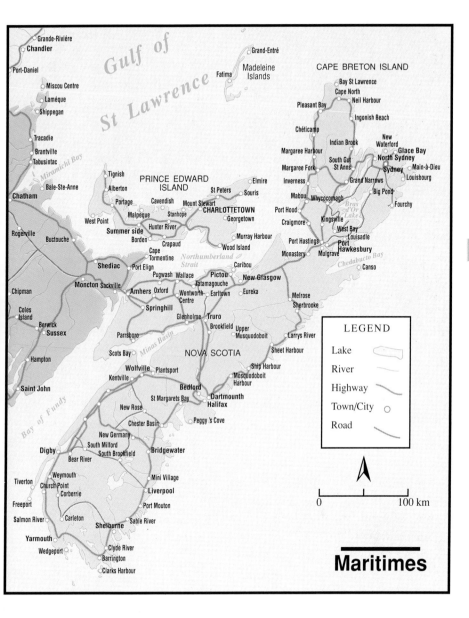

Maritimes

counter the strong French presence in **Cape Breton**.

Highlighting the other end of the square is the Victorian-style **City Hall** where the Mayor and Town Crier welcome visitors to tea.

The provincial government meets at the sandstone **Province House** described by Charles Dickens as "a gem of Georgian architecture." The 1842 opening of Canada's smallest legislature building was, according to the writer, "like looking at Westminster through the wrong end of the telescope."

Harbor at Halifax.

Down by the waterfront are the 1913 steamship *CSS Acadia* and the *HMCS Sackville*, a World War II convoy escort corvette float, outside the interesting **Maritime Museum** of the Atlantic with its graphic depiction of the Halifax Explosion. During World War I, a French munitions ship collided with a Belgian relief ship, causing a blast that devastated large parts of the city and killed about 2,000 people. A few survivors still draw pensions for their injuries and Halifax continues to send a Christmas tree to Boston in gratitude for its relief assistance.

Along the docks where press gangs roamed, looking for men to impress into His Majesty's Navy, and where privateers – licensed pirates of the British crown – stored their stolen cargo is known as **Historic Properties**. The restored 19th-century warehouses have become an attractive seaside setting of shops, outdoor cafes and restaurants.

The gentry of the time stayed clear of this area, preferring to walk around the lovely **Public Gardens**. The continent's oldest and finest formal Victorian gardens was designed by a gardener to Ireland's Duke of Devonshire and, until the 1960s, was cared for by his descendants.

Privacy and quietude at Smuggler's Cove, Nova Scotia.

Nova Scotia has one of the oldest Black populations in Canada, starting with a black man who accompanied Samuel de Champlain in 1605, followed by many Black Loyalists after the War of Independence and slaves who took advantage of the war's chaotic situation to be free. Many lived in Halifax's **Africville** until the 1960s when the city relocated the residents and demolished the poor housing for other projects. The **Black Cultural Center** outside of Dartmouth in **Westphal** preserves their history and heritage.

South Shore Treasures

The scalloped coastline of Nova Scotia curls around rocky coves, fishing villages, long stretches of sand dunes and beaches, and an old lighthouse. The one

An enactment of a New Scotland farmer on his daily route at a heritage park.

in **Peggy's Cove** serves as a post office. Weathered, shingled houses the colors of the rainbow hover around the barren granite boulders of this fishing village immortalized by several photographers and artists.

The Atlantic coast has many large old houses built by those who became wealthy from shipbuilding and privateering. Among the Victorian houses in **Mahone Bay** is the manufacturing and design firm of **Suttles and Seawinds**, well-known throughout Canada for its vibrant Nova Scotian-crafted clothing, quilts and accessories.

The legend of pirate Captain Kidd burying his treasure chest in 1700 on **Oak Island** in Mahone Bay continues to lure fortune seekers. The unearthing

of a complex system of tunnels and shafts, which scientists estimate men using 16th-century tools took 100,000 hours to construct, has given credence to the legend. Another source of uncovered wealth is **Ovens Natural Park** where stairs lead down the vertical-shale cliffs to oven-shaped caves, the site of an 1861 gold rush. The park rents and sells gold-panning equipment.

Lining the narrow streets in the historic area of **Lunenburg** are many examples of the ornate architecture of German Protestants brought in by the British after driving out the French-speaking Acadians. Liverpool with its grand houses dates back to New England Loyalists. The largest number – about 10,000 – settled in **Shelburne**, creating a population that eclipsed Montreal and Quebec City.

Evangeline Trail

At the southwestern end of Nova Scotia is the busy and thriving seaport town of **Yarmouth** where you can catch a ferry to **Bar Harbor** or even Portland, Maine. At the scallop fishing center, **Digby**, daily ferry service sails to **Saint John**, New Brunswick.

This coastal drive is named the **Evangeline Trail** for Henry Wadsworth Longfellow's epic poem about the British expulsion of the French-speaking Acadians from Nova Scotia after they refused to swear allegiance to the British Crown. Many of the Acadians returned years later to communities around **St. Mary's Bay**.

Annapolis Royal

Canada's first European settlement was **Annapolis Royal**, called **Port Royal** by the French. The chimneys of the Officer's Quarters rise above the earthworks of **Fort Anne**, a site where the British and French fought more than 12 battles

until the Treaty of Utrecht awarded it to Britain in 1713. Winding pathways lead through the quiet retreat of **Annapolis Royal Historic Gardens**, with its theme gardens, including one exhibiting new trends in garden techniques and another, an old Acadian garden.

Numerous historical buildings add charm to this one-traffic-light town protected from the high Bay of Fundy tides by the original French-made dikes. The **Annapolis Royal Tidal Power Project** displays the unique harnessing of tides for hydroelectric power.

Across the causeway lies **Port Royal National Historic Site**. A palisade encloses fortified black buildings with steeply pitched roofs that form a rectangle around a courtyard in the style of 17th-century France. Authorities based the reproduction of the original French fur trading post on the picture plan of Samuel de Champlain.

After the British takeover of Port Royal, the Acadians moved inland to Grand Pré, about 4 km outside the Acadia University town of Wolfville in the Annapolis Valley. Sheltered by mountains, this fertile valley has long been famous for its apples. When French troops attacked the British in 1774, the Acadians were once again expelled. Today the **Grand Pré Historical Park** has a bronze statue of the fictional

Alexander Graham Bell

The Alexander Graham Bell Museum.

museum chronicling his life and the history of the telephone – he made the world's first long distance telephone call from Brantford to Paris, Ontario.

Alexander Graham Bell, the inventor of the telephone, turned a tiny Nova Scotia village into a world center for scientific research. Born in Edinburgh, Scotland in 1847, he assisted at his father's speech laboratory, becoming a specialist in correcting speech problems at the age of 19.

When the family moved to **Brantford**, Ontario in 1870, Bell joined them and with his father worked as speech therapist for the deaf, using his unique Bell system of teaching the deaf to speak correctly. His future wife was, ironically enough, one of his patients. She was totally deaf, but Bell's technique successfully improved her speaking ability.

In Brantford, he conceived the idea of making an electric current vibrate to sound. In what is now the **Bell Homestead** in Brantford – a

After inventing the telephone at the age of 29, while a Vocal Psychology Professor at Boston University, Bell founded the **Bell Telephone Company** and moved to Washington, D.C. to watch over his business interests. His patent for the telephone made him wealthy, but Bell disliked Washington's humid summers and social whirl. On a visit to Newfoundland, he stopped at Baddeck in Cape Breton. The scenery of rugged hills and the deep blue of **Bras d'Or** lake reminded him of Scotland and he built *Beinn Bhreagh*, Gaelic for "Beautiful Mountain," a turreted castle-like home, which still belongs to the family. Across the bay, the **Alexander Graham Bell National Historic Site** houses many of his inventions.

From early spring to late fall, Bell, often

Evangeline and a little church with stained glass windows depicting the expulsion of the Acadians. Nearby is the province's pioneer wine operation, **Grand Pré Vineyards**.

The British gathered together the Acadians at Fort Edward in Windsor for shipping to the American colonies. Today's Cajuns of Louisiana are their descendants. All that remains of this

fort, last used as a training ground during World War I, are the earthworks and a wooden blockhouse.

In the village, the 1836 **Haliburton House** was the home of Judge Thomas C. Haliburton, author of the humorist Yankee clock peddler, *Sam Slick*, and originator of such phrases as "facts are stranger than fiction."

The tide from the Bay of Fundy

accompanied by research associates sat on the verandah overlooking the sea, discussing research problems until late at night. At other times, dressed in a tweed jacket and knicker-bockers with knee-length woollen stockings, Bell roamed the wooded hills, his mind actively jumping from idea to idea.

Bell worked on an extraordinary number of projects – the iron lung, the surgical probe, desalination of seawater, the phonograph and, what was preoccupying inventors around the world, aerial flight.

With some young scientists, he formed **The Aerial Experiment Association.** They pledged to devote a year of their lives to building a prototype flying machine. Bell began by working with giant man-lifting kites assembled by craftspeople in the 'kite house' on the shore near his Cape Breton home, producing one which was complex and strong enough to carry a man nine meters into the air. Eventually, the group turned to gasoline-powered biplanes. The *Silver Dart* became the first manned flight in Canada, taking off from Baddeck Bay in February 1909 and flying 64 km an hour.

Bell and his associates also created the *HD-4* (HD for hydrodrome), a hydrofoil that roared down the waters of Baddeck Bay at 114.04 km/hour in 1919, the fastest man had ever travelled on water, establishing a record that was not broken for more than a decade.

Bell died in 1922 at the age of 75. Both he and his wife are buried on the grounds of his Baddeck estate.

rushes into the **Salmon River** at Truro creating a tidal bore that can vary from a ripple to well over several feet. An unusual thrill are the various raft trips riding the tidal bore.

Cape Breton

The inventor of the telephone, Alexan-

Statue of Evangeline adorns a park.

der Graham Bell, who summered at **Baddeck** on Cape Breton said, "I have seen the Rockies, the Andes, the Alps and the Highlands of Scotland, but for simple beauty, Cape Breton outrivals them all." Not to be missed is the 300-km **Cabot Trail** going around the northern portion of the island. Named after John Cabot who first sighted Cape Breton, this is unquestionably one of the most beautiful drives in North America.

It's best to go clockwise for the security of hugging the cliffs. Start in Baddeck (see box on Bell), go through **North East Margaree** where the **Museum of Cape Breton Heritage** displays local handicrafts of the Micmac Indians, Acadians, and Scots, and the **Margaree Salmon Museum** pays homage to the

Cape Breton's gentle waves wash the beaches at Cabot coast.

great salmon fly fishing along the **Margaree River**. A sideroad leads up to the **Margaree Valley** where its river pierces deep gouges through the **Cape Breton Highlands**.

The **Acadian Fishing Village** of Cheticamp has whale-watching tours and the **Dr. Elizabeth LeFort Gallery & Museum**, the area's best-known weaver. Tapestries by 'Canada's Artist in Wool' hang in the Vatican, the White House and Buckingham Palace.

The 106-km drive from Cheticamp to **Ingonish** sweeps, twists and turns around wooded mountains that rise 455 m above the sea to a large plateau of forests, lakes, bogs and tundra inhabited by moose, bald eagles and deer, much of it within the boundaries of

Cape Breton Highlands National Park.

Scottish festivals are held throughout Nova Scotia. However, Cape Breton is where you'll find a good many people speaking Gaelic, often learned at the **Nova Scotia Gaelic College of Arts and Culture**, the only Gaelic college in North America. **South Gut St. Ann's** also hosts **The Gaelic Mod**, a seven-day festival of Celtic culture usually held during the first week of August. In **Iona**, the **Nova Scotia Highland Village Museum** has homes dating back to the first days of the Scottish settlers.

At **Glace Bay**, past Sydney, retired miners give visitors a chance to experience the work of a miner by leading tours down a coal mine by the **Miner's Museum**. A similar museum can be

The Micmac

Before the Europeans arrived, the Micmac were spread out over the Gaspé peninsula, Prince Edward Island, Nova Scotia and New Brunswick. The Europeans named them Micmac, after noticing they were always saying *nikmaq* to each other. This word was a traditional Micmac greeting meaning 'my kin friends' in the vernacular.

The Micmac lived mainly in the coastal areas and depended on the sea for much of their food. They caught fish using various simple but effective methods. For large fish, such as salmon, they would use a leister – a three-pronged spear-like device with one shorter prong in the center to spear the fish and a barbed prong on each side to hold the fish.

The Micmac normally hunted beaver, whales, seals and moose. Although moose was hunted all year, the best time to catch them was in February and March when the snow was soft and hunters could spot the moose tracks in the snow. Using dogs and wearing snowshoes, they could catch the moose fairly effortlessly. The panicked moose kept sinking into the deep snow and soon was tired. The animal was killed with either a spear or an arrow.

The most common way to cook meat was by roasting it over a fire; however, the Micmac also boiled their food. They made containers of birchbark that were sewn together with spruce roots and waterproofed with spruce gum at the seams. Using wooden thongs, the Micmac picked up red-hot rocks from the fire and placed them in the container. When the rocks cooled down, more hot rocks were put in. The Micmac also made 'wooden kettles' hollowed out of tree trunks. These kettles were used to make butter from crushed moose bones.

Birchbark was an all important material for the Micmac. Canoes and baskets were made from it as well as the wigwams they lived in. A wigwam was built by covering a group of poles with birchbark and stitching the birchbark together with spruce roots. The most common design of the 17th century wigwam was conical-shaped, similar to a teepee. Wigwams were very practical for the nomadic Micmac since they were very light and portable. An early observer noted that when the Micmac had to move they just rolled up the birchbark like a piece of paper and carried it away on their backs thus making the relocation very simple.

The basic piece of clothing for the Micmac was the loincloth. During the colder months the Micmac wore leggings, moccasins and robes commonly made of beaver pelts. The pelts were stitched together using a needle, made out of bone or copper, and thread, made of animal sinew. Did you know that the word toboggan is derived from the Micmac word *taba'gan*? Toboggans weren't built to provide the Micmac with some form of winter recreation, rather they made the transporting of goods through the snow easier.

---

seen at **Springhill** along with costumes and memorabilia belonging to its native superstar daughter at the **Anne Murray Center**.

About 25 minutes south of Sydney, go over the drawbridge and enter the mighty **Fortress Louisbourg**, built by the French during the early 1700s. After numerous battles over the years, the French surrendered this biggest French fort in North America to the British.

Inside this huge complex, you can drop in to eat lunch with the "townspeople," but you'll only be offered a spoon and you have to share a knife, just like they did in the 1700s.

If you are following the Eastern shore back to Halifax, drop into **Sherbrooke Village**, a former lumbering and shipbuilding town restored to look as it did 100 years ago. The layout has an authentic finish and is impressive.

Newfoundland

Life revolves around the sea in Newfoundland, shaping the people and their culture, giving it a distinct character, notably different from the rest of Canada. On the **Rock**, the locals' name for Newfoundland, time seems to stand still. People on the rocky island mainly live in tiny fishing villages, some set in mountains and fjords more spectacular than Norway. Labrador remains a practically untouched wilderness of rivers and mountains, a haven for fishing and hunting, edged by a wild, rocky coast.

Springtime in Newfoundland's countryside is spread with fall maple hues.

Economic necessity has long forced many to leave for better jobs on the mainland, yet Newfoundland has Canada's highest return rate of people to their home province. The strong family ties pull them back as does the lure of living in a small community among people known for their warmth, folk music, and good humor. They are the butt of *newfie* jokes throughout Canada, but many of the best are

173

told by the Newfoundlanders themselves. Their sharp wit is evident in the names given to some of the villages – or *outports* – places like **Stinking Cove**, **Dildo**, **Come By Chance**, and **Blow Me Down**.

St. John's

The capital of the province sits snugly protected inside a large, nearly land-locked harbor. Only a small gap, called the **Narrows**, reveals the Atlantic beyond. Painted wooden houses, some in the Irish and English styles of their ancestors, intermingle with modern buildings on the hills beyond rising from the sea. There is a lively nightlife with cosy British-style pubs and toe-tapping fiddling music.

Attacks by pirates, battles and fire destroyed many buildings over the decades, although a few survived. Period costumed guides show visitors through the gracious clapboard 1819 **Commissariat House**. The white limestone **Colonial Building**, the seat of government from 1850 until 1960 when the legislature moved into the **Confederation Building**, stands high above the city. The **Murray Premises**, an 1847 office and warehouse complex, now houses **Newfoundland Museum** exhibits on the province's sea trade and its natural and military history. The main museum documents the varied living styles of settlers and townspeople as well as the native population.

One of the oldest settlements in

North America, St. John's, dates its beginnings to 1497 when John Cabot landed in Newfoundland. His news about the flourishing fishing grounds brought ships from France, Portugal, England and Spain on the long, arduous journey. Wanting full control of this

Newfoundland boasts picturesque riverside cycling paths.

resource, Queen Elizabeth sent Sir Humphrey Gilbert in 1583 to claim the island as a British possession. The British and French fought for centuries over ownership of the island. The British won the final victory when they recaptured St. John's in 1762.

This clash, the last battle of the Seven Years War in North America, was fought at **Signal Hill**, a natural lookout

There's always an abundance of salmon, rainbow trout and brook trout.

situated on the steep cliffs at the mouth of the harbour. Outside of the fortifications built by the British in the 1800s, the **Signal Hill Tattoo** re-enacts colonial military exercises in the summer. Nearby, the 1897 **Cabot Tower** has exhibits on signalling and communications with a section devoted to Guglielmo Marconi. Below the tower, Marconi received the first transatlantic wireless signal in 1901.

On the precipitous cliffs on Signal Hill's north side, overlooking a narrow inlet to the village of **Quidi Vidi**, is **Quidi Vidi Battery**, a small fortification built by the French in the Seven Years War. Captured by the British and rebuilt in 1780, it was manned by British forces until their withdrawal from Newfoundland in 1870.

St. John's Regatta, a fixed-seat boating race held on the first Wednesday in August at **Quidi Vidi Lake**, is considered the oldest continuing sports event in North America. As the small museum at the boathouse proves, the race has been held since at least 1826. On shore, live music and games of chance add a carnival atmosphere to the regatta.

Outports of Newfoundland

Among the numerous attractive outports bearing names that reflect their heritage, a few outshine the others. **Trinity** in the Eastern Region is called a national treasure for its historic 19th-

The National Historic Sites and Parks have friendly animals as in this deer.

century houses tucked into winding lanes. Further south, **Grand Bank** with its attractive homes reflects the past wealth of the Grand Bank's fishing industry, an era on display at its Southern Newfoundland Seamen's Museum. The charm of **Brigus** on the **Avalon Peninsula** inspired American artist Rockwell Kent in the early 1900s to set up a summer residence and studio.

Fishing

While little in the island appears to have changed in over 50 years, underneath lies the harsh reality of the collapse of the cod fishing industry. The major northern cod fishery off the northeast-ern coast of Newfoundland was closed in 1992.

In 1994, the Canadian government banned cod fishing in most Canadian waters. Even recreational cod fishing has been halted off the northeast and south coasts.

Overfishing, record cold water temperatures, growing seal populations, mismanagement and unknown environmental factors are blamed for the 95 percent decline in northern cod stocks in the last three years.

Fishermen continue hauling in lobster, scallops, shrimp and other species, but the importance of fishing to the economy has dropped and has been replaced by logging and mining.

Yet, recreational fishing for other

St Pierre & Miquelon

These tiny islands 20 km off the coast of Newfoundland are all that are left of France's once mighty North American empire. The islands are represented in the Parliament in France by one deputy and senator respectively. The 6,400 inhabitants remain proudly French, keeping the traditions and way of life of their ancestors.

Actually, this corner of the old world actually consists of three main islands – **St. Pierre**, **Langlade**, **Miquelon** – and, in the harbor of St. Pierre, the tiny Sailor's Island.

Old World Ties

The tall old-fashioned stone buildings fronting St. Pierre's harbor, the winding, narrow streets, and vividly painted wooden houses, convey the feeling of stepping directly into Europe. The one small museum has relics relating to the islands' colorful history.

Discovered by Portuguese explorer Joao Alvares Fagundes in 1520, St. Pierre was claimed by Jacques Cartier for France in 1636. French fishermen and Acadians deported from Canada by the British settled the island. For over 100 years, the French and English fought over possession until the Treaty of Paris awarded the islands to France in 1815.

The American prohibition was the islands' most prosperous era. Bootleggers like **Al Capone** used the islands as the transfer point between the distilleries of Scotland and the wine producers of Europe. The liquor traffic came to an abrupt end in 1935 and just the small trafficking with Newfoundland continued. When New-foundland joined Canada in 1949, and prices of food and other products were raised to balance the budget, smuggling increased. It is a trade that continues to this day, despite the tremendously heavy fines.

The French wine, perfume and other goods in the duty-free shop entice many visitors, as do the numerous good restaurants, which befits a region of France. Recently, North Americans have been coming here to learn French in a typical French environment. Air St. Pierre flies here regularly and a passenger ferry service travels to Newfoundland.

The majority of the population lives on the eastern side of St. Pierre which is sheltered from the winds continually sweeping the islands. An isthmus of sand joins Miquelon to the island of Langlade. The isthmus only began to appear about 200 years ago. It was formed by the action of sea current, helped by the wreck of ships trapped in the sand.

The islands have a rough and wild charm, with its rocky land of peat bogs and marsh. A sandy beach and towering cliffs distinguish the coast of the largest island, the summer vacation spot of Langlade. After two centuries as a fishing village, **Sailor's Island** is now inhabited only during the summer.

The islands' economy depends entirely on fish and the Canadian government's cod fishing freeze in the **Grand Banks** stunned them. Now, the islanders are trying to develop scallop fishing and increase tourism. A new airport is being built, to be completed in 1998, and plans are being made to erect a casino. This will ensure that tourism will increase in the future.

species continues to flourish. The province's small population – about 570,000 – ensures abundant supplies of salmon, rainbow trout and brook trout for individuals fishing in the lakes and rivers, including in St. John's itself. For a preview, the **Newfoundland Freshwater Resource** has nine windows allowing visitors to see fish in their natural environment. North America's only public **Fluvarium** also has aquariums and displays of freshwater ecology.

People throng to the beaches near St. John's in late June and early July for the annual *capelin scull*. The small, smeltlike fish spawn in the shallow wa-

Newfoundland has many beaten tracks leading to fishing coves.

ters and the tide carries them right onto the shore, ready to be scooped up by buckets, nets or any other container.

Oil

The hope for future employment of people in the fishing industry rests on the natural gas and oil off the coasts of the island and Labrador. During the past 25 years, companies have found 25 significant oil and gas deposits.

In the northeast corner of the Grand Banks alone, the discoveries total 1.6 billion barrels of oil, 4 trillion cubic feet of natural gas and 237 million barrels of natural gas liquids.

Less than one percent of the off-shore area has already been explored, and low world prices in recent years have depressed exploration. However, already the largest Grand Banks field, **Hibernia**, is scheduled to start production in 1997. Located 315 km offshore, it contains an estimated 615 million barrels of crude petroleum.

Cape Spear

A short drive from downtown St. John's is **Cape Spear National Historic Park**. This is a good spot to spy whales and the ethereal, ghostly shapes of icebergs as they drift by a two-story wooden light-house. The continent's oldest surviving lighthouse was erected in 1835. During

Snow geese flock the skies of Newfoundland.

World War II, two gun emplacements were installed in this easternmost point of North America to protect the city against Nazi submarines.

The German submarine, U-190, surrendered during the last days of the war at **Bay Bulls**, the repair depot for Allied warships. Tours from the town go within hailing distance of the **Witless Bay Ecological Reserve**. This reserve is home to the largest nesting colony of puffins in North America.

Along Hwy 13, large boulders known as glacial erractics, sit where dropped by the retreating glaciers thousands of years ago. These glaciers had carved the presently seen two deep bays on either side of the narrow neck of land that joins the Avalon Peninsula to the rest of the island.

Placentia was the French capital of Newfoundland. The French erected fortifications on the forested hills flanking the large beach. From **Plaisance**, the French name for the village, **Pierre Lemoyne d'Iberville** led numerous attacks against the English. After the **Treaty of Utrecht** in 1713 awarded the island to the British, they renamed the town and, during the Seven Years War upgraded the defences.

Castle Hill National Historic Site displays some remains of the fortifications along with an exhibit dealing with the hardships faced by the early settlers. This is described in graphic detail tracing the settlement problem to the peaceful period.

Isolation

These first fishing families depended on a single commodity, dried salted cod fish, which was subject to violent price fluctuations. On an island where rocky soil and a harsh climate made farming nearly impossible, a life of debt was practically guaranteed.

As the population increased, people settled hundreds of communities along the 10,000-km coast. The bleak terrain kept them glued to the coast. For many living in outports even today, the only way to reach another community is by boat.

Originally, England prohibited settlement: their merchants feared competition from a resident population. The ban was rescinded when France founded a colony at Placentia. However, emigration was discouraged. England largely ignored the residents, only bowing to appeals for law and order in 1729 by giving the commander of the naval force the additional duties of Governor. A year-round governor was eventually appointed in 1815.

The colony's continually fluctuating economy finally dwindled during the 1930s depression. Decreased exports and the increase of people on relief had bankrupted the country.

To get Newfoundland out from its hole, a British commission was set up in 1934 to rule the island. After the war, two referendums resulted in a slim margin voting to join Canada in 1949.

Language

The isolation from other countries and between communities helped develop the Newfoundlander's love of storytelling. The tradition of passing along the stories of their colorful history has also created pride in their past and in their distinctiveness from the rest of Canada.

Their language, in particular, the colorful expressions and accents that haven't been heard since Shakespeare's day sets them apart. There are more than 60 dialects and subdialects spoken, a combination of southern Irish brogue with southwestern English dialect that can vary from community to community, depending on the homecountry of their ancestors back in the 17th century.

Scenic Beauty

The island's top attraction is **Gros Morne National Park**. Named a UNESCO World Heritage Site for its geology, the park has Newfoundland's most dramatic scenery. Continental drift and glaciers sculpted its deep fjords and ponds.

This is referred to by Newfoundlanders as fresh water lakes, raised mountains formed the **Tablelands**. This is a lunar-like plateau of yellowish rocks that was originally an ancient sea bed before being pushed up by forces below the earth's crust. A highlight of any visit is a boat cruise to **Western Brook Pond**

Getting Around Newfoundland – Transportation

Getting around Newfoundland and Labrador can be a challenge and since some outposts can only be reached by boat or plane, trips require advance planning.

The "Newfie Bullet," the ironically-named Newfoundland train service was abolished years ago and replaced by a bus service, CN Roadcruiser. From **Port aux Basques**, one bus goes to **Grand Falls** three days a week, another daily to **St. John's**. Smaller bus lines, called outport taxis, regularly serve other communities as well.

If you want to take your car to Newfoundland, it's advisable to make reservations in advance, especially from the most popular transit point, North Sydney, Nova Scotia. From here, car ferries make about a six hour daily journey to Port aux Basques, Newfoundland. In the summer, another twice-a-week ferry heads to Argentina, the closest port to the capital city of St. John's, a 14-hour voyage.

A car ferry runs from **Happy-Valley Goose Bay** and Cartwright, Labrador, to Lewisporte, Newfoundland, just a few times a week and from June to September only. Another, between Blanc Sablon, Labrador, and St. Barbe, Newfoundland makes two round trips a day, from May to December, on a first-come, first-served basis.

The one major highway, the **Trans-Canada**, starts in St. John's at a sign reading, "Canada Begins Right Here." The 905-km road crosses east to west, ending at **Channel-Port aux Basques**. Other highways are good, although there are some rough, unpaved roads leading to the smaller outports. Some can only be reached by private boat, while continuous ferry services regularly land at others. These are for passengers and cargo only. Tourism Officers can give you the number to telephone for the specific line serving the outport you want. Ferries from **Fortune** go to the French island of St. Pierre in the warmer months.

Roads in Labrador are practically non-existent. The highway from **Baie Comeau**, Quebec, to the modern mining towns of Labrador City and Wabush is only partially paved. From there to Happy Valley-Goose Bay is a seasonal gravel road. The **Quebec North Shore** and **Labrador Railway Company** travels from **Sept Iles**, Quebec, through some marvellous landscapes to the **Iron Ore Mining Company** town of **Schefferville**, on the western edge of Labrador.

There are small stretches of roads along Labrador's coast, but to reach the more than 24 communities further north, you have to hop aboard a coastal boat. The boat takes passengers and cargo from **Lewisporte** to **Nain**, a trip that can take two weeks because it stops at so many communities and passenger space is limited. Reservations for this service can be made only from within the province.

surrounded by cliffs and waterfalls.

Early Beginnings

The central region of the island offers a completely different landscape, a forest wilderness, inhabited by moose and caribou. This was the winter home of the Beothuck, now-extinct aboriginal people who decorated their faces, bodies, garments and utensils with red ochre, earning the name Red Indians.

The two last-known Beothuck were captured in 1823. Grand Falls has a small reconstructed **Beothuck Village** and the **Mary March Regional Museum** with displays on their history and traditions.

Outdoor Adventures

Across the channel that funnels the

An elk bull displays its stately horns.

Labrador current into the Gulf of St. Lawrence is **Labrador**. It has a nearly uninhabited wilderness of superb rivers for white-water canoeists and fishing, mountains to climb and ski as well as big game hunting. There are over 6,000 black bears, 100,000 moose and the largest caribou herd in the world which number about 600,000. There is never a lack for big game hunting in Labrador.

Labrador

Labrador is just across the Strait of Belle Isle from Newfoundland's Great Northern Peninsula. On, a clear day it is visible across the 17.6 km wide strait.

Southern Labrador is the traditional home of the summer fishermen whilst coastal Labrador is still a wilderness filled with rugged seacoast, fast running rivers and totally breathtaking mountain ranges. The interior of Labrador is mainly a vast wilderness with an area of 293,347 sq km and a total of 29,000 permanent residents. There are recent pockets of modern industrialization that house descendants of European settlers.

Their native Inuit fellow men with their *Naskapi-Montagnis* traditions and lifestyles resist the encroachment of modern society in their coastal habitats. It is a community of friendly, independent spirits in a region which offers an unforgettable experience in the wilderness.

Prince Edward Island (known as P.E.I. and locally as the island) is a colorful world of green hills, multi-hued sandy beaches, red sandstone cliffs, and brilliant blue waters. Canada's smallest province is also the most rural. The neat tidy farms, the small towns, the undulating landscape, the unhurried pace of life and the sociable inhabitants impart a feeling of tranquillity, a sense of calm that has long distinguished the island. "Compressed by the inviolate sea, it floats on the waves of the blue gulf, a green seclusion and haunt of ancient peace," wrote Lucy Maud Montgomery, author of *Anne of Green Gables.*

Thyme fields are a refreshing treat for Prince Edward Island's nature lovers.

The major drawing card for international visitors, particularly Japanese tourists, is Montgomery's famous fictional character, Anne Shelby. This best-seller about the freckled, red-haired little girl is now an international television series.

The island's isolation helps it maintain its calm

Prince Edward Island

rural lifestyle. Car ferries travel year-round from Cape Tormentine, New Brunswick to Borden, a 45-minute trip, and May to December from Caribou, Nova Scotia to Wood Islands in just over an hour. After decades of debate, however, approval has just been given to construct a bridge to the mainland, much to the dismay of many environmentalists and residents who fear losing their way of life. The bridge is expected to be completed in 1997.

Land & Sea

This tiny 224-km long crescent-shaped island where you're never more than 16 km from the sea has a unique geological feature, red soil. The color comes from the iron oxide trapped in the bedrock underneath, producing a red so rich that in some places it appears to have been poured straight from a paint can.

Grain, cereal, and hay crops for the dairy industry flourish in this soil, but this is "**Spud Island**," an image boosted by popular Canadian country singer Stompin' Tom Connors. His song, *"Bud the Spud,"* starts with, "It's Bud the Spud, from the bright red mud, roll' down the highway smilin'."

Over 800 farms grow more than 70 varieties of potatoes, producing one fourth of all the potatoes grown in Canada and exporting more potato seeds than anywhere else in North America. Road-side stands start selling new potatoes in July while recipes for an astonishing number of ways to cook potatoes are available all the year round. There's even a new **Potato Museum at O'Leary**.

The province also takes advantage of the influx of tourists by promoting another important economic mainstay, fishing. At campgrounds, parks and special events in the summer, cooks demonstrate how to barbecue seafood. The island is also known for its lobster suppers, a tradition started by churches. But be aware: these informal meals often serve only cold lobster.

One small fishing village that retains much of its 19th-century atmosphere is Victoria, a short drive east of the ferry terminus at Borden along a road marked by signs displaying a blue heron. **Blue Heron Drive** is one of three scenic drives following the island's coastline.

Canada's Birthplace

With its Victorian architecture, pink-bricked buildings and tree-lined streets, Charlottetown remains much as it was during its golden era, the 1800s. Even the population hasn't greatly changed: rising from 12,000 in 1901 to 20,000 today. This seaside colonial town is where Canada was born, at the Charlottetown Conference at **Province House**. You can tour this three-story sandstone structure, still the island's legislature building, and see the original room where representatives of the colonies met to discuss union in 1864.

Charlottetown's houses always make a pretty picture.

When agreement was finally reached and Canada formed in 1867, P.E.I. did not join. The independent minded islanders waited until 1873 when the Canadian government sweetened the deal for them. Even so, Lord Dufferin, Canada's Governor General said the islanders agreed "under the impression that it is the Dominion of Canada that has been annexed to Prince Edward Island."

Next door is the modern Confederation Center of the Arts where the musical, *Anne of Green Gables*, is per-

*The receding tides sprinkle the beaches of
Prince Edward Island with misty grey puddles.*

formed each summer in one of two theatres. The center's art gallery highlights Robert Harris, a renowned portrait painter who collaborated with his architect brother in creating the pretty chapel in tiny **St. Peter's Cathedral**. W.C. Harris also designed the 1877 Vic-

torian mansion **Beaconsfield**, restored with 1900 Edwardian-style furnishings.

Restoration of the wharves has recaptured the era when they bustled with sailors and ship building. The waterfront **Victoria Park** is home to the handsome white southern-style mansion,

with a wooded trail bypassing birch-bark wigwams, a smoke house, sweat house and a museum of artifacts.

Prince Edward Island National Park

The 40 km long **Prince Edward Island National Park**, along the island's north shore, encompasses seven beaches. The island's so packed with beaches that they've been divided into categories A to C. The C classification indicates limited beach area at high tide, but these are usually good spots for clam digging. B have less sand than top-rated A beaches. A large number of the "A" beaches are in P.E.I. National Park. At the eastern edge of the park, sand dunes surpass 25 m in height. The marram grass growing out of the dunes act as a safety net, gripping the dunes to prevent the sand spreading over the fields and into the harbors. The east edge of park is also where you'll spot a summer "cottage" built for an oil magnate in 1896, the magnificent Victorian-style **Dalvay-by-the-Sea**, the island's only seaside hotel.

At **Orby Head**, on the park's western edge, red sandstone cliffs rise sharply from the water to a height as high as 30 m. The eroding cliffs has turned the white sands a pinkish-colour.

The Land of Anne

The tour of *Anne of Green Gables* land

Government House, residence of the island's lieutenant-governor. From the park, there's a good view across the water to the ruins of **Fort Amherst**, built in 1758 by the British after they expelled the French-speaking Acadians. Before the Acadians arrived, this was Micmac land and the Micmac Indian Village at nearby **Rocky Point** recreates that life

The undulating plains of Prince Edward Island
that inspired Anne of Green Gables.

begins in the park, by Cavendish, at **Green Gables House**. (See box). Near the farmhouse through the dark spruce forest of The Haunted Woods is the new location of the "little low-eaved" schoolhouse Montgomery attended as a girl. All that remains of the home where she lived are the foundations, around which are quotes from her journal.

The area is still owned by her family. A similar house has been relocated and restored and is now the **Green Gables Post Office**. The nearby Cavendish United Church is where Montgomery met the minister whom she married. They are both buried in the nearby cemetery. In New London, 11 km from Cavendish, the modest white house where the author was born in 1874 contains many of her personal effects, such as her wedding dress.

At Park Corner, Montgomery's descendants still own the house she loved best and where she was married. She used the house, now the **Anne of Green Gables Museum** at **Silver Bush**, and its surroundings, including the **Lake of Shining Water** across the road, in her book *Anne of Green Gables*.

Summerside

People living on the island's south shore claim the waters are warmer on this side of the island, the "summer side." At the town of **Summerside**, the second-largest community on the island, stately

Anne of Green Gables

Anne of Green Gables is a story about the orphan, Anne Shirley, who was taken in by Matthew and Marilla Cuthbert, a kindly but strict brother and sister who lived on a farm called Green Gables on the outskirts of Avonlea, P.E.I. They had originally wanted a boy, but received Anne by mistake.

Lucy Maud Montgomery's story of this red-haired, freckle-faced girl has enraptured millions including Mark Twain who called Anne the most lovable childhood heroine since the immortal Alice – of Alice in Wonderland. It was an amazing success for a book first published in 1908, after being continually rejected by publishers. Discouraged, the author, had hidden it away in an old shoe box. When Montgomery found it a couple of years later, she decided to give one final try. Within six months, six editions were published and it became one of the most popular children's books ever written.

Montgomery published seven sequels to Anne as well as other books, short stories and poems. But it was Anne who captured the hearts of people in stories that have been seen on television around the world.

Thousands of people come to P.E.I. to see the secret haunts Anne spoke about and to see her home and other places mentioned in the books. Leading the list is Green Gables House,

on the western end of **Prince Edward Island National Park,** which picturesquely evokes the rural 19th-century atmosphere of the book. Built in the mid-1800s, the charming two-storey white and green farmhouse belonging to the author's cousins was the main setting for *Anne of Green Gables.*

In 1936, the federal government preserved the house and surrounding farmland within the Prince Edward Island National Park. They restored the home and furnished it with authentic 1890 pieces, using descriptions in the book for reference, and allotted bedrooms for each of the main characters.

You can also stroll through the farm's woodland haunt and perhaps derive the same benefit as Montgomery. **Lover's Lane,** which figured prominently in the book, was a favorite sanctuary of the author. She wrote, "This evening I spent in Lover's Lane. How beautiful it was – green and alluring and beckoning! I had been tired and discouraged and sick at heart before I went to it – and it rested me and cheered me and stole away the heartsickness, giving peace and newness of life."

From Lover's Lane, a path winds along a shady babbling brook in **Balsam Hollow Trail**. Signs point out the natural beauty spots of this area which inspired Montgomery.

wooden homes reflect its era as the centre of fox ranching. The **International Fox Hall of Fame and Museum** tells the story of this industry that saw the price of a pair of silver foxes rise to $35,000 in 1920.

Acadians

From Summerside, Lady Slipper Drive enters the Evangeline Region, in which French-speaking Acadians had settled

in. They had escaped into the forests when the British began deporting them.

This area of brightly painted houses with Acadian flags has a French-language theatre and, at **Mont-Carmel**, an **Acadian Pioneer Village**. There is an altogether French atmosphere in this area. The Acadian Pioneer Village in particular captures the essence of the bygone era. This is actually a reproduction of their ancestors' 1820 log settlement. An adjoining restaurant specializes in Acadian cuisine.

Nouveau lobster – a feast for the palate and the eyes.

PEI Oddities

At **Cap Egmont**, you can see the unusual hobby that occupied one retired fisherman. Edouard T. Arsenault cemented over 25,000 bottles of all shapes, sizes and colors to build the **Bottle Houses**. It is a glass world consisting of a six-gabled house chapel complete with altar and pews. There is even a tavern made out of bottles.

At times, it appears that nearly every farmhouse you pass has a Bed & Breakfast (B&B) sign, but the most unusual is the old lighthouse keeper's residence at the 1875 West Point Lighthouse where the museum documents the history of lighthouses. Just outside is the beautiful white sandy beach of **Cedar Dunes Provincial Park**.

Irish Moss

Storms churn up purplish seaweed from the ocean floor and carry it to the shores which horse-driven carts collect. The Irish moss, when processed, is used in ice cream, cough syrups and other foods as you will learn at the **Irish Moss Interpretative Center**, which is aboard a fishing vessel at **Miminegash**.

Fittingly enough, this tiny island has an equally small railway. The 1/8-scale **Prince Edward Island Minature Railway** near **Kildare** carries passengers on a 20-minute ride through a rural landscape of meadows and forests, not far from one of the island's 30 provincial parks. **Jacques Cartier Provincial Park** was named for this first European to sight the island. In a letter back to the King, Cartier raved, "...the fairest land 'tis possible to see!"

Malpeque Bay

The land becomes more hilly around **Malpeque Bay** where the famed Malpeque oysters are harvested before being shipped off to oyster gourmets. It takes five years before the oysters are plump enough to harvest.

On Lennox Island, more than 50 Micmac families, descendants of the first peoples in P.E.I., live on a Reserve.

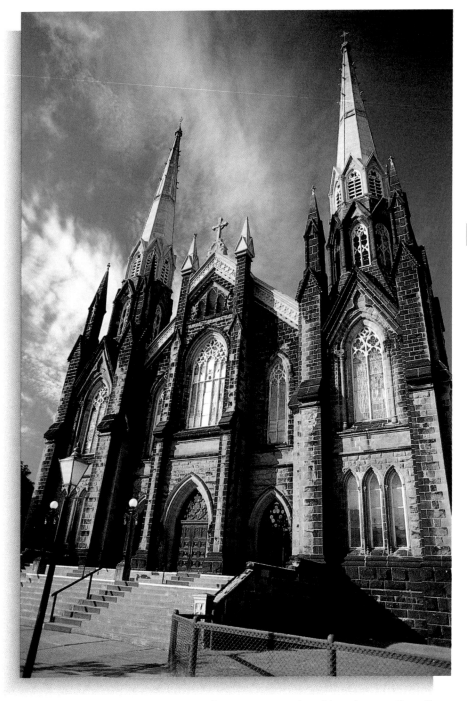

A Scottish church looms majestically against sapphire blue skies at Orwell Corner Historic Village.

A fisherman with his catch at Malpeque Bay.

Their **St. Anne's Church**, named for the Micmac patron saint, displays native artifacts and paintings. The shop, **Indian Arts and Crafts of North America**, sells ash splint baskets, pottery, masks, animal hides, drums and other handmade Indian crafts.

Shipbuilding dominated the island's economy in the 1800s. James Yeo, Jr. had his shipyard and home on the bay at **Port Hill**. **Green Park Shipbuilding Museum** traces the industry with photographs and tools while the 1865 steeply gabled Victoria home of this wealthy

settled by Scottish and Irish pioneers, the roots of the majority of the islanders today. The growth of larger towns and better transportation doomed these small commercial centres. On this site of a farmhouse, community hall and other restored buildings, a *Ceilidhs* musical concert of fiddling and stepdancing takes place on Wednesday evenings every week.

The **Sir Andrew MacPhail Homestead** nearby features the home of this author/physician as well as trails through a peaceful reforestation woodlot and lovely gardens with heritage plants.

A boardwalk at **Buffaloland Provincial Park** takes you near to herds of buffalo and white-tailed deer. At **Murray River** and **Montague**, seal-watching tours are popular.

The Kings Byway passes through some of the island's most reddish soil and richest farmland. Morrell celebrates a **Strawberry Festival** in mid-July and in August, **St. Peters** has its **Blueberry Festival** and **Homecoming**. This area is also known for its Island Blue mussels. Those rows of buoys you see sticking out of the bays mark the spots where lines of these cultured mussels are growing.

Souris, a busy fishing port where ferries travel to Quebec's Magdalene Islands in the Gulf of St. Lawrence, is near some fine white sandy beaches while just north, on a bluff overlooking the Atlantic, the **Basin Head Fisheries Museum** has a reconstructed fish shack and lobster cannery.

owner shows how the prominent shipbuilding family in that era lived.

The Living Past

Orwell Corner Historic Village, east of Charlottetown, via **Kings Byway**, recreates the rural crossroads community

British Columbia (or B.C. as it's usually known) is called Canada's **Lotusland**, a name given in recognition of its spectacular scenery and laid-back attitudes. People are more relaxed than in the rest of Canada, more open to new experiences and enjoying life to its fullest.

This is a mindset attributable to several factors. Their ancestors were the more adventurous who heeded the call to "Go West." They have also been influenced by their proximity to California as well as all the recreational opportunities offered by the province's diverse topography and, in southern British Columbia where most of the approximately 3 million population live, Canada's mildest climate.

The Pacific Ocean and towering mountains define B.C. Forests cover nearly three-quarters of the province, both huge inland forests intersected by raging rivers and dense rain forests along the jagged mountainous coastline with its hundreds of islands.

Windsurfing on the glassy sea at British Columbia.

British Columbia

This grandfather's clock at a busy shopping mall conveys much of British Columbia's link with the past.

Indian Heritage

Isolated by the province's diverse and rugged terrain, the 10 linguistic groups of indigenous people – called the First Nations – developed their own cultures.

Some of their civilizations were highly sophisticated and unique to British Columbia. While a few indigenous people continue to live by the skills of their ancestors through hunting and fishing, suppression by missionaries, government and disease has taken its toll.

The J W Jerome statue captures the thriving outdoor spirit of British Columbia.

Evidence of their rich legacy can be found at various museums throughout British Columbia.

More than 20 gathering of nations or *pow wows* are held throughout the province. *Pow wows* are partly social and partly religious celebrations that went underground in the early 1900s until the government passed a religious freedom act in 1955. You can see one of these colorful displays of dance and music as well as exhibits of arts and crafts during mid-August on the banks of the South Thompson river.

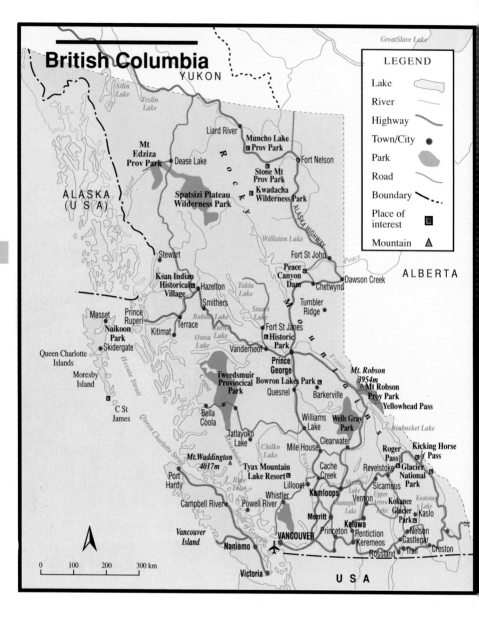

British Columbia

YUKON

Atlin Lake
Teslin Lake

GreatSlave Lake

Liard River

Muncho Lake
Prov Park

Mt Edziza Prov Park
Dease Lake

Fort Nelson

Stone Mt Prov Park

Kwadacha Wilderness Park

ALASKA (USA)

Spatsizi Plateau Wilderness Park

ALASKA HIGHWAY

Williston Lake

Stewart

Fort St John

Peace

ALBERTA

Ksan Indian Historical Village
Hazelton

Peace Canyon Dam
Chetwynd
Dawson Creek

Takla Lake

Smithers

Babine Lake

Stuart Lake

Tumbler Ridge

Masset
Prince Ruperi
Terrace

Burns Lake

Fort St James
Historic Park

Naikoon Park
Kitimat

Ootsa Lake

Vanderhoof

Skidergate

Prince George

Queen Charlotte Islands

Hecate Strait

Tweedsmuir Provincial Park
Bowron Lakes Park

Mt Robson 3954m
Mt Robson Prov Park

Moresby Island

Quesnel
Barkerville

Yellowhead Pass

C St James

Bella Coola

Williams Lake
Wells Gray Park

Kinbasket Lake

Tatlayoko Lake

Chilko Lake

Mile House
Clearwater

Roger Pass
Kicking Horse Pass

Mt Waddington 4017m
Tyax Mountain Lake Resort

Cache Creek

Revelstoke
Glacier National Park

Port Hardy

Lillooet

Sicamous

Campbell River
Powell River

Whistler

Kamloops
Vernon
Kokance Glacier Park
Kaslo

Merritt

Kelowna
Princeton
Penticton
Keremeos

Nelson
Castlegar

Vancouver Island

VANCOUVER

Rosland
Trail
Creston

Naniamo

Victoria

USA

0 100 200 300 km

LEGEND

Lake	
River	
Highway	
Town/City	●
Park	
Road	
Boundary	
Place of interest	▣
Mountain	▲

Secwepemc

Secwepemc Native Heritage Park at **Kamloops** was built on a 2,400-year site of the inland Secwepemc whose culture varied greatly from the coastal tribes.

The park has a reconstructed full-scale winter village and replicas of pit-houses – circular wooden homes on top of a pit. The most impressive Indian villages were built by the coastal Indians, who were renowned for their artistic accomplishments. Unique to these First Nation people are totem poles, columns of cedar wood carved in detail with animals, humans, birds and mythological figures representing a family or clan, which stand guard outside of '**Ksan**, a reconstructed **Gitksan village** near **Hazelton** in the north.

The village has seven log longhouses that were usually occupied by 20 or more families, a salmon smokehouse and a wood carving house. There are dancers performing the extraordinary "transformation mask" dance on Friday nights in summer.

On the **Queen Charlotte Islands**, a six-hour voyage from Prince Rupert, the Haida Indians successfully forced the banning of logging. They have lived in these islands since 1500 BC. Bald eagles soar above the mist-shrouded forests, one of the few places where original totem poles remain standing. These poles outside the old Haida villages inspired the bold, disturbing paintings of Emily Carr, one of Canada's foremost artists.

From June to September, a ferry travels between Prince Rupert through the **Inside Passage** to **Port Hardy** on Vancouver Island. This is a 15-hour trip through some tremendously majestic mountainous coastlines.

Victoria

When the Spanish

A coastal Indian woman carves a totem out of cedar wood.

began exploring the west coast in 1774, the British quickly asserted their interest by sending Captain James Cook. He landed at Vancouver island, where he bought some furs from the Indians.

At the same time, others were crossing the Rockies and setting up numerous trading posts, bringing an end to the traditional life of the First Nations.

After the **Hudson Bay Company** (HBC) built Fort Victoria at the southern tip of Vancouver Island, the city mushroomed as gold seekers

A fleet of yachts at British Columbia's harbor.

poured into the port on their way to the **Fraser River**. Even though Victoria is the capital of British Columbia, the small decorous downtown gives the impression of a city not yet fully grown. It is the pace of life that appeals to the many retirees who are attracted by its mild weather and its British heritage. The HBC employees tried to recreate a bit of their homeland here.

Tudor houses, lamp post flower baskets and the afternoon tea still served at the turreted **Empress Hotel** assert this influence. At the head of Victoria's harbor are the Parliament Buildings that when built in 1859 were described as "something between a Dutch toy and a Chinese pagoda." It is a description particularly apt at night when over 3,000 lights outline the building and add a touch of fantasy for strollers along the harbor's boardwalk.

The highly rated **Royal British Columbia Museum**, just a few hundred feet away, charts the province's human and natural history. It has a priceless collection of Northwest Coast Aboriginal art and dioramas on their way of life. A much smaller museum displays the works of Canada's best known female artist, Emily Carr. The museum has been named the Emily Carr Gallery in her honor. A former gravel pit has been transformed into a floral wonderland. This is the **Butchart Gardens** which is 20 km away. It is a magnificent mixture of shrubs, trees and flowers, including a Japanese garden, an Italian garden, and rose gardens.

The unusual architecture and front facades
of the market square fascinate these children.

Nature has a lot to offer fishermen at the northern part of Vancouver Island.

Vancouver Island

The civility of Victoria disappears as you go further north into fishing hamlets and wild, mountainous interior. Heavy rainfalls produce rain forests as dense as it is along the Amazon. From **Port Alberni**, you can take a ship or drive along twisting roads winding west to one of the province's jewels, the **Pacific Rim National Park**.

The park has three very distinct sections. At **Long Beach**, surfers take advantage of the huge waves crashing into the smooth hard-packed sand, strewn with gnarled pieces of driftwood. A narrow 11 km-strip of land framed by mountains, Long Beach lies between **Tofino** and **Ucluelet**, villages where you can join whale-watching expeditions for close-up views of the approximately 20,000 whales that annually migrate past here on their way to the **Bering Sea** in March and April and to Mexico in late September.

A favorite of experienced canoeists is the **Broken Group Islands**. These 100 islands, habitat of seals and sea lions, can only be reached by boat. The **West Coast Trail** is a demanding 72-km trail of bogs and rainforest which is often rain-soaked.

Recreational Activities

Fishermen head to the northern part of

Moss covered trees along the West Coast Trail reveal an unearthly charm.

the island, on the **Campbell River**, for salmon weighing up to 10 kg. Like many of the fishing areas in British Columbia, the only way in is by plane or boat. Another fish that lures people into British Columbia is rainbow trout, particularly in the trout-teeming lakes of the **Thompson-Nicola** region on the high central plateau. More easily accessible are the lakes in the **Kootenay** region in southeastern B.C. where caviar-producing sturgeon grow to 600 kg.

British Columbia's climate and topography makes it an outdoor paradise for all types of recreational activities. Boats can be rented to sail or cruise the coast. **Squamish** calls itself the windsurfing and rock climbing capital of Canada. At **Porteau Cove Marine** Park, not far from Vancouver, scuba divers can explore three sunken ships or dive around the **Gulf Islands**, home to brilliant orange sea cucumbers and abalone. The Gulf Islands, lying on the ferry route between Vancouver and Victoria, are populated by many art and craft people. Hikers and climbers have a wide choice of mountains. British Columbia's Rocky mountains include Canada's highest, 3,956 m **Mount Robson**.

White-water rafts bounce down the **North Thomson River** and along the Fraser River. At **Hell's Gate**, tramcars take passengers directly above the turbulent 34.4 m gorge of the Fraser River.

Whistler

An Alpine-village at the base of two mountains has been voted the number one North American ski resort by *Snow Country* magazine the last two years in a row. The chic **Whistler Resort**, about 2 hours outside of the north of Vancouver, attracts an international clientele. Over 200 varied runs cover its two mountains, **Whistler** and **Blackcomb**. Blackcomb alone provides 1,600 m of continuous skiing – the highest rise served by lifts in North America. In the summer, heli-skiing companies take skiers to the glacial mountain tops.

Vancouver

Vancouver may be Canada's third larg-

The Minter gardens are an outdoor treat for the family.

est city, but its setting between the Pacific Ocean and majestic mountains leapfrogs it into the ranks of the world's most beautiful cities.

Named after Captain George Vancouver, the British officer who surveyed the land in 1792, the city only started to grow when coal and timber were discovered in the mid-1800s. Once the Canadian government promised a rail link to the rest of Canada, the colony joined Canada and Vancouver has blossomed into the west's most sophisticated city.

The most impressive heritage left by the early settlers is **Stanley Park**. Set aside in 1886, this 400-ha oceanfront oasis of trees and playgrounds is on the edge of downtown Vancouver. Surrounded by beaches, this restful retreat is also the site of the huge **Vancouver Public Aquarium**.

Within sight of the distinctive white-sails roof of Canada Place, built for Vancouver's hosting of the 1986 World's Fair, Expo 86, is **Gastown**. Cobbled sidewalks, gaslamps and charming old buildings converted into boutiques and restaurants mark this original site of Vancouver, named after "Gassy Jack" Deighton who built a saloon here to serve sawmill workers.

Chinatown

Within walking distance is **Chinatown**. Its wide streets make Chinatown appear less frenetic than its counterpart in

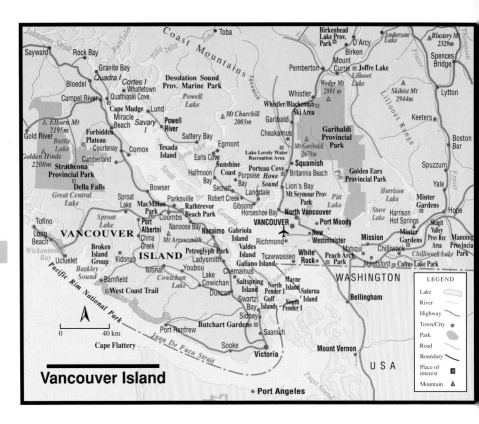

Vancouver Island

LEGEND

Lake
River
Highway
Town/City
Park
Road
Boundary
Place of interest
Mountain

USA

Toronto, yet it is the third largest in North America.

For a peaceful moment away from the restaurants and shops, head to the **Dr. Sun Yat-Sen Classical Chinese Garden**. The only authentic classical Chinese garden outside of China was constructed by artisans from China. Its ornately decorated arched garden 'gazebos', in the Oriental style, convey a uniquely Eastern atmosphere.

The lush garden setting complements this ornately classical structure. A visit soothes the senses with its tranquil pond, handcarved mahogany pavillion, and rocks and pebbles turned into works of art.

Sites Of Interest On The North Coast

Across **English Bay**, on the picturesque ocean-side campus of the **University of British Columbia (U.B.C.)**, the renowned Vancouver architect Arthur Erickson created the glass and concrete **U.B.C. Museum of Anthropology**. Totem poles and large wooden carvings are among the extensive collection of Northwest Coast Native artifacts.

Before returning to downtown Vancouver, either take a ferry or drive to **Granville Island**, a bustling maze of charming craft and art galleries, thea-

Eau de violet cascades silkily down at Derek Falls.

tres, a market and restaurants. There are several items which are affordable.

Underneath Vancouver's skyscrapers is the city's 1910 neoclassical courthouse, home to the Vancouver Art Gallery and a good collection of the works of Emily Carr.

Grouse Mountain, the northshore mountains dominating the skyline, offers another panoramic view of Vancouver once you take the Skyride 1,128 m to the top. Night skiing in winter is a unique experience as you traverse down the mountain with Vancouver's lights

Asian Settlements in Vancouver

The 77-log bridge at Vancouver's Asian settlement.

Long before other cities in Canada had any sizeable Asian community, Vancouver was home to the Japanese, Chinese, and East Indians, predominantly Sikhs. There was a natural result of the province's dependence on these immigrants. Over 100,000 Chinese were imported to build the transcontinental railway in the 1880s. Japanese and East Indians were brought to work in fishing and logging.

But it wasn't an easy life for these early immigrants. They faced discrimination, were paid less than white workers, and forced to live in ghettos. An influx of Japanese in 1907 caused residents of Vancouver to riot, a protest that embarrassed the Canadian government which recompensed Japanese losses. But, at the same time, the government negotiated an agreement with Japan to limit immigration into Canada. In 1923, the government banned Chinese immigration. During World War II, even second and third generation Japanese were rounded up and sent to live elsewhere in Canada, away from the coast.

It wasn't until 1967 that the government removed immigration restrictions based on racial origins. Vancouver's location as the closest Canadian city to the Pacific Rim countries, and its climate made the city a natural destination for Asians. After 1967, Chinatown expanded dramatically with stores, restaurants, theatres, and community organizations setting up shop in both new and heritage buildings. Structures were erected in the early 1900s with typically Chinese architecture of recessed balconies and decorative railings. On weekends, this third largest Chinatown in North America, after San Francisco and New York City, is thronged with shoppers.

There's a small **Japantown**, on nearby **Powell Street**, with grocery stores, fish stores and restaurants. **Little India**, on **Main Street** between 48th and 51st Avenues, has shops selling spices, saris, and restaurants. The majority of Asians, however, live scattered throughout Vancouver. The suburb of **Richmond** at **Aberdeen Center**, which is owned by a Hong Kong family, lays claim to the title of having North America's largest Asian mall.

Asia accounts for about two-thirds of Vancouver's recent immigrants. And signs of their presence are everywhere. At the University of B.C., a leading Japanese landscape architect designed the beautiful **Nitobe Memorial Gardens** with flowering cherry trees, restful bowers and Japanese maples.

In South Vancouver, a silver filigree onion dome glitters above a white Sikh temple. A red

shimmering at your feet.

South of the skyride is the **Capilano Suspension Bridge**, spanning 140 m across a river canyon at a height of 71.9 m. This awesome walk takes you across the longest and highest suspended foot-

British Columbia's famous
market square.

The Lions Gate Bridge.

and gold decorated Chinese Buddhist temple was installed in Richmond. Many of the immigrants from Hong Kong are from wealthy families insuring a retreat when China takes over the colony in 1997. Along with the Japanese, they've invested millions in Vancouver, buying businesses and buildings.

Vancouver's largest ethnic and cultural festival is **The Powell Street Festival**, which is dedicated to the history, arts and culture of Asian Canadians. Another event, the **Canadian International Dragon Boat Festival** in June, pits dragon boat teams from all over the world in the competition to win the Canadian International Championship.

bridge in the world to **Capilano River Regional Park**.

Its rugged trails direct hikers along

the granite cliffs that line the canyon. The steep granite cliffs are a constant temptation to climbers.

Interior B.C.

Convoluted highways to the east lead through sagebrush country to B.C.'s fruit belt, the **Okanagan Valley**. Orchards and vineyards are stretched along the string of valleys punctuated by lakes and rivers.

If you miss the **Okanagan Wine Festival** in early October, 11 wineries in this fertile region offer tours. Cattle and sheep ranching are mainly in Cariboo country, south-central B.C.

In the lush forests and valleys of the

Whistler has been voted the number one North American ski resort.

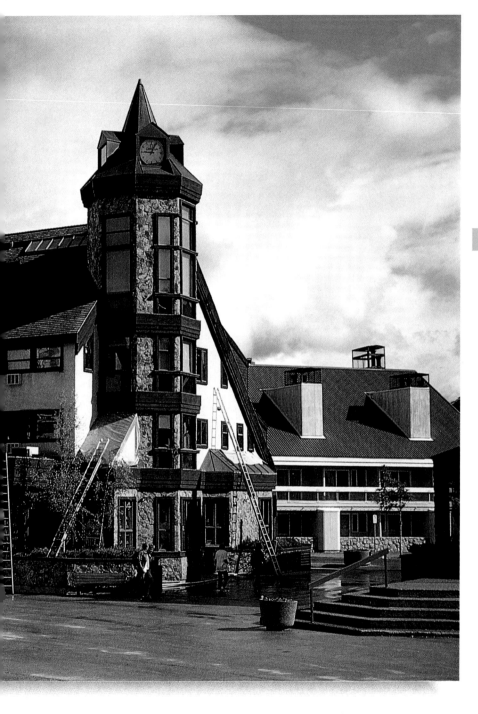

Oriental splendor at Dr Sun Yat-Sen Classical Chinese Garden.

A clown entertains the lunch-time crowd at the "Gassy Jack" Deighton statue.

The Capilano Suspension Bridge stretches to 140 m.

Kootenay region is **Castlegar** where the **Doukhobor Heritage Village** duplicates the communal lifestyle of these Russian pacifists who lived here until the 1930s. The heritage town of **Nelson** celebrates its roots as a silver and iron mining town in the late 1800s by preserving over 350 buildings in a picturesquely appealing setting on **Kootenay Lake** amidst the steep **Selkirk Mountains**.

  Barkerville is a restored 1870s gold rush town with board sidewalks and dirt streets where you can try your hand panning for gold and watch melodramas of the period. Of the thousands who mined the Fraser River and the Cariboo, about one third made fortunes, one third made some profit, and the remainder were totally ruined.

Deflection of one of Vancouver's skyscrapers.

The stetson is still proudly worn in Alberta, even if it's only for special occasions. This cowboy hat recalls the frontier days, the era of rugged individualism – the spirit responsible for, at times, pitting Alberta against the Federal government.

Alberta's oil and gas deposits, the richest in Canada, has been the source of much of the friction between the fiercely independent Albertans and the Canadian government. On an individual basis, however, the people are friendly and welcoming, both in the countryside and in the cities.

Most Albertans live in either Edmonton or Calgary. The sparsely populated rural area encompasses a breathtaking diversity, a semi-arid south where dinosaurs once roamed, rich farmland with vast wheat fields and cattle ranches, a northern wilderness and, of course, what Alberta is best known for – the spectacular **Rocky Mountains**.

The lyrical beauty of Banff's Bow River Valley.

Alberta

219

Calgary

Calgary originated in 1875 as a North-West Mounted Police post

Two 'conversing statues' at Alberta's downtown shopping mall.

intended to curb the illegal whisky trade at this Indian campsite on the confluence of the Bow and Elbow Rivers.

Ranchers in search of better grazing land also gravitated to this area, earning Calgary its nickname, **cowtown**. This heritage is celebrated in early July at the **Calgary Stampede**, a non-stop 10-day party, highlighted by a rodeo.

Cowboys still continue to herd cattle at Alberta's huge ranches, but it was the oil boom which brought an influx of Americans and American oil companies. They greatly influenced Calgary's emergence as an energetic, glass and steel, modern metropolis.

The revolving restaurant and the observation deck at the top of the 190-m **Calgary Tower** downtown affords a panoramic view of the city, the treeless surrounding plains, the snow-capped peaks of the Rockies and the distinctive saddle-shaped roof of the **Olympic Saddledome**, built when Calgary hosted the 1988 Winter Olympics.

The outstanding museum in Calgary is the **Glenbow Museum** with its historical displays, including an excellent array of Albertan Indian and Inuit clothing and carvings.

Heritage Park, Canada's largest historical village, a short distance from downtown, immerses visitors in pioneer life with over 100 restored buildings and exhibits, which authentically portray an 1880 settlement, a 1910 town and the Banff Mounted Police barracks.

The large **Calgary Zoo**, straddling

Chinatown's cultural center.

the **Bow River**, takes you even further back in time. The **Prehistory Park** returns you to the days when dinosaurs lived in Alberta.

Calgary to Banff

The major gateway to the Rockies is Calgary. The 120-km drive west along the **Trans-Canada Highway** passes another legacy of the 1988 Winter Games. On the edge of the city is **Canada Olympic Park**, where you can see the ski jump, bobsled track, and a film showing the footage of historical Winter games at the **Olympic Hall of Fame**.

In the foothills of the Rockies is **Kananaskis Country**, an outdoor recreation center usually bypassed by people anxious to reach Banff. Yet, within this area sports enthusiasts will find many of the same activities: horseback riding, hiking, and skiing – both at **Nakkiska**, developed for the 1988 Olympic alpine events, or on the much smaller and easier slopes of **Fortress Mountain**. Want to sleep in a teepee? **Sundance Lodges** has hand-painted *Sioux*-style teepees set in secluded sites near the **Kananaskis River**.

The Rocky Mountains are Alberta's top tourist attraction and it's not hard to understand why. The spectacular scenery combines towering peaks, multicolored lakes, rivers, treed valleys, and flower-coated meadows through which elk, bears, moose and other animals

Skiing at Nakkiska.

freely roam.

Banff

Banff is the most popular destination in the Rockies. Despite the flock of people, during summer at the peak of the tourism season, Banff maintains the characteristics of an alpine village, helped by its location, cramped between mountains, and by building restrictions. The height of the chalets and buildings along its main street is limited. **Banff Avenue** is packed with restaurants and boutiques, many displaying signs "We speak Japanese," a reflection of the huge number of visitors from Japan.

Across the bridge at the end of Banff

Avenue, past a replica of a fur trading post, is the **Luxton Indian Museum**, which exhibits dioramas of Indian life. The Cave and Basin hot springs is also situated here. Originally, it was a peace meeting site for Indian tribes. After its discovery by white men in 1883, disputes arose over ownership and the government stepped in to mediate. They resolved the dispute by creating Canada's first national park, **Banff National Park**. The stone building surrounding the mineral-rich waters have been restored to its 1914 appearance. Even the swim suits for rent are replicas from that era.

Southwest of the bridge, looking like a Scottish baronial castle, stands the **Banff Springs Hotel** in splendid isolation. The terrace restaurant of this hotel built in 1888 has a great view of the glacial-green Bow River and the snow-capped mountains.

Higher up the road is **Sulphur Mountain** where an eight-minute gondola ride whisks riders to the 2,285 m summit with its birds-eye view of the Bow and Banff Valley. Competing with the view are bighorn sheep roaming around the summit. Wear a jacket if Banff feels chilly because it's probably snowing around the summit, even in July and August.

To reach the legendary **Lake Louise**, take either the more scenic but slower **Bow Valley Parkway** or the **Trans-Canada Highway**. A detour from the highway leads to a five-km gondola ride past waterfalls, canyons and sheer

Banff Springs Hotel – a fairy tale-like castle.

mountain face up to **Sunshine Village**, the highest ski resort in Canada. From there, a chairlift goes to the 2,400 m peak where 20 km of trails wind through meadows strewn with alpine flowers. The last ice carved the mountains into towering peaks and dug deep basins that when melted, created lakes of which the most beautiful is Lake Louise.

The emerald-green Lake Louise backed by glacier-draped mountains could be a fairy tale setting, complete with a storybook castle, **Chateau Lake Louise**. The **Lake Louise Gondola Lift** gives an unparalleled view of the area as well as the opportunity to hike trails surrounded by alpine flowers.

The Icefields Parkway to Jasper is a mind-boggling scenic drive through the Rockies highest and most rugged mountains, waterfalls, canyons and glaciers. The Columbia Icefields is worth a stop. This is where *snocoachs* take groups onto the 325-sq-km area of ice. **Athabasca glacier** was formed from snow falling as long as 400 years ago.

Jasper

Fewer tourists visit Jasper than Banff, partly because it is more remote from a big city. The village has a low-key atmosphere without all the expensive boutiques of Banff and tourists spilling into the streets. Even the mountains play their role by appearing less intimidating because they're further back from

Calgary at dusk.

the village than in Banff. The Whistlers' mountain, reached by the **Jasper Tramway**, Canada's longest and highest cablecar ride, gives a spectacular view of the town, the giant peaks and deep blue lakes.

Many people consider the variety of ski runs, from beginner to expert slopes, at nearby **Marmot Basin** better than those at Banff. In the summer the pre-eminent activity is hiking to such beauty spots as **Maligne Canyon**, the Rockies's longest gorge where you might see a bear, sheep, deer and moose.

Stop also for a boatride or chance to match wits against the fighting trout at **Lake Maligne**. Since Jasper sits in the middle of the home range of an elk herd, these animals frequently wander through the town.

Edmonton

Edmonton was named capital of Alberta because it's smack in the middle of the province, straddling the fertile farmlands in central Alberta and the vast, resource-rich northern hinterland.

The city grew up around the North Saskatchewan River which winds its way past miles of parkland in the valley under a bluff lined with skyscrapers.

Edmonton's northerly location – meaning long cold winters – has made it a city of malls and, fittingly enough, Edmonton is home to the world's largest indoor mall. The West Edmonton Mall,

Calgary Stampede

The Calgary Stampede is a riotous, rollicking celebration.

A vaudeville trick roper staged a pioneer day in 1912 that's grown to become what Calgary calls "the greatest outdoor show on earth." The 10-day celebration in the middle of July is when residents and visitors alike don stetsons, jeans, western shirts, and cowboy boots, and let down their inhibitions for a non-stop party that recalls the romance of the wild west.

The combination **Exhibition and Stampede** kicks off with a colorful parade of marching bands, native people in traditional dress, cowboys and cowgirls, and decorated floats. The nightly $2^1/_2$ hour **Grandstand** show always starts with **The World Championship Chuck Wagon Races** where chuck wagons follow the cattle drives, carrying the food and cookware to feed the cowboys. The four-horses chuck wagons speed against each other in a dangerous half-mile race, followed by a stage show of song, dance, comedy and variety.

The highlight of the Stampede is the daily **Half Million Dollar Rodeo** held in the afternoons at **Stampede Park**. In this display of unabashed machismo, riders try to stay on bucking broncos and vicious Brahma bulls. Other events promising cash prizes are calf-roping, wild cow milking, and Indian buffalo riding.

Wander through an Indian village set up on the grounds of Stampede Park, where there's also a western town, championship livestock shows, a blacksmiths' competition, a casino, stage shows, and a midway with plenty of rides.

Each morning during the Stampede, city officials fry up free flapjack and pancakes breakfasts to dispense from chuckwagons set up in different locations in Calgary.

The festivities continue throughout the day with square dancing on the streets and mini-parades. In the hotels and saloons, bars continue the western theme, playing country and western music that always has the effect of propelling dancers onto their feet.

An idyllic boat ride at Lake Louise.

a combination mall and amusement park, has more than 800 stores and 19 movie theatres that sustain attractions for nearly every age and interest. These include a 2-ha water park with 22 waterslides, a triple-loop roller coaster, bungee jumping, a skating rink, various animals and marine life, such as live dolphin shows, sharks, penguins, a life-size replica of Christopher Columbus' *Santa Maria*, a bingo hall and a casino. If that's not enough to amuse you, there's also a hotel in the mall with some rooms decorated in motifs ranging from Classical Rome, to an Igloo.

Fort Edmonton dominated the western fur trade and a full-scale replica of this 1846 huge wooden fortification lies in **Fort Edmonton Park**. The park also depicts the city's growth with roads leading past buildings representing the years 1885, 1905 and 1920.

The **Ukrainian Cultural Heritage Village**, about 53 km east on Hwy. 16, portrays the turn-of-the-century homes, lifestyle and traditions of the Ukrainian settlers, Alberta's largest non-British immigrant group.

In July, Edmontonians dress up in 1890s garments for **Klondike Days**, a celebration of Edmonton's burst of prosperity during the Yukon gold rush. Thousands of people bought supplies here before heading to find their dreams of wealth in the Klondike. Many of those same people returned to Edmonton broke and disillusioned.

A long-lasting boom occurred in

Jasper National Park is a treat for animal lovers.

1947 when black crude oil gushed from the **Leduc Number One Well** about 40 km southwest of Edmonton and gave the city the title of "**Oil Capital of Canada.**" While the first oil in Alberta was found rather close to Calgary, the majority of wells are now within 60 km of Edmonton.

Most oil companies have their head office in Calgary, while Edmonton is technology-based. Fluctuating oil prices have forced both cities to attract other investments and helped spur the intense rivalry between Edmonton and the slightly smaller populated Calgary. Oil has supplanted agriculture as the dominant source of Alberta's economy. At **Fort McMurray** in northern Alberta, the **Oil Sands Interpretative Center** illustrates the history and innovative technology used to extract this black gold from the **Athabascan Tar Sands**, considered the world's largest oil deposit.

The South

Around **Drumheller**, northwest of Calgary, wind and water have carved Badlands, an eerie landscape of heavily scarred bluffs, mushroom-shaped *hoodoos* or rock pillars and deep gullies. When the area was swamp and marshland 70 million years ago, dinosaurs reigned here. The **Royal Tyrell Museum of Palaeotology** has one of the world's largest collection of dinosaur remains, from nests intact with

Giant chairs at Edmonton bring one right onto the mountains.

eggs to full-grown dinosaurs.

More complete skeletons have been found at **Dinosaur Provincial Park** than anywhere else in the world. Trails through this UNESCO-designated World Heritage Site led to the discovery of preserved dinosaur bones.

South of Calgary, through the rolling grasslands flourishing with wheat and other crops that partially account for Alberta contributing 20 percent of Canada's agricultural output, detour from Hwy 2 onto 785 to reach **Head-Smashed-In Buffalo Jump**, where the Plains Indians stampeded herds of buffalo over the cliff and then used their remains for food and clothing. Native guides explain the lifestyle and customs of these Indians.

Return to Hwy 2 south to **Fort Macleod**, Alberta's oldest settlement, a town that has preserved many of its architecturally interesting old buildings. Inside the North-West Mounted Police fort, costumed guides give visitors a sense of life in and around the fort for the Mounties, the Indians and the pioneers.

Further East

Further east at **Lethbridge Indian Battle Park**, where the Blackfoot and Cree fought one of the area's last great Indian battles, is **Fort Whoop-Up**, legendary as the major whisky American trading post with the Indians. The **Nikka Yuko Japanese Gardens**, built in 1967 as a

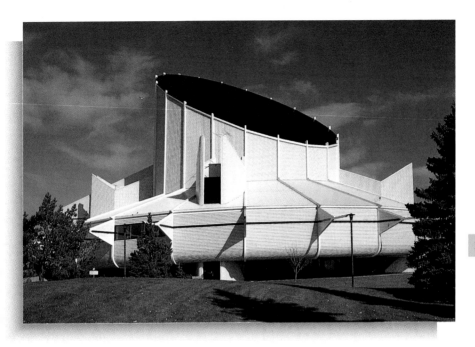

Edmonton's famous Space and Science Center.

friendship center, is a soothing meditative park of water, rocks, and green shrubs, and a stark contrast to the first Japanese community in Lethbridge. They were interred here during World War II when the Canadian government forcibly moved anyone of Japanese ancestry from the west coast.

From Lethbridge, drive past **Cardston**, the first Mormon settlement in Canada, to **Waterton Lakes National Park**. Situated in the Rockies near the Montana border, this beautiful park has 183 km of hiking and wildlife-spotting trails, scenic boat cruises across the border and many other activities.

A "must-see" is **Red Rock Canyon**, with its rusting iron deposits in the earth which colored the rocks red.

An Indian staying near Fort Whoop-Up.

As the central Prairie province, Saskatchewan lives up to the image of seemingly endless wide open spaces filled with vistas of grain only interrupted by brightly painted grain elevators against one of the bluest skies you'll ever see. It is a panorama unlike the nearly uninhabited northern half of the province, a wilderness of forests and thousands of glacial lakes and rivers.

It is the fertile nearly flat plains of the south that has shaped the people and the province – land that the Métis under Louis Riel fought for in the last military conflict on Canadian soil, the North West Rebellion of 1885. After their defeat, the Canadian government mounted a huge advertising campaign that brought settlers by the thousands across the Atlantic.

Drought and crop failure along with the depression in the 1930s badly hurt the farmers, but they remained on their farms. Their tenacity kept them going on as did their willingness to help each other and

Saskatchewan

231

A prairie dweller re-lives his triumphant past through the hard won badges of his youth.

The prairies are mostly composed of flat plains that seem to go on endlessly.

work together, a spirit still evident in their hospitality and warm-heartedness.

Regina

In the midst of the flat plains, **Regina** suddenly pops out of the landscape. Back in the days when it was called **Pile O'Bones**, you would have seen a huge pile of buffalo bones, left by generations of Indians. Renamed in honor of Queen Victoria and made the capital, after the railroad came through, Regina has become a graceful, tree-lined small city with an onion-domed Legislature regally sitting surrounded by formal gardens in **Wascana Park**.

Regina's cultural and recreational activities center around the 930-ha Wascana Park, one of the largest urban parks in the world.

It was developed around a muddy creek – the only body of water around – that was dammed to make Wascana Lake, the focus of this marvellous park, which has a bird sanctuary, mainly populated by the Canada Goose, horsedrawn carriage rides, and, Can $2.00 ferry rides take picnickers to **Willow Island**.

Buildings in the park include the **Museum of Natural History**, with dioramas in its new **First Nations Gallery** that bring alive, with sounds, smells, and dialogue, the history and the life of the province's Indians. The struggle of the Plains Indians, the clashes

The Mounty with his horse is probably the most famous symbol of Canada.

with the British and the eventual formation of the First Nations is retold with vigour and charity. The **MacKenzie Art Gallery** is an excellent showcase of western Canadian art and also where the *Trial of Louis Riel* is staged in the middle of the summer. One of the longest running shows in Canada, this play re-enacts the dramatic events surrounding Louis Riel's capture after the North West Rebellion of 1885.

The troops that defeated Riel and his ragtag army included members of the North West Mounted Police, or as

Saskatchewan's palatial provincial legislature building.

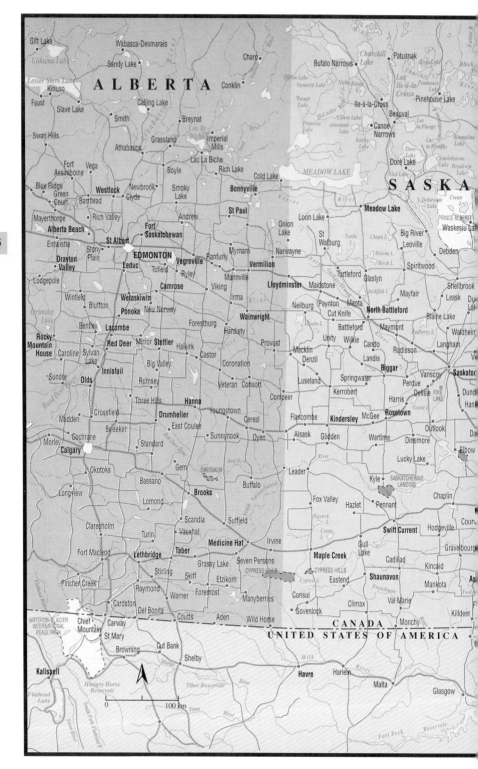

SASKATCHEWAN

ALBERTA

SASKA

SASKATCHEWAN

Gift Lake
Wabasca-Desmarais
Charo
Bufalo Narrows
Patuanak
Churchill Lake
Ulkuna Lake
Lesser Slave Lake
Kinuso
Sandy Lake
Conklin
Dillon Lake
Vermette Lake
Nisku Kaoan
Lac Ile-à-la-Crosse
Pinehouse Lake
Faust
Slave Lake
Calling Lake
Watapi Lake
Ile-à-la-Cross
Pinehouse Lake
Smith
Breynat
McCusker
Canoe Lake
Beauval
Swan Hills
Grassland
Imperial Mills
Primrose Lake
Arsenault Lake
Canoe Narrows
Lac la Plonge
Athabasca
Lac La Biche
Keeley Lake
Fort Assiniboine
Vega
Boyle
Rich Lake
Cold Lake
MEADOW LAKE
Doré Lake
Sled Lake
Smoothstone Lake
Wapawekka Lake
Blue Ridge
Green Court
Westlock
Newbrook
Smoky Lake
Bonnyville
SASKA
Crean Lake
Barrhead
Clyde
Meadow Lake
Delaronde Lake
PRINCE ALBERT
Mayerthorpe
Rich Valley
St Paul
Loon Lake
Waskesiu Lak
Alberta Beach
Fort Saskatchewan
Andrew
Onion Lake
St Walburg
Turtle L.
Chitek L.
Big River
Leoville
Debden
Entwistle
Stony Plain
St Albert
EDMONTON
Narwayne
Helene L.
Spiritwood
Drayton Valley
Leduc
Vegreville
Ranfurly
Myrnard
Vermilion
Neg L.
Tortleford
Glaslyn
Birch L.
Lodgepole
Tofield
Ryley
Mannville
Lloydminster
Maidstone
Jackfish L.
Mayfair
Shellbrook
Winfield
Camrose
Viking
Irma
Neilburg
Paynton
Meota
North Battleford
Leask
Du Lak
Bluffton
Wetaskiwin
New Norway
Wainwright
Cut Knife
Blaine Lake
Bentley
Ponoka
Forestburg
Hardisty
Battleford
Maymont
Waldhei
Rocky Mountain House
Lacombe
Red Deer
Mirror Stettler
Halkirk
Castor
Provost
Unity
Wilkie
Cando
Radisson
Langham
Caroline
Sylvan Lake
Big Valley
Coronation
Macklin
Denzil
Landis
Biggar
Vanscoy
Saskato
Innisfail
Olds
Rumsey
Veteran
Consort
Luseland
Springwater
Perdue
Delisle
Dund
Sundre
Three Hills
Hanna
Youngstown
Compeer
Kerrobert
Harris
Rosetown
Han
Madden
Crossfield
Drumheller
Cereal
Flaxcombe
Kindersley
McGee
Goose L
Cochrane
Beiseker
East Coulee
Sunnynook
Oyen
Alsask
Glidden
Wartime
Outlook
Da
Morley
Calgary
Standard
Lucky Lake
Elbow
Okotoks
Gem
DINOSAUR
Red D
Leader
River
Bassano
Buffalo
Kyle
SASKATCHEWAN LANDING
Chaplin
Longview
Lomond
Fox Valley
Hazlet
Pennant
Claresholm
Scandia
Vauxhal
Suffield
Bigstick L.
Swift Current
Hodgeville
Cour
Turin
Medicine Hat
Irvine
Crane L.
Gull Lake
Gravelbourg
Fort Macleod
Lethbridge
Taber
Maple Creek
Cadilad
Kincaid
Pincher Creek
Stirling
Grassy Lake
Seven Persons
CYPRESS HILLS
Eastend
Shaunavon
Mankota
As
Raymond
Skiff
Etzikom
Cypress L.
Frenchman
Twelv
Cardston
Warner
Foremost
Manyberries
Consul
Val Marie
Del Bonita
Coutts
Aden
Wild Horse
Govenlock
Climax
Killdeer
WATERTON-GLACIER INTERNATIONAL PEACE PARK
Chief Mountain
Carway
St Mary
CANADA
Monchy
Browning
Cut Bank
Shelby
UNITED STATES OF AMERICA
Kalispell
Hungry Horse Reservoir
Shelby
Milk
Flathead Lake
Tiber Reservoir
River
Havre
Harlem
Malta
Glasgow
Fort Peck
Reservoir

0   100 km

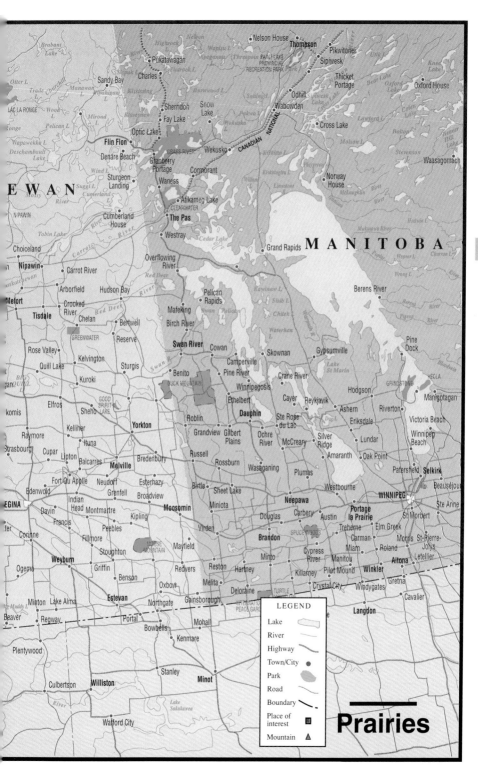

MANITOBA

Prairies

LEGEND
- Lake
- River
- Highway
- Town/City
- Park
- Road
- Boundary
- Place of interest
- Mountain ▲

The Big Muddy Badlands which used to be a favorite spot for outlaws.

they're better known today, the Royal Canadian Mounted Police (RCMP).

With their red jackets, gleaming horses and stetson hats, the Mounties are probably the most famous, photographed symbol of Canada.

Every new recruit spends six months at Regina's RCMP Training Academy where the official **RCMP Centennial Museum** has mementos from its dealings with Sitting Bull and Riel and other artifacts which trace the history of this police force created to keep law and order among the settlers, the Indians and the Métis in the prairie provinces.

Try to be on the RCMP grounds around 12:45 p.m. when recruits march in the **Sergeant Major's Parade** from Monday to Friday. On Tuesdays in the summer, they perform the stirring **RCMP Sunset Retreat Ceremony.**

Regina Retreats

A popular resort area northeast of Regina is the beautiful **Qu'Appelle Valley,** a lush, green valley with a series of lakes and attractive villages, such as **Fort Qu'Appelle.** The original 1864 **Hudson Bay Company** trading post is joined to a museum stocking relics of its trading days as well as Indian artifacts.

Southeast of Regina is an island of forest in the middle of the prairies. **Moose Mountain Provincial Park** is a huge natural refuge for beavers, bald eagles and numerous birds, along which exist

Prehistoric Indian carvings at St Victor Petroglyphs Provincial Historical Park.

a beach, waterslides, golf course, and horseback riding.

Cannington Manor Provincial Historic Park reveals the sojourn of an eccentric British colony. In 1880, Captain Edward Pierce bought a huge tract of land cheaply and, after building himself a mansion, sold some of the remainder to other wealthy English who imported foxhounds, played cricket and held fancy dress balls. After 15 years of trying to duplicate life in England, the colony failed.

The Badlands

In the days of the wild west, the **Big Muddy Badlands,** south of Regina, were a favorite hiding spot for American horse thieves and stagecoach robbers. This rugged and forbidding landscape of windswept sandstone buttes and rounded hills conceal canyons and gulches that made it an ideal hideout for outlaws like Butch Cassidy. Cassidy laid out an escape route from Canada to Mexico, known as the "Outlaw Trail." Station Number 1 of the trail was near **Big Beaver** in these badlands. Tours from Coronach travel the area, pointing out such sights as the caves used by the Nelson-Jones gang, caves that were originally wolf dens.

Etched into the sandstone cliff at nearby **St. Victor Petroglyphs Provincial Historical Park** are prehistoric Indian carvings of faces, animal tracks

Homes on the Prairies

Prairie dwellers in their home.

Battleford's Heritage Farm and Village. The street also has a bank, Co-op store, and other homes including a working farm where hired hands actually still use equipment and techniques from the 1920s.

A large appropriately furnished 1904 turreted house in Grenfell, gives an idea of how the more wealthy lived as do the homes of upper class British at Cannington Manor Provincial Historic Park. The various ethnic groups often congregated in the same area and built homes in the same style. Mormons first settled in 1887 at Cardston, Alberta, where the founder's one-story log house still stands. Mennonites originally erected sod houses lengthy enough to accommodate livestock as well as people, as can be seen at the Mennonite village museum in Steinbach, Manitoba. This is a tradition they continue to this day by adjoining barns to their wooden homes, enabling them to do their chores without going outside. These homes were built to last: logs were squared, then joined with oak pines to make a solid, long-lasting wall. Bales of straw piled against the house provided insulation.

Houses built by the *Hutterites* were larger, since they were shared by two or more families. A house would have a separate living space for each family and one large dining hall where everybody ate all their meals.

Distinctive Slavic designs and decor exemplified the *Doukhobours's* wooden homes, although the home occupied by the leader Peter Veregin in 1917 is an impressive three-story wooden house with Victorian trim on its exterior pillars. This house, a bathhouse and several other buildings can still be seen at Veregin, Saskatchewan.

"Buy 160 acres of prairie land for $10" – that advertisement brought over 2 million immigrants to the prairies between 1896 and 1913. Many were peasant farmers from the poverty-stricken plains of central and eastern Europe who came without any money. Some, like the English cockneys led by Reverend Barr, lacked basic skills such as the construction of tents supplied by the Immigration department. This was about the only help offered to newcomers.

The government added one stipulation: settlers had to build a house within three years. As soon as they claimed their land, the settlers gathered whatever material they could find to build homes as quickly as possible, not only to meet the government deadline but also to weather the harsh prairie winters when snow could completely blanket a home.

The first homes often had walls made from bricks of sod on frames of scarce poplar or willow with canvas covering the windows. A recreated sod hut is located in the **Regina Plains Museum**.

Some built tarpaper shacks. When timber was available, log cabins were built. The **Heritage Cultural Center** at **Lloydminster** tells the story of Barr and his colony and displays a log cabin furnished in early 20th century style.

The Ukrainians livened their log homes by painting the clay plaster in bright colours. An Ukrainian home with a thatched roof is part of the 1920s prairie town recreated at **North**

The Trans Canadian Highway cuts through the barren prairies.

and footprints.

To evade the large military force being gathered in the United States to avenge Colonel George Custer's death and the defeat of five regiments at the Battle of Little Big Horn, Chief Sitting Bull and 5,000 followers scampered across the border to the grasslands of **Wood Mountain**. For five years, they lived here until dwindling food supplies forced them to return to the United States. The **Wood Mountain Post Historic Site** recaptures that era with displays and two reconstructed Mountie posts from 1874-1918. This is ranching territory and the **Wood Mountain Rodeo and Ranching Museum** conjures up the old west with models of bunkhouses, an adobe building and ranch scenes. In July, present-day cowboys and cowgirls ride broncking bulls at Canada's oldest continuous rodeo.

After **Grasslands National Park**, a preserve of shortgrass prairie land, badlands and river valleys populated by rattlesnakes and prairie dogs, you reach **Cypress Hills Interprovincial Park** on the border with Alberta. In the middle of the prairies, deer, elk and lynx roam freely among the park's forested hills, the highest point of land between Labrador and the Rockies. This was "Whoop-Up" country, where whisky was illegally traded for buffalo hides. Liquor was the major cause of the Cypress Hills Massacre of 1873. The slaughter of 20 Indians by American whisky traders and wolf hunters brought the Mounties who

Saskatoon – the economic hub of Saskatchewan.

patrolled this area from Fort Walsh. Along with the reconstructed fort is **Farwell's trading post**, one of the so-called whisky posts.

Heading back towards Regina along the Trans-Canada Highway, the road travels through prime ranch land and the "old cowtown of Maple Creek," with its 19th-century historical storefronts.

Historical murals splashed on buildings in **Moose Jaw** recalls some of this town's colorful past. During the American prohibition, liquor was bootlegged from Moose Jaw to the United States

since World War II because the nature of farming has been changed. It has inevitably become less dependent on labor and more reliant on capital. Agriculture, however, remains the main industry with Saskatchewan farmers producing about 60 percent of Canada's wheat as well as other grains and cattle ranching. More recently, the province has benefited from natural gas, crude oil and other natural resources.

Saskatoon

The American Prohibition would certainly have pleased the first settlers of Saskatoon, a temperance colony from Ontario, although the newest attraction, **Wanuskewin Heritage Park**, pays homage to the original inhabitants who camped along these buffalo hunting grounds for over 5,000 years. About 8 km of trails connect the 19 archaeological sites, teepees, and a log buffalo pound used to ambush these large animals. To really absorb the culture, try its restaurant specializing in authentic Northern Plains food, including the staple of natives and traders, *Pemmican*, a mixture of fat, berries and dried meat.

Saskatoon grew up in the rolling parklands around the gently bending Saskatchewan river to become the economic hub of the province and its largest city with a population of about 185,000. Across one of the seven bridges is the **University of Saskatchewan**, home of the **John Diefenbaker Center**

and, supposedly, Al Capone hid out here during those days. Tunnels underneath many of the downtown buildings help keep this past alive, but it was more likely Chinese railroad workers who used these tunnels to avoid the government-imposed "head tax."

The number of rural communities in Saskatchewan has been dwindling

A prairie house adds color to the dry land.

It contains his personal belongings and a duplicate of his office while he was the Prime Minister of Canada. He and his wife are buried on the grounds.

The Western Development Museum (WDM) recreates a typical prairie town of 1910 with an authentic reconstruction of a street lined with a church, theatre, Chinese laundry, hotel and about 30 other buildings.

Numerous museums in the province reflect the strong presence of Ukrainian settlers: Saskatoon's **Ukrainian Museum of Canada** has a small gift shop selling the traditional decorated Ukrainian Easter eggs. A local magnate's collection fills the **Mendel Art Gallery**, including a good display of Inuit sculpture along with contemporary and historical artwork and, an unusual touch for a gallery, a conservatory with changing flower displays.

Between Regina and Saskatoon, near **Watrous**, is **Little Manitou Lake** where you can swim in water more salty than the ocean and so dense, it's almost impossible to sink. The recently opened **Manitou Springs Mineral Spa** is helping to return this resort community to its popularity in the 1930s.

The All Saints Anglican Church at Watrous has a magnificent medieval stained glass window. During the 1640's Civil War between King Charles 1 of England and Oliver Cromwell, the windows were buried for safekeeping against Puritan vandalism. Following the restoration, it was replaced in the church in

Wiltshire, England, until another memorial window was installed. The first Vicar brought it to All Saint's in 1912.

Métis Country

Saskatoon is the jumping off point for the sites of the North West Rebellion. The first battle was at **Duck Lake** where the Métis defeated the North-West Mounted Police. The Mounties retreated across the rolling hills to Fort Carlton, 26 km north, but they realized the wooden palisade fur trading post couldn't be adequately defended and in their haste to evacuate, fire broke out and destroyed the fort.

The rebuilt fort has four buildings with the fur and provisions store giving you a chance to closely inspect the different animal pelts traded by the Indians for guns, beads, and other goods.

About 88 km northeast of Saskatoon, at Batoche, in the valley of the South Saskatchewan River, the Métis leader, Louis Riel declared a provisional government in 1885. The decisive battle was fought on what is now the **Batoche National Historic Park**. The government troops, armed with a gatling gun overwhelmed the Métis defending the village from trenches and foxholes. Costumed guides will point out the bullet holes on the exterior of the restored

rectory, the original altar items in the tiny church while at **Caron House**, you'll hear about the Métis farming lifestyle. French remains the dominant language in many of the tiny villages. In **Bellevue**, northeast of Batoche, **Le Rendezvous Cultural Centre** serves traditional French dishes, such as tourtière and sugar pie. At St. Laurent, a French missionary erected a grotto with the **Statue of Our Lady of Lourdes**. Since 1905, the site has drawn pilgrims for two days in mid-July and mid-August.

The North-West Mounted Police built Fort Battleford in 1876 on the top of a steep bluff overlooking the river valley which was between the Cree and Blackfoot Indians. Some 500 settlers sought protection here from Indians coming to complain about the lack of government help. Negotiations failed and the battle at **Cut Knife Hill** ensued. At **Prince Albert National Park**, the prairie of the south turns into a forest of conifers and hardwoods dotted with lakes, many with sandy beaches and facilities for horseback riding, steamboat rides, golf and tennis. Hidden inside, on **Ajawaan Lake** is the simple cabin of **Grey Owl**, the naturalist well-known for his writings and his environmental preservation work. Only after his death in 1938 was it discovered that Grey Owl was really an Englishman captured by Indians since childhood.

Midway between the Pacific and Atlantic Oceans is Canada's heartland, Manitoba. It is a province blanketed by forests in the north and crossed by rivers and thousands of icy lakes except in the most northerly section where subarctic tundra surrounds Canada's largest inland seaport which is Churchill.

The populated area is south, in the large sweep of flat fertile prairie dotted with little communities that still reflect the ethnic diversity that developed Manitoba. The northern area of Canada is relatively unpopulated and is largely composed of wilderness, mainly land and innumerable icy lakes.

Over the years, large groups of people migrated from the farms and small towns, mainly going to Winnipeg, where they have maintained the simplicity of their rural heritage.

Manitoba

247

This fisherman is raring to catch fish at Lake Winnipeg.

The rosy facade of Winnipeg's skyline.

Winnipeg

Winnipeg is a dynamic, cosmopolitan city, the fourth-largest in Canada, with a core of marvellous turn-of-the-century warehouses in the **Exchange District**.

The theatre district has numerous art galleries and buildings as ultramodern as the half-pyramid rose-colored glass exterior of the **Royal Canada Mint** and as unique as the **Winnipeg Art Gallery**, which is triangular shaped, similar to the prow of a ship sailing the prairie sea.

oped Chinatown. There are alcoves of hand made items and cul de sacs of ethnic knick-knacks that can be found.

Winnipeg grew up at the junction of the **Red and Assiniboine** rivers where the terraced grounds of **The Forks** now sits. A massive redevelopment project, a combination entertainment and historical 56-acre park has been completed at this site. This is a year-round gathering place for modern Winnipeg.

A food and craft market building, shops and restaurants and an outdoor amphitheatre overlooks boats docked at the pier, including a water taxi that goes to other docks. One section has archaeological digs that have uncovered spearheads, copper tools, and pottery of the aboriginal people who lived here as much as 6,000 years ago. Besides interpretative tours of these summer excavations, **The Wall Through Time** chronicles the history of this site.

Fur traders who ran the posts built here were upset when Lord Selkirk established an agricultural colony in 1812 around The Forks at Red River. While the competition between traders was fierce, the worse conflicts were against the settlers, Scottish crofters who'd been kicked out of their homes.

The fur traders were hostile to any agricultural expansion that could destroy their livelihood. In 1816, employees of the North West Company massacred 20 agricultural settlers. Hiring about 100 Swiss and German mercenaries, Lord Selkirk's private army arrested the offenders and restored peace.

Just south of downtown is trendy **Osborne Village**, with boutiques, restaurants and clubs in large old homes that house the wealthy.

Brick sidewalks and colorful flower pots hang outside the antique clothing stores and Mediterranean restaurants of **Little Italy** while an ornately wrought Chinese gate leads to the newly devel-

The onion-domed Ukrainian church.

The peaceful period lasted until 1869 when the Métis (children of fur traders and Indian women) under Louis Riel rebelled. (See Box on p. 257).

This rebellion was squashed and the settlers went on to build Winnipeg, creating the impressively wide principal thoroughfares, Portage and Main Streets. These roads were supposedly built large enough for ten Red River carts, the main means of transportation for the settlers, to drive abreast. Portage and Main intersect is known as Canada's coldest and windiest corner. A network of over-

Métis children share a joke.

head walkways and underground passages enables pedestrians to protect themselves from the long, cold winters. Summers are lovely with dry heat that averages a maximum of 27°C.

Down the riverbank from The Forks is Manitoba's **Legislature Building**, a harmonious neo-classical structure made of local limestone in 1919, with a dome topped by the four-meter tall **Golden Boy**, the work of Parisian sculpture Charles Gardet. Sheathed in 24-carat gold, the boy carries a torch of progress in one hand and a sheaf of wheat in his left hand.

While wheat remains the main crop followed by barley, canola, other grains and cattle, manufacturing now outranks agriculture as Manitoba's main indus-

try. The **Canadian Shield** in the north yields copper, zinc, gold, and 25 percent of the world's supply of nickel. **Inco** has regular conducted tours of its integrated nickel mining and processing complex at Thompson.

The rich pelts of the region's animals, however, was the first resource developed. **The Manitoba Museum of Man and Nature** has a walk-on full size replica of the boat, *Nonsuch*, that sailed into Hudson Bay in 1668 and returned to England with a cargo of furs, spurring the founding of the Hudson Bay Company. It is a name prominent in Canada because it's now a reputable national chain of stores.

While the museum draws applause for such exhibits, Winnipeg's huge, tree-

Heavily forested area north of Winnipeg.

filled **Assiniboine Park** has native animals as well as a section for kangaroos and other Australian animals, and a statue of Winnie-the-Pooh, the famous, lovable storybook animal named after Winnipeg. A restful spot is outside the Tudor-style pavilion, the sculpture garden with its large bronze statues donated by renowned Winnipeg artist Leo Mol.

The French

From The Forks across the Red River, the French quarter of Winnipeg, **St. Boniface**, retains its heritage with French restaurants, a French cultural center and Le Musée Saint-Boniface. Built for the Gray Nuns as a convent and hospital, this hand-hewn oak log building, the largest in North America, contains artifacts dating back to the Red River colony days and mementoes of Louis Riel. The "Father of Manitoba" was born here and after his execution in Regina, Saskatchewan, was buried outside the impressive neo-romanesque facade of St. Boniface Cathedral.

While many of the Métis moved to Saskatchewan, many of their ancestors fell victim to diseases brought by Europeans. Smallpox eradicated entire tribes of Cree, Ojibwa and Assiniboine Indians. Their numbers decreased, the remaining Indians now mainly live on reserves in central and northern Manitoba. In Winnipeg, the annual

Louis Riel

Louis Riel is one of Canada's most controversial historical figures. Even today, people debate – was Louis Riel a rebel or a hero?

Born in Manitoba in 1844, Louis Riel was a Métis – descendent of mainly French-Canadian fur traders and Indian women. When the Hudson Bay Company (HBC) gave their land to Canada, the Métis were worried that the Canadian government would kick them off their already settled lands in favor of the British Protestant settlers. They refused to allow a government survey unless the Canadians consulted them. To back up their demands, about 400 Métis, under the leadership of Riel, seized control of Fort Garry. An easy task since the HBC trading post had no militia and could not challenge the takeover.

Riel proclaimed the establishment of a provisional government with the task to negotiate union with Canada. A HBC representative agreed to a French-English provisional government with Riel as president, but when two prisoners of the Métis escaped and were recaptured, Riel made his fatal mistake. He commuted the death sentence of one, but not the other. Incensed by Thomas Scott's taunts about his mixed blood and threat to assassinate him, Riel put Scott on trial: Scott was executed by firing squad. **The Red River Rebellion** was over. That death eliminated any chance of the government dealing with Riel.

Although Riel fled and was in hiding, he was nominated twice to Canada's Parliament. While Riel suffered a nervous breakdown, many of the Métis decided Saskatchewan might be a better place to maintain their traditional lifestyle. But after settling the area around the North and South Saskatchewan Rivers, the same problem occurred: the Métis were told they had no right to the land. The government ignored their complaints about the survey. Once again, they called upon Riel.

And again, he declared a provisional government, demanding the Mounted Police surrender nearby Fort Carlton. They responded by attacking the small community of Duck Lake, but the police lost and were forced to retreat. Within weeks, 5,000 troops poured into the area, ready to put down the Northwest Rebellion. Eventually, the troops overwhelmed the poorly-armed Métis defending the village of Batoche. A few Métis leaders escaped to the United States, including Gabriel Dumont, Riel's second-in-command. He became one of the star attractions of **Buffalo Bill's Wild West Show**. After he was given amnesty, he returned to live peacefully at home in **Batoche**.

Riel surrendered and, despite the outrage of French Canadians, was hanged in Regina in 1885. His body laid in state at the family home near the Red River in St. Vital. This is a tiny log Red River Frame house, which is open to the public, and he was buried on the grounds of St. Boniface Cathedral.

Thunder Bear Pow-Wow in May brings members of the various tribes to compete in 12 difference dance competitions. Paddlewheel riverboats cruise between The Forks and Lower Fort Garry in the summer, about 32 km north of Winnipeg, near Selkirk.

Inside this magnificent stone fur trading post, the oldest is still intact in North America, costumed guides act the roles and perform the tasks of the Governor and Hudson Bay Company's employees who inhabited this fort.

Lake Winnipeg

In the middle of Canada lies some of North America's finest white sand beaches, at Lake Winnipeg. Canada's seventh largest lake is also a great location to windsail and fish. Private cot-

A sea plane is set to start at Pelican Lake.

tages line its southern end while along its eastern shore are Winnipeg Beach, Victoria Beach and Grand Beach with dunes as high as eight meters.

Agriculture

In the 1800s, the Canadian government, worried about a possible annexation by the Americans, advertised heavily in Europe for settlers. The ads promised "the best wheat land and the richest grazing land under the sun." A legacy that was bequeathed was **Lake Agassiz**, a glacial lake that covered most of south-central Manitoba 8,000 years ago. The duration of this ice age produced a markedly flat land with some of the province's most fertile farmland.

People came by the thousands, grabbing the opportunity to obtain their own land at low prices. They were determined to escape class systems, religious prosecution, and famine in Europe and Eastern Europe.

The homesteaders faced many problems. Drought, depressions that greatly lowered the price of their crops, and a short growing season of only 90 days forced many adults and children to give up and leave when the farms could not support too many mouths.

Brandon

The handsome old homes in Brandon

Trapper Don's Lodge is preserved as a historic site.

testify to the prosperity of this area's wheat industry. Manitoba's second-largest city, 197 km west of Winnipeg, was named after the nearby Brandon Hills.

During World War II airmen and women trained here and the two-level **Commonwealth Air Training Plan Museum** at Brandon airport honors their memory by maintaining 13 planes used for their training as well as numerous photographs and memorabilia from that period.

A bison kill area, dating back 1,200 years when bison by the thousands roamed through here, is located about 10 km west of Brandon.

Archaeologists have found bones and artifacts at **Stott Site**, located in **Grand Valley Provincial Recreation Park**, where a viewing platform looks over a reconstructed bison enclosure and prehistoric encampment.

Steinbach

Mennonites from Russia were among the many who settled in Manitoba. Their 40-acre **Mennonite Heritage Village** at Steinbach, 61 km southeast of Winnipeg is definitely worth a visit. This living history museum is spread out like a typical Mennonite village before the turn of the century. It has numerous buildings of which an example of the first crude homes, a log home lived in until 1985 and a combination house-barn with the typical central brick heater

Bison and its young at Riding Mountain Park.

to warm the entire place.

Riding Mountain National Park

Northwest of Winnipeg at what is now **Riding Mountain National Park**, fur traders exchanged their canoes for horses on their trips west. The 3,000 sq km park is a lush wilderness that suddenly rises from a sea of farmland. It is part of the Manitoba escarpment, a ridge extending from North Dakota through Mani-

ers, cyclists and horse riders lead through the diverse landscape.

At the edge of the park on **Clear Lake** is the summer resort town of **Wasagaming** with its scenic golf course, tennis courts and a Summer Arts program from mid-May to mid-September with art and craft classes for all ages.

On the northern slopes of the park is **Dauphin**, the permanent home of Canada's **National Ukrainian Festival**, celebrated with dance, music, crafts and food every August. A restored homestead and church of the **Ukrainian Heritage Village** acknowledges the waves of Ukrainians who settled around this area while the **Ukrainian Homestead Museum** at **Winnipeg Beach** has log buildings and agricultural equipment used by this ethnic group.

Directly west of Winnipeg, Austin has a **Homesteaders' Village**, simulating village life in the late 19th century. It includes typical log houses, an elegant clapboard home with a ballroom, and general store.

Churchill

"The Polar Bear Capital of the World" is an apt description for this community on the shores of Hudson Bay. So many bears inundate the town that it has a polar bear alert system and children learn at a young age how to avoid them.

The bears, weighing as much as 600 kg, spend the winter hunting on the frozen bay. They retreat into the

toba to Saskatchewan. The forested slopes rise to a highland plateau, where stands of white poplar open onto meadows of wildflowers. Large herds of elk feed in some meadows while in the woodlands, lynx stalks its prey. Beavers inhabit most of the waterbodies while Northern pike is the main fish taken from its deep cold waters. Trails for hik-

The vastness of Riding Mountain National Park extends to the horizon.

wilderness when the bay melts, then return from October to November back to the refrozen bay.

Since the bears have no natural enemies and no fears, the safest way to see them up close is by the **Tundra Buggy Tour**. You should make a reservation at least two weeks in advance. The high buses, with windows about sniffing height for a standing bear, travel throughout the tundra – depending on the time of year. The sight of a large polar bear standing on its hind legs is rather amazing. The put up a rather formidable front and it is just as well as to keep the windows wound up! The bears, the 200 species of migratory huge birds, and the abundant cold-tolerant plants color the spring and fall landscape in red, violet and yellow.

Churchill is nearly as famous for the thousands of beluga whales that congregate in the estuary of the Churchill River. In July and August, these huge mammals play in the river, often approaching scuba divers and tour boats. Whale-watching tours also often stop at the **Prince of Wales Fort**, built by the Hudson Bay Company in the 1700s which, despite its thick stone walls, was captured by the French without a struggle in 1782. A French priest established the **Eskimo Museum**, an impressive collection of Inuit artifacts and detailed carvings that date as far back as 1400 BC. No roads lead to Churchill, but there are flights from Winnipeg and a regular train service.

Sled dog racing at snow encrusted Manitoba.

I n the most northeastern section of Canada is the Yukon, a land of spectacular beauty. It is a pristine wilderness of glacier-coated mountains, forested valleys and crystal clear waters. With its small population of about 30,000 people, of twice the size of Great Britain, the Yukon is one of the few places left in North America where you can see wildlife in their natural habitat.

Yukon

261

The haunting beauty of the Emerald Lake.

History of Gold

News of vast gold finds first awoke the world to the Yukon's resources and spawned settlements which were left to decay, becoming ghost towns when rumours of larger finds lured people away. While the yellow metal still bewitches some, most visitors come to hunt and photograph big game such as moose and caribou. They canoe down to some of its 50 rivers, fish in lakes where northern pike average 3 kg, or just enjoy the solitude along numerous hiking trails.

Dawson City General Store is the provincial one-stop shopping experience.

Bonanza Creek

In 1896, a prospector with two Indian companions discovered gold in **Bonanza Creek** off the Klondike river. The word spread like wildfire and people from as far away as Germany streamed into the area, making it the greatest and the last gold rush in North America. Within a year, some 60,000 men and women had actually made the arduous trek to the **Klondike Valley**.

Some 80,000 people streamed into the area in search of gold until the rush ended in 1904. They extracted over $100 million worth of gold from the valley's rivers and streams, but no gold mines operate today.

However, rockhounds can pan for gold on the legendary streams, like Bonanza Creek, as well as search for jade, amber, topaz and other semiprecious stones and minerals.

Jewellers use local gold nuggets to craft stick pins to necklaces: those made in the territory carry "Product of the Yukon" logo.

Dawson City

Dawson City was an Indian salmon-drying station sheltered in the valley of the **Yukon River** at the mouth of the Klondike River. The gold seekers transformed this shanty town of timber shacks and canvas tents, boosting the popula-

The cabin of Robert Service, an English poet.

tion to some 30,000 people and erecting 20 blocks of commercial buildings to create the largest city west of Winnipeg, the San Francisco of the North.

Everything that money could buy was available – fine food, brandy, cigars and women. Prostitution was illegal in Canada, but authorities in this wide open city turned a blind eye. Elaborately gowned Belles, worked in the numerous saloons and taverns that had been made rich by the gold rush. Card sharks and con men flowed in right behind, anxious to relieve weary miners of their new-found wealth.

When the gold petered out, the miners left, followed by the cancan dancers, professional gamblers and everyone else who was trying to make a living off the miners. Dawson's population dwindled down to 1,000 people.

A visit to Dawson City allows you to relive these gold rush days. Its wooden sidewalks and restored clapwood buildings keep the spirit of 1898 alive. In the evenings you can enjoy the diversions popular in those days in entertainment centres, such as the restored **Palace Grand Theatre** built by Arizona Charlie Meadows in 1899. The flamboyantly decorated theatre/saloon has reincarnated Klondike Kate and the Gaslight Follies. The casino, **Diamond Tooth Gertie's Gambling Hall** – named after the Belle with a diamond between her two front teeth – captures the atmosphere of the time with its shows similar to those when Dawson City was the gold

The Search for Gold

Some families still live in cabins in Yukon's 'gold' country.

The cry of "Gold" on August 17, 1896, at Bonanza Creek on the Klondike River, sparked the world's last great gold rush. The following year, when a steamer arrived in Seattle with nearly three tons of gold dust and nuggets from the Klondike Valley, the race was on. In six months, more than 60,000 people had passed through the Chilkoot Pass, drawn by the tales of riches to be found.

What many didn't realize, however, was that to reach the Klondike, they had to conquer treacherous terrain in a subarctic climate. Most arrived by steamer at Skagway, Alaska, then they faced their first test, going over the Chilkoot

Pass. In winter, they had to climb ice steps cut into the nearly vertical cliff in a temperature that averaged 30°C in January, while daylight was only four hours long.

To ensure the survival of these prospectors, the RCMP demanded that each bring a year's supply of food of 800 kg over the Pass. It was a journey that took weeks and as many as 20 trips to carry all these supplies to the top.

Once this trail of human ants arrived at Bennett Lake, they had to wait – if it was winter – until the ice melted because the only way to reach the Klondike was by boat. Trees by the hundreds were cut down to make anything that could keep their unwieldy cargo afloat. The fearless pushed on, only to meet other challenges on the Yukon River. First, they had to pass

capital of the world.

Robert Service

The Englishman **Robert Service** was one of the many seeking his fortune and, like most, he was unsuccessful, but he left a rich legacy of ballads and poems about the hard life of the miners.

As an actor recites the poems, you can practically feel the spirit of Robert

Service echoing through his log cabin.

A stone's throw away is the cabin that housed the other writer whose work popularized and romanticized the Yukon, the American short story author Jack London. Readings from his *Call of the Wild*, are also given daily during the warmer months. River cruises go down the Klondike as far as Alaska while other tours travel to various gold fields, including the site of the first gold find, the **Bonanza Creek Discovery Claim**, through the tricky whirlpools of the narrow passageway at **Miles Canyon**, then tackle the White Horse Rapids. By June 1898, more than 7,000 craft had left Lake Bennett and over 100 fell victim to the canyon and the falls.

Rather than risk their lives on the rapids at Whitehorse, at what is today Whitehorse, many instead opted to portage their goods before venturing back onto the waters. However, they still faced another navigational hazard, the Five Finger Rapids, before reaching Dawson City.

Fortune seekers who came later had an easier time, travelling by narrow-gauge railroad from Skagway, Alaska, to Whitehorse, then by steamboats downriver to Dawson.

Once in Dawson City, everybody faced the same problem – finding a claim to stake. Some struck it rich, discovering huge nuggets in the creeks off the Yukon and Klondike rivers, but many found nothing. Many families living in the Yukon today are descended from those who fell under the spell of the Yukon.

Most left the Yukon, at least those who survived the journey in and out. Throughout this area are graves of those who fell victim to the weather, to scurvy, and to attacks by grizzly bears and other animals. As Robert Service wrote in his *The Law of the Yukon*, "This is the Law of the Yukon, that only the Strong shall thrive; That surely the Weak shall perish, and only the Fit survive."

and often offer a chance for visitors to pan for gold themselves. The myth of the Klondike Motherlode still lures some. According to them, all the gold claimed during the gold rush in the Klondike creeks had a source somewhere above that hasn't yet been found. This has naturally provoked a great many 'golddiggers' into eagerly panning different parts of the creek for gold. This, of course, is a fruitless task that sees scores of people attempting it anyway.

Whitehorse sprang up as a camptown for miners who had to portage around the White Horse Rapids on the Yukon River when making their way to Dawson City. The city again spurted in 1942, when Canadian and U.S. Army personnel poured into town during the building of the Alaska Highway. This government town – the capital of the Yukon was moved from Dawson City to Whitehorse in 1953 – maintained links to its roots with numerous musical revues and, at the **MacBride Museum**, displays of prehistoric mammals, Indian relics, minerals of the territory and **Sam McGee's** 1899 cabin, the man immortalized by Robert Service in his ode, *The Cremation of Sam McGee.*

Until 1900, Yukon residents relied on steamboats to connect them to the outside world and until 1952, when a road was built, sternwheelers hauled silver, lead and zinc on the Yukon River. At the Whitehorse dock is the restored *S.S. Klondike,* the largest and one of the last sternwheelers.

The **Whitehorse Rapids Dam** is the site of one of the world's longest fish ladders. From glass windows in late July or early August, you can watch *Chinook* salmon as they migrate through the city's rapids and read the Interpretative displays of this migration.

Winters can be bitterly cold and daylight short in the Yukon, but you can warm up by taking a short drive north to

A shopper at a general store at Whitehorse.

the **Takhini Hot Springs**. At 36°C, these natural hot springs enable people to swim all year round.

In this land of the midnight sun, winter evenings are often dramatic with the northern lights illuminating the night skies with streaks of colors. In June, snow can still cover the highest mountains, although in Whitehorse, between June and September, temperatures can rise to 30°C and daylight is nearly 24 hours long.

This is a challenge to gardeners, but people do grow vegetables as you can see in the experimental part of the Yukon Gardens, the testing grounds for new strains of vegetables suitable for this climate. Pathways through the 9-ha of the garden also lead past wild and domestic flowers, trees, and shrubs.

According to oral tradition, the Yukon Indian people have lived in this land since Crow made the world and all living things. Archaeologists estimate that the original inhabitants came from Northeast Asia about 30,000 years ago, crossing when the two continents were joined during the last Ice Age.

Many Indians have maintained the traditional ways. They are still relying on trapping, hunting and fishing for their livelihood. Furs brought the first Europeans into the Yukon who set up trading posts by the 1800s, but the major influx came when gold was discovered. After the gold rush, the fur industry rose to prominence again, only to be subdued by the anti-fur campaigns.

The Yukon Mountains

Yukon's landscape is mostly rugged, mountainous terrain. Along the eastern hypotenuse of this triangular-shaped territory, stretching north to south, are the British, Richardson, MacKenzie, Hess and Logan mountains. Along the south are the Pelly Mountains and in the southwest, the Saint Elias Mountains with the highest Canadian mountain, Mount Logan at 5,950 m.

Between the mountain ranges are plateaus, the Peel, the Porcupine and the Yukon – named for the rivers that run through it. The largest, the **Yukon Plateau**, with its own mountain areas and deep valley is unique among geological areas in North America because it was left untouched during the last glacial age.

The Yukon river is the fifth longest river in North America. Beginning at **Tagish Lake** on the Northern British Columbia border, it flows across Yukon and Alaska to empty into the **Bering Sea**. Except during spring floods, this slow-moving river is good for canoeing because there are few rapids. Government campsites are located along its banks, as are relics of the gold rush – abandoned mine workings and crumbling log cabins.

The Alaska Highway

The major entry into the Yukon is the **Alaska Highway**. Built in nine months because the Americans wanted a safe land route to Alaska, as the Japanese had invaded their islands off Alaska, the highway is 2,400 km long. The first town it passes in the Territory is **Watson Lake** which recalls the building of the highway with a slide-show at the **Visitor Center** and a recreation of a World War II USO show in an army tent. The Canteen Show is the type of entertainment presented to the Canadian and U.S. soldiers working on the highway.

In 1942, a homesick U.S. soldier, Carl Lindley, who was working on the highway put up a sign for his hometown, Danville, Illinois outside the town. It was an idea that caught on and now **Signpost Forest** has over 17,000 signs.

Next stop, **Teslin**, originally the summer home of Tlingit Indians from coastal Alaska and British Columbia whose descendants make up one of the Yukon's largest First Nations communities. This powerful and wealthy tribe controlled trade between the ocean coast and the interior.

The Chilkoot Trail

The famous **Chilkoot Trail** of '98 attracts hikers from around the world. Every summer, some come to retrace the steps of the miners on their route from Alaska to Dawson City. The trail starts 15 km from Skagway, Alaska, at **Dyea**, originally a Tlingit Indian community. Until the stampede of gold rush seekers

Yukon's Bennett has little ponds and clumps of bushes gently dotting its land.

The city center is rather laidback at Bennett.

overwhelmed them, they prevented both whites and other natives from using the Chilkoot Pass.

The historic trail, leading to **Lake Bennett**, winds through landscape that changes dramatically. It begins at tidewater, passes through a rain forest and climbs above the treeline into an alpine tundra, reaching the summit at 1,122 m before descending into a boreal forest with a series of lakes. Along the trail lies evidence of the various hardships suffered by those infused with gold fever – collapsible canoes, wagon wheels, and worn-out boots.

The trek to Lake Bennett, where miners boated up to the Klondike, takes most hikers three to five days to cover the 53.1 km. While both the Canadian and United States Park Services regularly patrol the trail, it can be treacherous, particularly at the summit.

Even in summer, hikers can run into snow, sleet, fog, hail, thunderstorms and rain. The White Pass & Yukon narrow-gauge rail service, operating from mid-June to mid-September, can return hikers back up to Skagway.

Crossing the Arctic Circle

The **Dempster** is Canada's most northerly highway and the only public highway to cross the Arctic Circle. Called "the road to adventure," this drive between Dawson City and Inuvik in the Northwest Territories takes you by

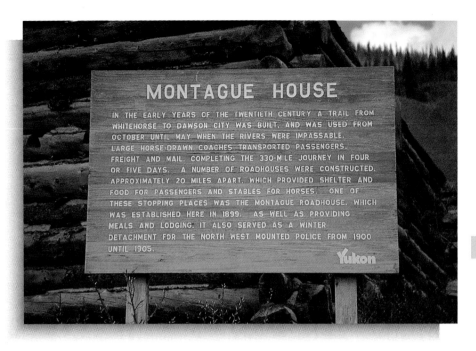

One of the 17,000 signs at Signpost Forest.

breathtaking views of mountains and strange, cone-shaped ice hills. These *pingos* form where the permafrost is hundreds of meters thick. Roaming throughout are bears, wolves, moose, grouse and, in June sometimes, migrating caribou herds.

Kluane National Park

Kluane National Park is a unique beautiful wilderness boasting the highest mountains in Canada, including Mt Logan (5,951 m), alpine meadows and the most extensive non-polar icefields in the world. The icefields, dating from the last ice age, cover more than half the park. The glaciers formed here melt in the lower valley, forming rivers and hanging valleys.

About 250 km of trails permit hikers to travel on day trips or overnight trips through this park with its salmon- and trout-filled lakes, grizzly bears, moose, and the rare peregrine falcon. To scale the mountains, climbers must be experienced and must register with the Warden Service before and after their climbs. Since much of the park is so remote, it's recommended everyone carry a compass and map.

Kluane National Park is accessible by car; however, much of the Yukon can only be reached by plane which you can charter or make arrangements with the numerous professional guides and outfitters available.

N

orthwest Territories (or NWT as it's usually written) is a land ruled by nature, a rugged bountiful land barely touched by humans. Its pristine wilderness, majestic scenery and wildlife makes NWT an outdoor paradise for photographers, artists, naturalists and anyone with adventure in their soul.

It's a land of legend, filled with stories of man against the elements. The loss of **John Franklin** and his two ships on their exploration of the Northwest Passage in 1845 riveted the world. The British sent more than six expeditions, consisting of dozens of ships and hundreds of men into waters where ice could suddenly enclose and crush ships. Franklin and over 100 men were never found until 1858 when one skeleton was discovered. The second was located, perfectly preserved, in 1984. The permafrost had preserved the fully-

A polar bear takes an icy break at the Northwest Territories.

Northwest Territories

273

Snowy beds of ice rest in the niches of jagged
granite rocks at the Northwest.

Arctic vegetation flourishes in this icy cold region.

clothed body, enabling scientists to conclude that the long-haired sailor had died of pneumonia.

One outcome of the tragedy was the mapping of this previously unknown land by the searchers. The NWT covers nearly one-third of Canada, a space half the size of the United States that spreads over four time zones, yet is populated by only 55,000 people.

They are a friendly, welcoming people with a long tradition of hospitality that is derived from living in a wilderness that can be harsh. The ancient people of these lands – the Dene Indians and Inuit (whom Southerners called Eskimos) – mostly live in small, usually widely separated communities. Many still continue the lifestyle of their ancestors, hunting and fishing, often supplemented by producing arts and crafts. Some communities have more artists per capita than anywhere else in the world.

Although communities are isolated, the people are fully aware of what's happening outside their world. In 1992, the NWT launched the world's largest aboriginal television network, Television Northern Canada (TVNC). Programming is provided in up to 12 aboriginal languages, as well as in English.

Geographical Features

The Métis, people of mixed European and Indian ancestry, and the Dene live

A large aerial of ice floes is a common sight at the Northwest Territories.

south of the treeline while the majority of the population, the Inuit, live north of the treeline, around the coast and Arctic Islands. The treeline extends from the **Mackenzie River Delta** in the northwest, near the mountainous border with the Yukon, to a point on Hudson Bay near the border with Manitoba.

North of the treeline is tundra, a bleak land in the winter that blossoms in the summer to a bright landscape of moss, lichen and colorful tiny flowers, vegetation that can thrive in this continuous permafrost zone. Along the coastal

waters are polar bears, seals, walruses and, at **Bylot Island Bird Sanctuary**, the rare peregrine falcon. North of the Arctic Circle, such small amounts of precipitation fall that the area's known as a polar desert. Instead of sand and cactus, the land is coated with ice and alpine vegetation.

Permafrost is soil frozen to a depth of 30 to 300 m. Around **Tuktoyaktuk** (**Tuk** as it's commonly known), permafrost has created cone-shaped ice hills up to 45 m high, called pingos. They form

Dall sheep thrive on the nipping cold of the subarctic boreal forest.

Life in an igloo

Inuit houses are built sturdily to keep out the cold.

The Igloo has to be one of the most unusual and fascinating dwellings in which humans have lived. It is hard to imagine having to live in a house of snow to keep yourself warm, but in the inhospitable climate of the central and eastern Arctic, snow was often the only building material at hand. Surprisingly, snow has excellent insulating properties.

An igloo is made of blocks of hard packed snow which were cut out of the ground using a bone or wooden knife. The cut blocks are between 61 to 91 cm long and 30 to 61 cm wide. The rows are laid one at a time from the inside with each row spiralling upward to maximize stability. Each row of blocks is drawn a little further in towards the center of the structure, achieving a dome. An improvised window is fashioned using a block of clear water ice to insert into the roof. The key snow block in the center of the roof gives the igloo its strength. The design of a long low narrow entrance way, possibly draped with an animal skin, helps keep out the cold air. A hole was poked in the top of the roof to let out smoke and improve the ventilation.

Temporary igloos were constructed when the Inuit were travelling or on hunting expeditions. These were smaller than the more permanent igloos and were normally less than 2 m high and 3 m wide.

where the permafrost is hundreds of meters thick, growing by as much as 1.5 m per year.

South of the treeline, in areas of poor drainage, melting of the permafrost by the sun's rays in the summer can result in string bogs and muskeg. In this subarctic boreal forest area of jackpine, spruce and poplar are huge herds of caribou and moose. Black bears and beavers also exist in this icy terrain.

The ice age 10,000 years ago shaped much of this land. The retreating glaciers stripped surface material down to the bare stone, carved deep fjords along the coast and gouged scars that made two of the largest lakes in the world; the **Great Bear** and the **Great Slave**. Innumerable other lakes remain unnamed because of their number.

Fossilized coral found on the eastern island of **Keewatin** is among the most unusual geographical feature. The community of **Coral Harbor** is named

The igloos inhabited all winter were more spacious and comfortable in design. The main room might be 3 to 4 m high and 4 to 5 m in diameter. Sometimes a series of domes were connected by passage-ways for storage and space for several families.

Inside the igloo a raised snow platform was built for sleeping. Shelves were carved out of the walls to store utensils and paraphernalia. Depending on the Inuit group, they may have used soapstone lamps, burning blubber to provide heat and light.

The sleeping platform along with the walls and ceiling were often covered with animal hides. Polar bear, caribou, seal and musk-oxen added an extra insulating layer to the igloo and also allowed the inside temperature to be raised without fear of melting the snow blocks.

Sleeping in something warmer than pyjamas was still necessary as the inside temperature ranged from just below freezing to temperatures slightly above.

When the igloo started to melt in the summer, the Inuit moved into tents and abandoned the igloo. The tents were made of caribou or seal hides stretched over poles to form a dome or teepee-like structure.

Today, igloos are still often used by the Inuit when they are travelling or out on hunting expeditions.

for this startling reminder of the island's once-tropical climate.

In the most northerly sections, winters are cold and dark with no sunlight at all in January. In June, there's 24 hour sunlight and about 20 hours in the southern regions. Temperature during the most popular tourist months (July & August) reach 21°C in July and 18°C in August in Yellowknife and go as low as 11°C, meaning you'd better pack a fall jacket with you. The further east you go, the shorter the summer.

Many communities can only be reached by plane. There are only eight highways in this huge land and very few paved portions. Even then, during the spring and fall when the ice roads along the river are not solid enough and the breaking ice makes it impossible to sail the ferries across the river, many communities cannot be reached by car, including the capital Yellowknife.

Yellowknife

Yellowknife with about 15,000 residents is Canada's most northerly city and the only city in the NWT. Attractively situated on pink granite rocks by Great Slave Lake, it was originally a trading post established by Alexander Mackenzie on his exploration of the river bearing his name. Today, Yellowknife is the transportation, government and service center – many outfitters make it their headquarters – but it still retains its frontier spirit. Dog teams, canoes, kayaks, boats and snowmobiles are as common as cars and trucks.

The city has two sections, the high rise office buildings, hotels and apartments of the new town and the old town of buildings erected during the goldrush. Prospectors on their way to the Klondike found gold in Yellowknife Bay in 1895, but Yellowknife's boom didn't start until 1936.

After the war, gold mining resumed on a large scale and the high prices for

Dettah Indian Village at Yellowknife Bay.

gold have kept two gold mines in business. In 1990, the **Giant** and **Nerco Con** produced 234,369 ounces of gold. Jewelry shops in town create rings, pendants and other gold nugget jewelry from Yellowknife gold.

Gem-size diamonds found trapped under glaciers about 250 km northeast of Yellowknife have recently spurred a diamond rush.

In 1989, Dia Met company started staking land, inciting the largest staking rush in Canada's history. Over 45 million acres have already been staked,

Short cruises around Great Slave Lake and across to Yellowknife Bay are available to view the Dettah Indian Village. Guides offer hands-on dog team rides, sightseeing of caribou, and trips to fish for trout and northern pike. To catch the famous salmon-like Arctic Char, you have to go to Great Bear Lakes or other lakes north of the treeline.

Purple wildflowers, which people pick and use in place of spinach, bloom everywhere in summer around Yellowknife. At night, the sky dances with the streaks of color of the *Aurora Borealis*, the northern lights. The lights are not as visible during the city's **Midnight Golf Tournament**.

Canoeing

Canoeists fly in from around the world to paddle the **South Nahanni River** in the strikingly beautiful **Nahanni National Park Reserve**, the first area in the world designated a UN World Heritage Site, in the southwest corner of the territory. The river, which whitewater rafting companies also use for travel, flows through the mountains bordering the NWT with the Yukon.

As the river descends, it drops more than 120 m on the 200 km trip between **Nahanni Butte** and **Virginia Falls**, winding past the tall trees, ferns and other lush vegetation growing around some hot springs and through large canyons with sheer cliffs before reaching the magnificent Virginia Falls, which

surpassing the land claimed in the days of the Klondike Gold Rush.

A simulated bush plane ride is the highlight of the brand-new **Northern Frontier Regional Visitors Center** while the Prince of Wales Northern Heritage Center looks into the past with historical and geological displays and exhibits on Dene and Inuit culture.

A brawny oarsman braves the Virginia Falls.

is more than twice the height of Niagara Falls. Near the falls, wild orchids blossom next to snow. Immediately downriver are 8 km of nearly continuous rapids and standing waves.

Of the four small communities in the area, Fort Simpson is the largest and the park's headquarters. It sits on a little island at the confluence of the **Liard** and **Mackenzie Rivers**.

Straddling the border with Alberta is **Wood Buffalo National Park**, the second largest park in the world. This subarctic wilderness has the world's larg-

Canada initiated a program to hatch the extra egg in incubators and raise the chicks in captivity.

While most of the park is in its original wilderness state, there are areas with camping, boating and swimming facilities. The **Reception Center** is just north of the Alberta border at Fort Smith, one of the main links in the chain of trading posts along the Mackenzie route to the Arctic. The **Northern Life Museum** makes a good introduction to the NWT with its accumulation of artifacts.

Time-worn trading posts dot the mighty Mackenzie River as it races through the **Mackenzie Mountains**. Alexander Mackenzie in 1789 noticed seeping liquid that looked like yellow wax around **Norman Wells**, but it was over 100 years later before a small well was drilled.

The United States government during World War II drilled a much larger well and built a pipeline as it was worried about oil supplies for Alaska. Norman Wells continues to be a major oil supplier, sending about 30,000 barrels per day south through a pipeline.

Inuvik can be reached by the Mackenzie River or from Dawson City, Yukon, by the Dempster Highway – the furthest north you can drive on a public highway. Inuvik was built in 1954 to replace nearby **Aklavik** which was sinking into the Mackenzie Delta's water. The planned town was to be "the first community north of the Arctic Circle built to provide the normal facilities of a

est free-roaming bison herd (about 6,000) and the nesting grounds of the rare and endangered whooping crane.

In 1941, there were only 21 whooping cranes left in the world. And today at least 130 return to the park to nest. Whooping cranes lay just two eggs, but only raise one chick. To increase the number of cranes, the United States and

modern Canadian town." All the buildings were erected on piles driven deep into the permafrost since buildings constructed directly on the ground could melt the permafrost. The town includes a Roman Catholic Church built in the shape of an Igloo and decorated by a native artist.

In the 1970s, gas and oil exploration in the area created a boom, which has since subsided, but the town remains an administrative center with numerous outfitters taking customers to see the whales and seals along the coast, and to the Mackenzie Delta to spot caribou, grizzly bear, mink and the migratory birds.

A charming little town in a sandpit at the edge of the **Beaufort Sea** is Tuktoyaktuk, more familiarly known as Tuk, the base for the oil and gas exploration on the Beaufort Sea. Unlike the igloos lived in by some natives, the Karngmalit Inuit of this region built sod houses and there is one you can view.

With its awesome glacier-topped mountains and deeply indented coast, **Baffin Island** is often described as the north's most beautiful island. Ice climbers come to tackle the sheer cliffs of its mountains while others come for its beauty, wildlife and art.

The soapstone carvings and prints of the Inuit artists on Baffin Island and particularly those in Cape Dorset are world famous. The influence of the whalers who used to ply these waters is evident in much of the art, especially in the delicately etched scrimshaw. Wall

hangings (embroidered, appliqued or woven) are a comparatively new art form for the Inuit.

Accommodation

Big city hotels can be found in Yellowknife as well as Bed & Breakfasts

Ice climbers are often attracted by the icy terrain.

(B&Bs), but your choices are more limited outside the city. Often, there's only one small homely inn with less than eight rooms, so it's best to reserve in advance. Numerous hunting, fishing and eco-tourism lodges are scattered throughout the territory as are outfitters and guides offering tours for everything from hunting caribou to trips by dog teams. Just make sure the business is licensed by the NWT Government. A consumer protection program guarantees the security of your deposits paid to licensed tourism operators.

Canadians take their sports seriously enough to have created a federal government department, Fitness and Amateur Sport. It was mainly set up to improve the country's success in international sports by funding athletes' training. Canadians are not normally flag wavers except when it comes to the Olympic Games or other international events when nationalism bursts out proudly whenever there's a Canadian win.

Skiing is a popular recreational activity at Calgary.

When Toronto's baseball team, the *Blue Jays*, won the 1993 World Series for the second year in a row, crowds paraded through the streets. Even in other cities, people spontaneously gathered together, honked car horns and waved the Canadian flag. The fact that only one Canadian played on the team was irrelevant.

On the other hand, the Canadian Football League (CFL) with teams from Montreal to Vancouver is being exported to the United States where franchises are planned for Sacramento, California and Shreveport, Louisiana. Canadian football

American football has slightly different rules from Canadian football.

varies from the American game: the CFL field is wider and longer, there are 12 players, not the American 11, and only 3 downs are allowed, not 4. Some sports experts call it a more exciting game than American football. Other spectator sports include basketball, baseball and, the most popular, hockey.

The National Hockey League (NHL) also has the most boisterous fans, particularly fans of the Montreal Canadians when their team is playing on home ice at Montreal's **Atwater Forum.** Hockey's popularity is such that thou-

Ice skating – Mum and son team.

Winter Sports

All ages take to their skates in the winters, trying to duplicate Canada's top figure skaters or to play hockey or just glide along on indoor rinks as fancy as the Calgary **Olympic Oval**, built for the 1988 Winter Games, or outdoor rinks, such as the frozen lake on top of Montreal's Mount Royal.

At Canada's premier outdoor rink, Ottawa's 5-km Rideau Canal, briefcase-carrying civil servants skate to work from about December to March. Absurd though this may sound, it is true. Recreational skaters can stop at the wooden huts situated along the canal to rent skates and rest with a steaming, hot

sands of young boys, and some girls, join minor hockey leagues as young as six years old. In fact hockey is a popular sport amongst school children and they are usually quite proficient at an early age. Heavy demand for ice time in some cities forces parents to wake up early enough for their children to start hockey practice at about 6:00 a.m. on weekdays.

Cross country Alpine skiing at Quebec.

chocolate drink.

Skiing is a way of life in Canada and many schools take students on one or two-day ski trips. Parklands throughout the country offer packed down trails for cross-country skiing. **Haliburton**, a resort area dotted with lakes and small towns with art galleries and restaurants, has a 250-km network of trails. The network connects a dozen lodges, most offering lodge-to-lodge ski packages.

Throughout the country are various sized hills for Alpine skiing, with the most challenging being in Quebec, the Rockies and British Columbia. Montrealers usually head north to the Laurentians while near Quebec City.

Mont-Saint-Anne caters to Americans and Europeans with such European-style facilities as an eight-passenger gondola and 214 km of groomed trails with nine heated cabins for cross-country skiing. Alberta's hosting of the 1988 Winter Games gave **Kananaskis** Country on the eastern slopes of the Rockies some excellent skiing facilities in addition to the peaks near Banff and Jasper. The two mountains at Whistler Resort are British Columbia's most prestigious ski hills; however, if you want untracked thick powder, there's heli-skiing at the province's many lofty peaks.

Horsing Around

A ride in winter on a horse-drawn car-

Dog sled trips are a popular diversion in the Saguenay Region.

riage filled with hay accords a leisurely tour of the country around Whistler. Some sleigh rides in Quebec are on old-fashioned sleighs, minus the hay, but horse-driven. A much faster way to tour is via snowmobiles, which are available at most resorts.

Horseback Riding

Horseback riding trips in the warmer months take you for hours or days up mountains and along rivers and lakes in the scenic backwoods of the Rockies. Alberta is horse country, a throwback to when horses worked and tamed the land. Their descendants, some 3,000 wild horses, still roam the foothills of the **Alberta Rockies**.

Horses are big business in this province, but they're also seen in the numerous rodeos, equestrian events, thoroughbred and harness races. There are guest ranches that give a taste of the Old Wild West with trail rides, pack trips and fun-filled camping trips.

The Rockies are a favorite destination for hikers and mountain climbers in summer and in winter for ice climbing. Each provincial and national park usually provides a number of scenic hiking trails. Experienced hikers test their endurance on the rugged **Chilkoot Trail**, the route over the mountains between Alaska and the Yukon that bonanza seekers travelled on their way to the Klondike in 1898. Another picturesque,

The Quebec Carnival

Trotting on ice during the winter carnival at Quebec city.

Canadians do not let the cold and snow of winter daunt them. Throughout the country, winter carnivals celebrate the season, with the largest held in Quebec City. For 11 days in early February, revellers enjoy themselves at the world's biggest winter party and its third largest carnival, after those in Rio and New Orleans.

Presiding over the festivities is **Bonhomme**, a large furry white snowman dressed in a traditional Quebec red toque and arrow-design woven sash belt. This mascot and host (his real identity is kept secret) makes his appearance the first Sunday in January when the Mayor turns over the keys of the city to him. This jolly snowman whose smiling face beams from post-

ers around the city dispenses cheer and presides over the celebrations, making speeches and telling jokes, a feeling enhanced by *caribou*, a fierce brew blended from alcohol and red wine, served in candy-cane shaped containers.

Bonhomme reigns from his **Snow Palace**, an ice castle built into the city's old walls, next to the main entranceway into the old city and opposite the Parliament Buildings. For years, the palace was made of snow. Over 9,000 tonnes of snow were compacted into blocks, which were then sculpted and laid side by side to form the immense structure. A team of 15 specialists took about two months to create the elaborate work of art – a castle with a 50-m facade, 20 m high and 20 m deep.

To everyone's delight, carnival organizers in 1993 converted the snow castle back to an ice

more accessible, hiking path is Ontario's 692 km **Bruce Trail**, which passes the Niagara Falls through farm country, **Niagara Escarpment** the **Caledon Hills** and on to **Tobermory** in the rugged land of **Georgian Bay**.

Curling dates back to Scottish settlers while the First Nations people gave Canada lacrosse, toboggans, snowshoes and canoes. Lacrosse has seven players per team who try to get a hard rubber

ball into the opposing team's goal by throwing the ball with large curved sticks with a pocket of netting or webbing. Its popularity has dwindled over the years.

The function of toboggans has changed, but they're found everywhere. In any city, wherever you see a hill with a clear run to its base, it's likely to be a tobogganing hill once it starts snowing. Quebec City has revived the old-fashioned man-made toboggan slide palace. Colored lights shimmering through its walls moulded from ice created a glazed luminescence. **Place du Palais**, as the castle and its grounds are called, is the site of many carnival activities, including dancing, aerobic workouts and the crowning of the Queen who presides at the opening ceremonies.

The most colorful part of Quebec Carnival is the brightly lit Saturday night parades. Marching bands, floats and clowns wind through the streets of Upper Town and Lower Town, starting at 7:00 p.m.

The highlight of the carnival is the canoe race. During this gruelling event, a dozen or so teams of canoeists half-drag and half-row their heavy boats across the partly frozen St. Lawrence River between Quebec City and Levis. On the Plains of Abraham, 20 teams of sculptors from around the world express some aspect of their nations' culture in the **International Snow Sculpture Competition**.

Since this festival's beginnings in 1894 (it only became an annual event in 1954) the number of activities has expanded to encompass all ages and interests. There are special exhibits at the museums, a reproduction of an Indian winter campsite, a **Sound and Light Show** in **Notre-Dame-de-Québec Cathedral**, car racing on ice, a 19th-century music concert, a *Mardi Gras* ball, speed skating, and one event guaranteed to send chills up your spine, rolling in snow wearing just a bathing suit.

Hiking at the Rockies.

and **snowshoeing** has become a sport practised by a few non-native hikers in the Canadian woods.

Canoeing

The canoe was the Indians main means of transportation, and the routes they used in Manitoba are now followed by recreational canoeists. With all the lakes and rivers in Canada, canoeists have a wide choice, from the **Bowron** chain of lakes in the Cariboo Mountains in British Columbia to Ontario's **Quetico** provincial park where bald eagles and osprey fly overhead. The **South Nahanni River** in the Northwest Territories is considered to be one of the most beauti-

outside the Chateau Frontenac.

Dogs dragged the Indians' toboggans through the snow, and today dog sled trips for people seeking this unique experience follow the paths of the trappers in Quebec's **Saguenay Region** as well as in other remote areas, including the Northwest Territories.

Snowshoes were an Indian invention for travelling around in winter, but now they prefer the speed of snowmobiles

The choppy waters of Ottawa prove to be a lure for canoeists.

Fly fishing at British Columbia.

ful and challenging rivers.

Whitewater rafting is felt by many to be an invigorating experience in many locations, including British Columbia's **Fraser River, Maligne River** in Jasper National Park and on the Ottawa River between **Pembroke** and **Renfrew** in Eastern Ontario.

Yachting

As expected, yachting is popular along both coasts. The Straits of Georgia are sheltered from the Pacific Ocean, giving this island-studded area ideal sailing conditions. **The Thousand Islands** on the **St. Lawrence River** is another scenic region as there are over 14,000 islands

on Ontario's **Lake of the Woods**, where an international sailing regatta features a seven-day race that starts and finishes in **Kenora**.

Fishing

Golf, tennis and cycling are popular, but Canada is better known for its bountiful fishing waters, especially in the northern wilderness from British Columbia to Labrador, areas which often can only be reached by float plane. The **Yukon** and **Northwest Territories**, known for Arctic char, harbor trout in its lakes weighing more than 20 kg. **Prince Edward Island** has deep-sea tuna fishing while the foremost salmon areas

The Ski-Doo

The persistence and inventive genius of Joseph-Armand Bombardier created the huge snowmobiling industry.

The **Ski-Doo** revolutionized winter transport, especially for the Inuit in the Arctic where the snowmobile quickly replaced the traditional dog team. Millions of people around the world have taken it up for sport and recreation. In North America alone, there are over 10,000 clubs and more than 150,000 km of snowmobile trails. Quebec, with over 25,000 km of trails, has more trails than any other province.

The Ski-Doo has made Bombardier Inc. one of Canada's most successful manufacturing companies. Not only does it control about 25 percent of the snowmobiling market, it is North America's largest manufacturer of rail equipment and the acquisition of several aerospace companies including Learjet Inc have made it Canada's largest aerospace company. Bombardier has manufacturing facilities in eight countries, employing over 34,000 employees.

Bombardier was born in Valcourt Quebec in 1907. Like most inventors he spent much of his childhood building and taking things apart. While most boys were dreaming about being a doctor or a hockey player, Bombardier envisioned building a machine which could travel on snow. Undoubtedly, he was inspired by the difficulty of winter travel in rural Quebec. Many communities were isolated during the long winter since only a few roads were cleared of snow. Often, the only transport was a horse drawn sleigh.

Bombardier's first snow machine was built when he was only 15 years old! The crudely built machine was basically a sleigh powered by a propeller attached to a ford engine.

Trying out a snowmobile.

waiting for a nibble. Not everybody sits protected from the elements when ice fishing, but it's decidedly more comfortable. In Quebec's Saguenay fjord, you can rent huts to try your hand at catching some 50 species of fish.

Ontario watersports

Ontario's location around all of the Great Lakes except Michigan and its numerous rivers and lakes gives it thousands of kilometers of sandy beaches with a variety of watersports. **Scuba diving** is great among the shipwrecks at **Fathom Five National Marine Park**. The exceptional clarity of the Georgian Bay waters helps preserve the wrecks and also

are the **Miramichi** and **Restigouche Rivers** in New Brunswick and the **Campbell River** on Vancouver Island.

There are tiny little huts on the frozen rivers and lakes in the winter, especially in Manitoba, Quebec and Ontario in which people patiently sit

Rafting requires team effort for a fun-filled experience.

favors underwater photography. At the nearby **Flowerpot Island**, snorkelling enthusiasts examine the pillars of the flowerpots. Flowerpot Island, in particular has sea-washed, spectacularly shaped rocks that invite speculation regarding its origin. Swimmers find this an especially cosy spot for a private beach picnic. Other shipwrecks attracting divers are by Manitoulin

Island and Parry Sound.

Boats and houseboats can be rented to travel the historic **Rideau Canal** between Kingston and Ottawa, where they can dock within sight of the Parliament Buildings, as well as along the historic **Trent-Severn Waterway**, the 386-km route linking the Bay of Quinte with Georgian Bay.

Sightseeing cruises are as varied as a 2-hour tour of **Lake Simcoe** and **Lake Couchiching** on a **Mississippi riverboat** to an 8-day cruise on a replica steamship sailing the St. Lawrence River.

Shopping in Canada's large cities is like venturing into a *souk*, for there are innumerable shops offering a great diversity of merchandise, all easily obtainable through credit cards and travellers' cheques.

Canada is world famous for its **furs, native art, sculpture** and **maple syrup** while Americans appreciate the wide selection of **china, silverware** and **woollen garments** from Great Britain.

■ ■ ■ ■ ■ ■

Beautifully donned mannequins make shopping irresistible.

Where to Shop

Canadians' passion for indoor malls, a boon in the winters, reaches its peak in Edmonton where the **West Edmonton Mall** reigns as the world's largest indoor shopping center. But you'll also find malls ringing every city in Canada. Most large cities will also have a mall downtown, often housing one or two department stores. The same chain stores seem to appear in all shopping malls throughout the country.

The main department stores found throughout Canada are **Sears Canada**, (primarily in malls outside the city centre), **Eaton's** with its glass domed structure where almost everything can be found and the **Bay** whose colorful and warm **Hudson Bay duffel coats** are a Canadian institution.

An underground shopping arcade.

Toronto

The Canadian shopping mecca is **To-ronto**, where **Bloor Street West** and **Yorkville** tantalize with luxury goods and *haute couture* (high fashion). The

Bay, at **Yonge and Bloor**, is the start of this stroll past **Tiffany's** and other expensive jewelry stores, boutiques with **Armani** and **Calvin Klein** and other designer names. They occupy a stunning marble and glass building, Canada's high fashion department store, **Holt**

Every city in Canada is ringed with indoor malls.

Country Town Markets

Fresh lobster can be found for a good bargain at country town markets.

Shopping at **markets** is a tradition that lives on in Canada. Unlike the bland, impersonal atmosphere of stores and malls, these markets are active, lively areas where customers pinch the fruit, pick up the vegetables and, sometimes, haggle over the prices.

Most markets abound in fruit, vegetables and flowers, but you'll also find gunny **sacks of pecans, cheddar cheese, spiced olives** and strolling musicians at Toronto's **St. Lawrence Market**. Locally caught shrimp are sold along with tomatoes grown around Quebec City at its **Old Port Market** (Marché du Vieux-Port).

Canada's oldest market building is in Saint John, New Brunswick. It was opened in 1876 as a showcase to the prosperity of the city. Inside the sturdy brick **Old City Market**, shipbuilders fashioned hand-hewn timbers and arched oak beams to resemble the inverted hull of a ship. Underneath this handsome ceiling, you can buy food for a picnic suitable for royalty – live and cooked **lobster, fresh pasta** and **berries**.

The market was nearly demolished in the early 1970s for lack of business, but market shopping made a tremendous comeback in

Canada, helped in Alberta and Saskatchewan by the provincial governments instituting programs to set up farmers' markets.

As markets grew in popularity in the late 1970s, entrepreneurs gravitated towards them and in Ottawa, **Bytown Market** became the trendy area. Chic restaurants and bars now surround the outdoor stalls of **vegetables, maple syrup, fish** and **meat**, while the market building houses local craftspeople.

Canada's most beautiful market is Vancouver's Granville Market, a spacious building with exposed industrial fixtures which create a high-tech feeling, and a glassed-in snack spot to eat the **fish chowder** or **grilled oysters** you can pick up from the food stalls after purchasing **fresh fish** and **vegetables**. Outside the market building are several galleries of **Inuit artwork** and **crafts**, making the entire island a popular tourist attraction.

Among the more than 80 markets in Ontario, the **Waterloo Farmers' Market** is distinctive. Along with local farmers and craftspeople selling their products, Mennonites display their home-made sausages, soaps, knitted sweaters, jams and quilts. The farmers' markets in both Waterloo and nearby Kitchener, which are located in a shopping mall, are open Wednesdays and Saturdays in the summer. They are open only on Saturdays the rest of the year.

Renfrew. For **handknit Aran sweaters**, sturdy men's **tweed jackets**, and **silk chiffon dresses** from Ireland, there's **The Irish Shop**.

The **Colonnade** is a two-level indoor mall with quality **leather goods** and clothing boutiques like **Chanel** on the south side of Bloor West.

Sidewalk cafes litter the busy shopping malls.

Squeezed into the narrow, multi-level **William Ashley** shop are a wide range of **English china** and **silver**, at competitive prices. Ask them about a specific china pattern and they will pull up a picture on a computer screen and let you know if it's available. **Yorkville** starts about a block north of Bloor and is also bordered by the three areas of Yonge, Bay and Scollard.

This is a delightful area filled with attractive old Victorian homes packed with more high fashion boutiques along with **antique shops**, **art galleries**, and **restaurants** which, in the summer, become outdoor cafes where you can sit and enjoy the atmosphere. There is a decidedly French feel to this place and it is also always flocked with tourists.

Electronic

Bay Bloor Radio was rated by England's "High Fidelity" magazine as one of the continent's top **hi-fi** shops. Inside its private sound booths, you can listen to CD players, speakers, and other equipment sold at good prices.

Two big chains, mainly located in the suburbs of Toronto and other large cities, are **Majestic** and **Future Shop**, which compete against each other in pricing their audio and video equipment, as well as computers, printers and other accessories.

As a result, some of the latest in hi-fi equipment can be found. The prices are rather reasonable as well.

Taxes

The **Goods and Services tax (GST)** is a national tax that is added on to nearly every transaction in Canada, the main exception being basic groceries. There are a few quirks with the GST. For example, while the GST is charged on one donut, it isn't charged on a half-dozen.

Non-residents of Canada can obtain a GST refund for short term accommodation and for goods taken out of Canada within 60 days. Unfortunately, there are no refunds for meals and restaurant charges, camper and trailer fees, alcoholic beverages and gasoline.

Rebate forms can be picked up at some border and airport duty free shops or from Revenue Canada (Visitors' Rebate Program, Ottawa, ON Canada K1A 1J5). Rebates are only given for amounts over $7.00.

Instant rebates can be obtained from some duty free shops. If the amount is over $500, you must apply to Revenue Canada. The GST rebate must be claimed within one year of the date of your purchase.

The above may soon be academic as the new Liberal government has promised to replace the GST with a hidden tax.

Of course, then there are also provincial **sales taxes** that are levied on restaurant meals and most goods – with the exception of Alberta,

the Northwest Territories and the Yukon.

Provincial sales taxes vary from 6 percent in British Columbia to as much as 12 percent in Newfoundland. Some provinces also have a tax on accommodations, for example: in British Columbia, the tax may even be as much as 10 percent; in Ontario and Alberta it is 5 percent while in Quebec it is 4 percent. This makes living in British Columbia much cheaper.

Provincial rebates similar to those on the GST are offered by Nova Scotia, Quebec, Newfoundland and Manitoba. Ontario doesn't have a rebate program anymore.

Vancouver International airport is the only airport in the country that charges a user **fee** for its **airport**. Charges for international flights are $15, national flights $10 and $5 for flights within British Columbia.

The user fee was introduced following the leasing of the airport to a non-profit company. The fee will eventually go towards financing a new runway and terminal.

The travel industry is not happy about this new tax and, as a result, airlines and travel agents have refused to collect the fee. This has forced the airport to set up booths outside the security gates to collect the money before people board the planes.

Antiques

Interior designers patronize Yorkville's antique shops when they need 18th century **French furnishings**, **art deco tables**, **Canadian mirrors** or other high quality furnishings and accessories.

More informal and with more unpredictable merchandise is the **Harbourfront Antique Market** where you can haggle with 100 exhibitors from Tuesday to Saturday. On the busiest day, Sunday, the number of dealers

increases by at least a 100.

Contemporary Canadian Fashion

Innovative, hip clothing by young designers, such as **Jim Searle** and **Chris Tyrell** who have a store displaying their **Hoax Couture** label, has helped make Toronto the nation's fashion center. Most of the shops are on **Queen Street West**, the city's avant-garde section, where you can find **Siren** with its nearly all-

Craft shops are laden with exquisite antiques at Old Montreal.

Black clothing and brocade corset tops at **Fashion Crimes**.

The clothing is more traditional at Toronto's garment center on **Spadina**. Generally, the clothing manufacturers open their small showrooms for bargains in dresses, blouses, fur and leather on Saturdays.

Yonge Street

On **Yonge Street**, cat suits flounced with organza are a signature at the temple to flamboyance, **Chapter II**, while secondhand baggy suits and tuques at **New York Connections** appeal to hardcore ravers.

The mix is more eclectic at the **Eaton** **Center** where 'Canada Geese' created by Michael Snow soar from its arching glass roof. The three levels of restaurants and stores offer a wide variety of low-cost goods as well as high priced couture clothing. Eaton's dominates one end of the mall while an enclosed glass passageway leads across Queen Street to another Bay.

Markets

St. Lawrence Market on **Front Street** is in a grand old building that was Toronto's first city hall. The food stalls sell **sausages, cheddar cheese** and anything needed for a picnic lunch from Tuesday to Saturday. The plain one-story building

Strolling down Sherbrooke Street.

across Front Street is filled with local produce on Saturdays only.

Kensington Market, just behind Spadina Avenue's Chinatown is a colorful display of **fresh fish**, **live chickens**, **vegetables**, **cheeses** on tables outside shops catering to the city's ethnic population. The little old houses around the area are now restaurants and shops selling inexpensive unique clothes and jewellery from around the world.

Montreal

Sherbrooke Street is where the elite shop and eat in Montreal. In the grand old mansions are some of the city's best art galleries, antique stores and bou-

tiques with the high fashions appealing to Montreal's chic dressers.

The largest shop on the street is **Holt Renfrew**, where clothes by Yves St-Laurent sell next to Gucci leather items. Just two blocks down the hill is another Montreal institution, **Ogilvy**, where a kilted piper weaves his way at noon around this store made up of well-known designer boutiques like **Valentino**, **Jaegaer** and **Aquascutum**.

A 29-km underground walkway leads to downtown malls, offering a mix of exclusive boutiques with moderately priced stores: **Place Montreal Trust**, with its tall glass walls overlooking McGill College, the four-level **Les Cours Mont-Royal**, **Center Eaton** (the largest indoor mall with Eaton's department store), **Place Ville Marie**, and **Les Promenades** de la Cathédral, underneath the neo-gothic Christ Church Cathedral. The Bay department store is across the street.

Off the beaten track is **Complex Desjardins** where several stores surround a stage for everything from the circus to rock music.

Furs

Mink, beaver, fox and other lustrous furs are primarily made into fur-fashion garments in **Montreal**.

Holt Renfrew and **Alexandor** are well-known retailers or you could head to the small workshops in the **Fur-Fashion Quarter**, bounded by **De Bleury**, **St. Catherine**, **City Councilors**

Prices are very affordable at open markets.

and **de Maissoneuve Boulevard.**
Shopping in the stores displaying work
by some of Montreal's leading designers
can be quite an expensive with its range
from ready-to-wear to *haute couture.*

Antiques & Crafts

Canadian pine rocking chairs, **Victorian furniture** and **European antiques**
are sold in the numerous shops lining
Notre-Dame east of Atwater. A more
eclectic mix of antiques and secondhand goods fills the **Marché aux Puces**
on **King Edward Pier** in Vieux-Montréal
(Old Montreal). Along **St. Paul Street** in
Old Montreal are craft shops, although
the **Canadian Guild of Crafts** on **Peel**

Street is more centrally located.

For the Home

Generations of families have bought
their china, silver, crystal and jewelry at
Birks, which has its main store on **St.
Catherine. Caplan Duval**, which has
two stores in malls outside of the central
core, has good prices for its china and
crystal goods.

Ultra-modern lamps, Quebec-made
glassware and locally designed clothes
can be bought in tiny shops among the
trendy cafes and restaurants on **St.
Denis**. The lamps and glassware are
quite original in design and make good
personal gifts.

A fur shop at Prince Edward Island.

Native Art

Vancouver has a good selection of native art galleries. The **Gallery of Tribal Art** on **Granville Street** handles such Northwest Coast sculptors as **Robert Davidson**. In North Vancouver, you can go directly to **Khot-la-Cha** on a **Salish Indian reservation** for locally made sterling silver and gold jewelry as well as ceremonial masks.

Victoria has many stores, including The Bay, selling the famous hand-made **Cowichan Indian** sweaters. They cater to people who use genuine rabbit fur, leather and 100 percent sheepskin for their *mukluks*, slippers and mitts.

Edmonton and Winnipeg are also known for **Indian artwork**, slippers, beadwork and exquisite jade sculpture as well as **Inuit soapstone carvings** and prints. All authentic Inuit work comes with a Government of Canada tag displaying an igloo.

Calgary has many **Western shops** where you can purchase leather cowboy/cowgirl boots, hats, belts and all the other gear to fit into the atmosphere of the Calgary Stampede.

Canadian Food

Pick up cans of **maple syrup** in the spring from markets in Quebec and Ontario or from sugar shacks in the countryside. **Smoked salmon** is a

Victoria has several Cowichan Indian sweater shops.

Nova Scotia has a good stock of handmade quilts at its folk art shops.

specialty in Vancouver. In Nova Scotia, you can arrange to air express **fresh lobster** or **shrimp** home. **Wild rice** and **cheese** are sold in numerous spots throughout Ontario and Manitoba.

Canadian Crafts

The **Mennonites** of Kitchener-Waterloo in Ontario are known for their **quilts**. The Atlantic Provinces have items that range from **pewter accessories** in Fredricton, New Brunswick, to handmade **sweaters** in **Prince Edward Island**. **Nova Scotia** is known for its **tartans**. Hand-made floor **mats** with scenes from everyday Newfoundland life hang in homes in many countries.

Window shoppers at Vancouver.

Canadian food has evolved from the basic meat and potatoes of the past to a smorgasbord of choices. A rich and varied cuisine reflects the different regions of the country and the influence of its diverse immigrant communities.

Toronto is one city where this is most noticeable, with about 5,000 restaurants representing 80 ethnic groups. Some ethnic restaurants are concentrated in certain neighborhoods – **Greek restaurants** on **The Danforth**, **Chinese** around **Spadina** and **Dundas**, **Italians** on **St. Clair Avenue West**, **East Indians** on **Gerrard Street East**. While this makes it easy to locate a restaurant in a specific ethnic group, you can also find them scattered elsewhere in the city along with **West Indian, Thai, Korean, French, Hungarian, Japanese, Spanish** and the list goes on.

The numerous restaurants mean that competition is extremely fierce, but as soon as one door closes, another opens, giving you a choice from white tablecloth

Feast your eyes on a luscious lobster dinner at Prince Edward Island.

Cuisine

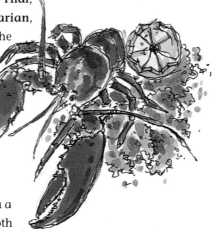

It is a busy nightlife at fruit-laden Chinatown.

elegance to a plain, six-table room.

The best dining rooms use European preparation techniques to combine indigenous ingredients with the culinary heritage of other countries to create a Canadian cuisine. Smoked venison is wreathed by mango-sparkling *macédoine* at one of Toronto's more expensive restaurants, **Orso**. At **Winston's** restaurant, a long-established gathering spot for the business elite, spicy bean curd comes with *crème fraîche*.

Food Courts, a collection of fast-food stalls around a seating area of two or four person tables are about the only choice for eating in most shopping malls. The inexpensive food is usually the most popular take-out food: **pizza**, **Chinese**, **Lebanese** and the **traditional chicken**,

Traditional English steakhouses always serve choice cuts.

There is never a lack of lobster and it is best served with sliced oranges and lemons.

hamburgers, and **french fries**. Except for teenagers who use Food Courts as their social center, people rarely linger, so if you can't find a seat, just wait a few minutes. The more chic hang out at espresso bars, sophisticated coffee shops which Vancouver introduced to Canada.

More upscale are **bistros**. The choice of dishes is limited, but since they employ some of the top chefs, the quality equals that in the more expensive dining rooms but at lower prices. Many bistros look to the past for their inspiration, to *homey* or comfort foods, described as refined, home cooking.

These would include recipes such as roast chicken with its crisp gold skin concealing rosemary, thyme and garlic.

Comfort food is a reaction against the excess of the 1980s, when food became an obsession in Toronto. People hopped from trend to trend, always wanting to experience the newest culinary art and restaurants tried to feed that appetite by serving novelties like **baby shark** in **blackberry coulis**. It was a spiralling fad burst by the recession that did have one benefit: Torontonians, who dine out more

Strawberry and kiwi fruit pie is the local delicacy of the Maritime provinces.

than other Canadians, now have a better knowledge and appreciation of food.

The trend throughout Canada these days is towards healthy foods, low-cholesterol and low salt dishes and fresh ingredients. This is being satisfied by grilling foods and by chefs looking into their own backyards.

Atlantic Canada

Nearly every city in Canada contains a minimum of one Chinese, Mexican, East Indian and Italian restaurant. Atlantic Canada can also add a great variety and amount of **fresh seafood**, much of it conservatively cooked.

Prince Edward Island is known for

its **lobster suppers**, often served by church groups. Usually, it's a choice of hot or cold lobster with drawn butter and salad, sometimes with potatoes, the island's main crop. Gourmets know P.E.I. for its **Malpeque oysters** but there are also mussels, oysters clams and mackerel, to name just a few of its beautiful harvest from the sea.

Chowders are the specialties of New Brunswick and Nova Scotia, where many north shore communities hold competitions for the best seafood stew. Nova Scotia is also known for its **lobsters** and **scallops**, but it's also an exporter of **_Chanterelle mushrooms_** that grow wild from mid-June until the cold weather. The German and Dutch gave **Dutch Mess** (codfish and potatoes) and _Salmi_

One of the upscale French restaurants in Quebec
that are always packed with people.

Gundi (pickled herring) to the Lunenburg area, while **oatcakes**, the heritage of their Scottish ancestry, fill breadbaskets in **Cape Breton Island**.

Unique to New Brunswick are *fiddleheads*, an edible form of the ostrich fern which, like asparagus, can be served hot or cold and are eaten in the spring. Another delicacy is *dulse*, a purple seaweed that is dried and eaten as a snack.

While these three Maritime provinces are justifiably proud of their **apples, cranberries, blueberries, strawberries** and Acadian dishes like **Poutine Rapée** (a potato pie made with salt pork or clams), Newfoundland boasts of **golden bakeapples** that grow in marshes and fresh catches of **skate, squid, Atlantic salmon**, and **crabs**. Just

ask for fish and you're served cod but now that even recreational **cod fishing** has been limited by the government, **sole, haddock** and a new local fish called grenadier may have to substitute in dishes such as **fish** and **brewis** (salt cod and hard biscuits soaked overnight, then fried). Other original dishes are **corned caplin, dried and salted bits of silvery fish**, and **flipper pie**, made from **seal flippers**.

Restaurants in Quebec City and Montreal have always been highly rated. Chefs duplicate the trends and dishes of France with local ingredients, such as **Brome Lake ducklings, lamb** and **cheeses** such as **Oka**, developed by Trappist monks, and **Ermite**, a **blue cheese** made by Benedictine monks. Their own

Canadian Dishes

A complete meal from Canada:
Bannock - a bread eaten by fur traders and settlers.

Red River Bannock
3 cups (750 ml) flour
1 tsp. (5 ml) salt
1 tbsp. (15 ml) sugar
2 heaping tsp. (10 ml) baking powder
1/2 cup (125 ml) dripping or lard
2 cups (500 ml) cold water
    Mix all into a ball of dough. Knead well for 5-8 minutes. Roll into a large round cake, about 2.5 cm thick. Cook 400°F (200°C) until light brown.

Baked Beans with Maple Syrup – an old traditional dish
2 1/2 cups (625 ml) small white beans
6 slices bacon, chopped in 2-inch (5 cm) pieces
1 medium onion, chopped
1/4 tsp. (1 ml) salt
1/2 tsp. (2 ml) dry mustard
1/2 cup (125 ml) maple syrup
1/2 cup (125 ml) rum
I pork hock (optional)
1/2 tsp. (2 ml) Worcestershire sauce (optional)
3 tbsp. (15 ml) brown sugar
3 tbsp. (15 ml) melted butter
    Cover beans with 8 cups (2 L) cold water. Soak overnight.
    Bring to boil, reduce heat and simmer under tender, one to one and a half hours. Drain beans, reserving 2 1/2 cups (625 ml) cooking liquid.
    Line casserole dish with bacon, top with baked beans.
    Combine together onion, salt, dry mustard, maple syrup, rum and 2 cups (500 ml) liquid. Pour over beans and push pork hock into center of casserole.
    Cover and bake in 325°F (160°C) oven for 3 hours. If too dry, add remaining 1/2 cup (125 L) liquid during last 30 minutes. Remove cover, top with brown sugar mixed with melted butter and cook an additional hour, until liquid has evaporated.

Salmon – the best cooking methods for salmon, as with most fresh fish, are simple ones. Decorate the dish with sauce, such as in this recipe.

Atlantic Salmon with Cucumber Parsley Sauce
4 Atlantic salmon steaks (1 inch/2.5 cm)
2 tbsp. (25 ml) olive oil
Sauce:
1/2 cups (125 ml) plain yogurt (or sour cream)
1 cup (250 ml) finely chopped cucumber
2 green onions, finely chopped
2 cloves garlic, minced
1/2 tsp. (2 ml) ground cumin
pinch of pepper
    Brush steaks with oil. Broil for 3 minutes one side. Brush with additional butter and broil

French-Canadian dishes, recipes handed down for generations, include **pea soup**, **cretons** (pork paté) and **Tourtière** (pork pie). As Canada's major **maple syrup** producer, syrup flavors **chicken** and **dessert** for a unique taste.

Upscale French restaurants in Montreal and Quebec restaurants often have a table d'hôte or menu de dégustation, a table d'hôte is a two-to four-course meal, a salad or soup and main course, while a menu de dégustation or gourmand is a more elaborate five-to-seven-course meal that, at the highly rated **Chez La Mere Michel**, could include pheasant with onion marmalade. Montreal is also known for its smoked meat sandwiches, a deliciously seasoned version of corned beef on rye best bought at delicatessens like **Bens**.

Many of the Greek and Vietnamese restaurants lining **Prince Arthur Street** encourage patrons to bring their own wine. Making it easier to choose a restaurant is the law requiring them to post menus and prices outside.

another 3 minutes. Or grill on a barbecue until it flakes easily with a fork.

Combine sauce ingredients and serve with salmon.

Nova Scotia Blueberry Grunt
Sauce:
4 cups (1 L) wild, fresh or frozen blueberries
$^1/_2$ tsp. (2 ml) nutmeg
$^1/_2$ tsp. (2 ml) cinnamon
$^3/_4$ cup (175 ml) sugar
1 tbsp. (15 ml) lemon juice
$^1/_2$ cup (125 ml) water
Dumplings
2 cups (500 ml) flour
4 tsp. (20 ml) baking powder
$^1/_2$ tsp. (2 ml) salt
1 tbsp. (15 ml) sugar
2 tbsp. (25 ml) butter or shortening milk
Whipped cream (optional)

Heat berries, spices, sugar, lemon juice and water in a skillet. Boil gently until well blended and slightly well cooked.

Sift flour, baking powder, salt and sugar into a bowl. Cut in butter and add enough milk to make a soft biscuit dough. Drop by spoonfuls into hot berry sauce. Cover tightly with a lid and simmer for 15 minutes (no peeking!). The dumplings should be puffed and well cooked through. Transfer cooked dumplings to serving dish. Ladle sauce over top. Serve with whipped cream.

Manitoba is known for Winnipeg **goldeye**, a red-gold delicate **smoked fish** as well as **golden caviar** made from **whitefish roe** and similar to Saskatchewan, **schnitzel**, **goulash**, and **perogies**, the heritage from the settlers of these prairie provinces along **whitefish** from their lakes. Alberta's cattle ranches produce thick, tender **steaks of prime beef**.

British Columbia is **salmon** heaven with five varieties of salmon as well as **black cod**, **shrimp**, **oysters** and **King**

Toronto's Chinatown's shops simply stretch into the horizon.

crab. Seafood is popular in Vancouver's trendy West Coast/California-style restaurants, such as **Bishop's** where **smoked black cod** comes with **sorrel** and **lemon** as it does in Asian restaurants. Pagoda-topped telephone booths distinguish **Chinatown**, the area centered on **E. Pender St.** between **Carrall** and **Gore**. **East Indian restaurants** are clustered between **48th** and **51st Avenues**.

There are so many Asian dining spots, from the small, unpretentious spot to an upscale restaurant that Japanese and Chinese businesspeople can find culinary skills equivalent to that in their home countries. The three-star **Tojo** could just as easily be in Tokyo, with its **pine-mushroom soup** and **chrysanthe-**

Barbecue dinners are becoming part of home cuisine.

mum blossoms and **tuna** with **sesame, soya, green onion** and **wasabi**.

Dim Sum, the assortment of Chinese appetizers usually served from carts which roam the restaurant, is popular for lunch especially on weekends when long lines form at some of the more popular Chinese restaurants.

Native Cuisine

Canada is known for its **cheddar cheese, maple syrup** and **seafood** but these days a few restaurants in major cities are offering more exotic indigenous fare-food from northern Canada, such as **muskox, caribou**, and the salmon-like **Arctic char**.

The interest in these foods was sparked by a team of First Nations people winning the Grand Gold for best overall performance at the last International Culinary Olympics in Frankfurt.

The Indians taught the settlers such cooking techniques as smoking **Chinook salmon** over applewood, as well as introduced them to **corn, squash** and **wild rice**. Wild rice is a **nutty-tasting rice** that grows in shallow marshes, predominantly in Ontario and Manitoba.

Canadian Eating Habits

Elaborate breakfast buffets are offered at hotels and restaurants on weekends and many business people hold breakfast meetings, preferring not to interrupt their day with a long lunch.

Lunch is often a rushed meal of a sandwich or soup and salad, unless it's a business meeting or a chance for friends to get together. Even then, the amount of drinking has gone down considerably, concerns about health and alcohol consumption induces many people to order a club soda or spritzer instead.

Dinner is the main meal and when eating out, people mainly choose a restaurant on the type of cuisine they want and price. Some restaurants offer "**Early Bird Specials**," that lower prices before 6:00 p.m. People dine later in major cities, usually after 7:00 p.m. and there are always restaurants that open late, often these are delicatessens and they are very well-stocked.

French styled sidewalk cafes have excellent salads and beer.

Toronto is the entertainment capital of Canada, an exciting, invigorating city that vibrates day and night. Events and activities can jampack your calendar all year long. The suburbs offer some entertainment, but the main action is in the city core.

Theatre

A dancer from the National Ballet of Canada uses every sinew of muscle to evoke the message of his craft.

Toronto's very active live theatre scene pushes the city into the ranking of top theatre centers in North America. Touring companies visit the city; however, the majority of productions are presented by local professionals.

Splashy **musicals** requiring elaborate sets are presented at the brand-new **North York Performance Center** where a revival of **Showboat** opened its new 1800-seat mainstage. Equally lavish and new is the $22 million **Princess of Wales theatre**, which inaugurated its 2,000-seat hall with the musical blockbuster **Miss Saigon**.

An open air play at St. John revives classical romance.

Christie's **The Mousetrap.**

There are three companies that concentrate on new Canadian drama: **Theatre Passe Muraille,** the **Factory Theatre** and the **Tarragon Theatre. Young People's Theatre** mounts productions for children whereas productions at **Buddies** in **Bad Times Theatre** tends to focus on gay, gender and sexual issues. The **Canadian Stage Company** presents its contemporary dramas at the **St. Lawrence Center,** which is also the venue for the **Toronto Operetta Theatre.**

The nearby **O'Keefe Center** is the home of the **Canadian Opera Company** and the **National Ballet of Canada** as well as the space rented by many touring companies and crowd-drawers like **Anne Murray.**

Dinner theatres solve the problem of finding a restaurant before or after the theatre. Diners sit back and watch Broadway musicals or comedies at the **Limelight Dinner Theatre** or **Harper's Restaurant** and **Dinner Theatre.** Guests at the Dinner Theatre at the **Royal York Hotel** attempt to solve a crime committed during dinner. Its mystery theatre dinners have been confounding patrons for seven years now.

John Candy and **Dan Aykryod** are among the comedians who went on to fame and fortune after performing at **Second City,** the city's prime and longest running comedy club. The other main comedy club is **Yuk Yuks,** with two stages in Toronto and one each in Ottawa and Edmonton.

The theatre is a few doors down from another Mirvish-owned theatre, the luxuriously fitted **Royal Alexandra,** which was resurrected to its former turn-of-the-century flamboyance by Ed Mirvish of the very popular "Honest Ed's" discount store.

Among the flurry of restorations that revived some old vaudeville houses on Yonge Street is the charming **Elgin Theatre.** It has just brought to its stage the $4.5 million Canadian-made megamusical **Napoleon.** Another beautifully restored theatre is **Pantages,** where the **Phantom of the Opera** has been running for five years.

It is a record that's been beaten by the **Toronto Truck Theatre,** now into their 17th year of presenting Agatha

A dinner theatre restaurant at the Royal York Hotel
where a 'whodunit' mystery is being solved.

Bars and Lounges

Bars and Lounges are scattered throughout the city with hotels having some of the most elegant decor. Overlooking the city, the **Park Plaza Roof Lounge** is for the debonair. The **Royal York's Library Bar** has the decor and atmosphere of a sophisticated private club. The action is more tumultuous in all the pubs in the area around the **Sky Dome**.

Among these havens for sports fans after the games are **Amsterdam** with its wooden floors and well-brewed beer on tap and **Loose Moose** with its pub games. The Sports Cafe takes it one step further, having tiny television sets on the tables and such games as table hockey and a cage where customers can dunk basketballs at will.

Throughout the city tiny pubs similar to **Queen's Head Pub**, supply the atmosphere, dartboard and imported beer of Great Britain. In the increasingly vibrant area of College Street, **Souz Dal** is a cool and inexpensive bar.

Music Clubs

Above the **Brunswick House**, an institution for hard-drinking university students, is the plainly decorated blues club, **Albert Hall**. Other places to listen to some live blues spots are **The Spoon** and the **Black Swan**.

Toronto's Jazz Festival has helped

Entertainment Industry

Christopher Plummer, Leslie Nielsen, Michael J. Fox, Donald Sutherland, – the list of Canadians who've found their niche in Hollywood goes on and on, all the way back to **Mary Pickford**. Yet, enough American film companies shoot on location in Canada for Vancouver and Toronto to vie for the title of "Hollywood of the North." So why haven't these people remained in Canada? It is because it's difficult to gain access to capital for production and there is an even more basic problem – Canada sits beside the behemoth United States.

The Canadian government quickly backed down in the 1980s to the threat of retribution if Canada tried to act like a foreign country instead of remaining part of the American domestic film market. The result: Canadian companies can only distribute foreign films, not any American film, so the approximately $550 million a year Canadians spend on watching American films goes to the United States. There isn't any requirement for Canadian theatres to run Canadian films either.

Despite these obstacles, there is a Canadian film industry, albeit a small one. **Alliance Communications,** producers of both television programs and films, reaped $2.8 million in Canada alone for the film *Black Robe*. Horror films have kept **David Cronenberg** busy. His *Naked Lunch* based on the William Burroughs novel of the same name, won numerous **Genie Awards**, the Canadian equivalent of the Academy Award Oscar. Another winner was Jean-Claude Lauzon's *Léolo*, a French-Canadian film which was also awarded the prestigious Golden Ear Award at Valladolid in Spain.

Not all Quebec films made the transition to English. People in Quebec enjoyed the slapstick humour of *Ding and Dong*, but that style of comedy is not a big seller in English Canada.

Montreal doubles for Chicago, Toronto for New York, and countless other Canadian locations form the backdrop for a number of American films. The lower Canadian dollar makes the country attractive and so do the highly skilled craftspeople.

Montreal's **Softimage** computer animators created many of the dinosaurs in *Jurassic Park*. Toronto's **IMAX** developed and manufactures the special cameras and projectors for simulation rides, such as the *Back to the Future* ride at Universal Studios in Florida, and for IMAX films along with producing its own movies. Their first feature, the Rolling Stones concert film *At the Max* grossed $13 million in just over a year after release. *Fires of Kuwait* was nominated for an Academy Award for Best Feature Documentary.

Canadian documentaries are synonymous with the **National Film Board** (NFB), the national film agency also recognized for its animated films. The revolutionary work of **Norman Mclaren** brought fame and an Oscar, a tradition continued to this day with another generation of animators. The NFB has been the training ground for many of the animators who are producing children's cartoon series and documentary film makers working in the industry today while the **Canadian Broadcasting Corporation** (CBC), the national radio and television company on the other hand, provided the training for Peter Jennings, Morley Safer as well as for numerous actors who still appear on prime-time T.V.

popularize jazz and the city now has numerous clubs, including the **Pilot Tavern**, **Montreal Bistro**, and the oldest jazz club, **George's Spaghetti House**. **Ella Fitzgerald** and many other big names, however, draw enough audiences to warrant **Roy Thomson Hall**, the city's premier concert hall.

Jazz and rock are showcased at the **Rivoli** while at **Hard Rock Cafe**, dancers swing to Djs spinning popular pop and rock from Thursday to Saturday and on Monday, guitarists jam on instruments once owned by Jimi Hendrix and Stevie Ray Vaughan.

Afro-beat, latin and reggae alter-

Canada's music festivals are always done on a lavish scale.

nate at the **Bamboo** on Queen West. Strictly latin music gets customers dancing at **Tapas** and **Copas** and jazz stirs them onto the dance floor at the **Top O'Senator**. The atmosphere is upscale at the **Berlin** where people dance to jazz and pop. Customers entertain themselves at the **Roppongi Restaurant's** karaoke bar and many other such bars throughout the city.

Film

The numerous cinemas offering the latest fare of classics at the **Bloor Cinema** explains the popularity of **Toronto's Festival of Festivals** in September. During this marvellous ten-day event,

about 250 films from all over the world are screened, some for the first time, to audiences that include people like **Faye Dunaway** and **Norman Mailer**.

For details about what is happening in Toronto, one could pick up the Friday edition of the *Toronto Star*, the *Saturday Globe* and *Mail* or one of the free tabloids.

French Entertainment

Montreal has many of the same type clubs and events as Toronto, including the **World Film Festival**, although here the cinemas screen English and French films. However, the city has a different atmosphere, a *joie de vivre* (joy of life) that is evident even within the affluent

Nightlife is always ablaze with color at Toronto.

areas. In Outremont, **Laurier Street** bubbles with lively chatter as people sip expresso and cappuccino in numerous chic sidewalk cafés reminiscent of those in Paris.

There are at least 10 French theatre companies, quite overwhelming the number of English theatres. The five concert halls offering theatre and musical productions for both langauge groups is Place des Arts.

A few blocks east is the Main, the anglophones' name for **St. Lawrence Boulevard**, Montreal's hip club section that appeals to both English and French. One usual gathering spot on the street is the eclectic all-night **Le Lux**, a bar cum magazine store.

While English speakers hover

around the central core of the city, drinking at **Sir Winston Churchill Pub** and **Grumpy's**, the favourite hang-out for the English media, young French café crawlers roam St. Denis Street with its minimalist decorated clubs, which seem to be continuously changing. Try Le Grand Café for jazz and blues. The predominance of English popular music in the western world has pushed both Quebec and France into actually creating laws compelling radio stations to play a set amount of minimum French music. Popular French music is therefore heard quite often in Quebec.

To further boost French music, a 10-day summer music festival in Montreal, **Les Franco Folies**, features an array of singing stars from France such as

Montreal's 'cinema wall' – a favorite with the younger crowd.

Ooh la la! – Les Franco Folies entertain at the summer festival.

Stephan Eicher, dynamic jazz singer **Liane Foley** as well as Quebec singers.

Montreal also hosts a bilingual comedy festival, the **Just for Laughs Festival**, an 11-day event featuring over 500 foreign and Canadian comedians who strut their best lines on indoor and outdoor stages around the city in July.

The English language, *Mirror* and the French language *Voir*, are the two tabloids with more information about Montreal's nightlife.

Montreal's hours reflect the more relaxed atmosphere in the city. Liquor is served until 3:00 a.m. and the minimum drinking age is 18. In contrast, Ontario has a minimum age of 19 and bars must stop selling liquor at 1:00 a.m. Naturally, Montreal has a more colorful nightlife.

Neon lights are alluring at Quebec's amusement park.

TRAVEL TIPS

ARRIVAL

By Air

The major international airports are at Vancouver, Toronto and Montreal. These three cities are well linked to other destinations across Canada. International flights also fly directly and regularly into Calgary, Edmonton, Halifax, Ottawa, St. John's and Winnipeg.

By Sea

Car ferrys run on both coasts. On the West Coast a ferry runs between Seattle and Victoria. A ferry connects Bar Harbour, Maine, and Yarmouth, Nova Scotia, on the East Coast.

Canada's long coastline and extensive inland transportation network makes the country a great one to visit by private boat. If, like most people, you don't have any access to a yacht or other boat, contact your travel agent and inquire about cruise ships sailing to Canada.

By Road

Many highways link the United States and Canada. Consult a map or your automobile association for the most convenient route.

If you don't feel like driving, you can always board a Greyhound bus. Greyhound buses travel daily between the United States and the larger Canadian cities.

Rail

Amtrak connects Toronto and Montreal to the major cities in the United States.

BUSINESS HOURS

Most stores are open from 9:00 a.m. to 6:00 p.m., Monday to Saturday. Stores usually have extended hours on Thursday and Friday nights, closing at 9:00 p.m. In some localities, stores stay open until 9:00 p.m. nightly.

All provinces, except Prince Edward Island, Nova Scotia and Newfoundland, permit Sunday shopping. Sunday shopping hours are usually limited, from 12:00 p.m. until 6:00 p.m.

Many convenience stores are open 24 hours.

CLIMATE

The weather varies greatly, depending on location and the season. In the southern parts of Canada, summers (June to August) are warm and often hot and humid, especially in central Canada.

Winter in southern Canada normally runs from mid-November to mid-March. The Pacific coast has wet and mild winters: the temperatures rarely fall below freezing. For the rest of the country, winter frequently brings freezing temperatures and plenty of snow. Spring and fall are generally characterized by mild day-time temperatures and cool nights.

CULTURE & ETIQUETTE

Canadians are generally very polite. If you accidentally bump into someone say "excuse me" or "I'm sorry."

It is illegal to drink alcoholic beverages in public. You may be fined by a police officer if you are caught drinking in a park or at a beach.

If you speak French, you'll notice that French Canadians are less formal in their speech than in France. The use of the familiar "tu" (you) is used more frequently, so don't be offended if someone addresses you in the "tu" form instead of the more polite "vous."

CUSTOMS

Visitors can bring in gifts free of duty and taxes, if each gift is worth less than $60. This doesn't apply to alcohol and tobacco.

Anyone 18 or older (this age may soon be raised to 19 in some provinces) can bring in duty-free: 200 cigarettes, 50 cigars and 400 grams of loose tobacco.

Visitors 19 or over (with the exception of Manitoba, Quebec and Alberta where the drinking age is 18) can bring in duty free: 1.14 litres of liquor or wine or 8.5 litres of beer.

Rifles and shotguns may be brought into Canada for hunting or sporting purposes; however, they may not let you bring in a gun if there isn't anything to hunt in season. Handguns and automatic weapons are prohibited, except under extenuating circumstances. If you wish to bring in a firearm, contact: Revenue Canada, Customs and Excise, Ottawa, Ontario K1A 0L5. Tel:(613) 993-0534.

Importing certain food products, plants and pets is also restricted.

ELECTRICITY

The electricity supply is the same as in the United States: 110 volts, 60 cycles. The plugs are flat and two-pronged.

FESTIVALS

It seems there is always a festival taking place somewhere in Canada, whether it's a festival celebrating the season, ethnicity, food or jazz.

HEALTH

Visitors do not need any vaccinations or health certificates to enter Canada.

HOLIDAYS

There are 10 National Holidays in Canada. Banks, post offices, government offices and stores normally close on national holidays; though, this varies with each province. Canada Day, on July 1, marks Canada's day of independence and is celebrated across the country.

MEDIA

The Toronto *Globe and Mail* is Canada's national newspaper. Newspapers from Europe, the United States and other Canadian cities are sold in magazine and tobacco shops in the large cities. *Maclean's* is Canada's weekly news magazine. Other Canadian magazines along with *Time* and *Newsweek* are widely available.

The Canadian Broadcasting Corporation (CBC), financed in part by the government, provides nation-wide television service in both English and French. The CBC also has a 24-hour cable news network and a radio network. The other national television network is CTV. There

are also many private local television stations.

Cable systems bring in American stations including NBC, CBS, ABC, PBS and CNN. The Toronto-based Much Music cable channel is Canada's 24-hour music station.

MEDICAL ASSISTANCE

It is highly advisable to invest in travel insurance before coming to Canada, in case some medical emergency arises. Prices are not as outrageous as those in the United States but costs can mount up rather quickly.

The larger cities usually have a 24 hour pharmacy.

MONEY & CURRENCY

The dollar is the basic unit of currency. Common denominations for dollar bills are: $2, $5, $10, $20, $50 and $100.

One dollar can be divided into 100 cents. Coins include: $1, 50¢, 25¢ (quarter), 10¢ (dime), 5¢ (nickel) and 1¢ (penny). The $1 coin is commonly called a loony because of the bird gracing the flip side.

Traveller's cheques can be cashed at banks, major hotels, money exchanges and bank kiosks located everywhere. Stores and restaurants will normally cash traveller's cheques if they are in Canadian dollars. American dollars and traveller's cheques are accepted by many businesses, but the rate of exchange is poor compared to the rates offered by the banks.

Most of the major credit cards are accepted across Canada.

ON FOOT

The only way to really appreciate a town or a city is by exploring it on foot. So make sure you pack comfortable walking shoes that provide good arch support.

It is easy getting around in most cities. There are street signs on every corner and local maps can always be picked up from the local tourist information centre.

If you do get lost, just stop someone on the street and ask for directions. Canadians are generally very friendly and happy to provide directions to visitors.

PASSPORTS & VISAS

Americans do not need a passport to enter Canada from the United States. A document proving American citizenship, such as a birth certificate, is all that is required.

People from other countries need a valid passport and, depending on their nationality, a visa. Citizens of the following countries do not need visas: Australia, Austria, Belgium, Denmark, Finland, France, Germany, Ireland, Italy, Japan, Netherlands, New Zealand, Norway, Spain, Sweden, Switzerland, United Kingdom and the United States.

Visa requirements may change; therefore, it's best to check with your travel agent, or a Canadian diplomatic mission, before setting out for Canada.

PHOTOGRAPHY

A wide variety of film is available in Canadian cities. Photo development is world class, so you shouldn't be in for any disappointments. If you are in a rush to develop your photos, some photo shops can process film within one to 24 hours.

There are generally no restrictions on taking photographs in Canada.

POSTAL SERVICES

Post offices are open Monday to Friday from 8:00 a.m. or 9:00 a.m. until 3:00 p.m. Some post offices are open as late as 6:00 p.m.

Stamps may be purchased from post offices, stamp machines, hotels and postal outlets located in some shops.

PRIVATE TRANSPORT

Car rental agencies have offices throughout t entire of Canada and at all major airports. The car rental companies include Hertz, Budget, Tilden and Avis.

You must be at least 21 years old in order to be able to rent a car.

The Canadian Automobile Association (CAA) has special agreements with the American Automobile Association (AAA) and other foreign automobile associations. Depending on the agreement, the CAA may provide affiliated members with maps, travel information and, possibly, roadside emergency service. AAA members are entitled to all of these services.

Depending on the province, a foreign driver's licence is valid for at least three months in Canada. If your licence is not in English or French, it is a good idea to get an international driver's licence. The province of Saskatchewan requires that all drivers must have a licence printed in either English or French.

Seat belts must be worn in all parts of Canada as a safety precaution.

PUBLIC TRANSPORT

Domestic airlines such as Air Canada and Canadian provide air service between the larger cities. Regional airlines and charter services connect the more remote locations.

The biggest passenger line in Canada is VIA Rail. VIA Rail has trains running across the country.

VIA Rail offers discounts to senior citizens and anyone 24 years old or younger.

VIA Rail has a Canrail pass which allows 12 days of unlimited travel within a 30-day period. Contact VIA Rail or your travel agent for more details. VIA Rail Canada: C.P. 8116, 2 Place Ville-Marie, Montreal, Quebec H3B 2G6: tel (514) 871-6000.

Greyhound and Voyageur are the two main bus lines in Canada.

Buses, subways and rail transport provide an excellent means of transport within Canadian cities. Exact change is normally required. Fares may be higher during the morning and afternoon rush hours.

TELEPHONES

A local telephone call costs 25 cents at a pay phone. Some pay phones accept credit cards, making long distance calling more convenient. You can dial other countries directly, if you know the proper area and country codes. If you don't, call the operator (dial 0).

To make a long distance call within Canada or to the United States, dial 1 + (area code) + telephone number.

Long distance rates vary, according to the time and day of the week. To take advantage of the lower rates, inquire before you place a call. Keep in mind that hotels usually add an extra charge for making long distance calls.

TIME ZONES

Canada covers six time zones.

Daylight Savings Time is in effect from the first Sunday in April to the final Sunday in October (except for most areas of Saskatchewan). During this period, clocks are one hour ahead.

TIPPING

Unless a service charge has been added to the restaurant bill, a tip of 15 percent is usually given to the waiter or waitress.

Barbers, hairstylists and taxi drivers are

normally tipped 15 percent.

Bellboys and porters should be tipped $1 for each piece of luggage. Maids receive $2 for each day of stay.

TOURS

There are a bewildering number of tours to choose from. Some tours will arrange your whole stay in Canada while others will only take you whale watching or on a city tour. Contact your local travel agent or a tourist office in Canada for more details.

WEIGHTS & MEASURES

Although Canada has been metric for some time, many people still refer to the old imperial system of measure. Supermarkets usually advertise prices for meats and fresh produce in both pounds and kilograms for easy reference.

WHAT TO WEAR

If you are visiting Canada during the winter, bring a warm coat, gloves and winter boots. Summers in Southern Canada are warm, so you might want to bring shorts, tee-shirts and a bathing suit. Bringing a bathing suit is a good idea even if you don't intend to go to a beach because many hotels and motels have swimming pools.

A good pair of comfortable walking shoes are a must because you'll probably end up doing more walking than you had planned. A collapsible umbrella will also come in handy.

A few expensive restaurants insist men wear jackets and ties.

DIRECTORY

ACCOMMODATIONS

The prices quoted are for two people sharing a bed during high season. Prices can drop considerably in low season. Some large city hotels offer reduced weekend rates.

ALBERTA
Banff
Banff Park Lodge & Conference Centre
222 Lynx St.
Tel:(403) 762-4433
$175

Banff Springs Hotel
404 Spray Ave.
Tel:(403) 762-2211
$165 to $337

High Country Inn
419 Banff Ave.
Tel:(403) 762-2236
$80

Calgary
Delta Bow Valley
209 4th Ave. SE.
Tel:(403) 266-1980
$130

International Hotel
220 4th Ave. SW.
Tel:(403) 265-9600
$126 to $158

Palliser Hotel
133 9th Ave. SW.
Tel:(403) 262-1234
$180

Prince Royal Inn
618 5th Ave. SW.
Tel:(403) 263-0520
$90

Skyline Plaza Hotel
110 9th Ave. SE.
Tel:(403) 266-7331
$150

Westin Hotel Calgary
320 4th Ave. SW.
Tel:(403) 266-1611
$139 to $206

Westward Inn
119 12th Ave. SW.
Tel:(403) 266-4611
$79 to $89

Edmonton
Best Western City Centre Inn
11310 109th St.
Tel:(403) 479-2042
$68

Edmonton Hilton
10235 101st St.
Tel:(403) 428-7111
$169 to $209

Fantasyland Hotel & Resort
West Edmonton Mall
17700 87th Ave.
Tel:(403) 444-3000
$140 to $170

Holiday Inn Crowne Plaza
10111 Bellamy Hill
Tel:(403) 428-6611
$125

Hotel Macdonald
10065 100th St.
Tel:(403) 424-5181
$155 to $185

Journey's End Motel
17610 100th Ave.
Tel:(403) 484-4415
$63

Radisson Hotel Edmonton
10010 104th St.
Tel:(403) 423-2450
$90

Ramada Renaissance Hotel
10155 105th St.
Tel:(403) 423-4811
$125 to $170

Westin Hotel Edmonton
10135 100th St.
Tel:(403) 426-3636
$92

Jasper
Sawridge Hotel Jasper
82 Cannaught Dr.
Tel:(403) 852-5111
$117

Jasper Park Lodge
Lodge Rd.
Tel:(403) 852-3301
$259 to $431

BRITISH COLUMBIA
Vancouver
Best Western Chateau Granville
1100 Granville St.
Tel:(604) 669-7070
$135 to $160

Best Western O'Doul's Hotel
1300 Robson St.
Tel:(604) 684-8461
$155 to $180

Bosman's Motor Hotel
1060 Howe St.
Tel:(604) 682-3171
$89

Delta Pacific Resort &
Conference Centre
10251 St. Edward's Dr.
Tel:(604) 278-9611
$109

Delta Place
645 Howe St.
Tel:(604) 687-1122
$185 to $225

Four Seasons Hotel
791 W. Georgia St.
Tel:(604) 689-9333
$210 to $310

Georgian Court Hotel
773 Beatty St.
Tel:(604) 682-5555
$119 to $170

Hotel Vancouver
900 W. Georgia St.
Tel:(604) 684-3131
$185 to $305

Hyatt Regency Vancouver
655 Burrard St.
Tel:(604) 683-1234
$185 to $250

Le Meridien-Vancouver
845 Burrard St.
Tel:(604) 682-5511
$200 to $260

Pan Pacific Hotel Vancouver
999 Canada Place
Tel:(604) 662-8111
$225 to $275

Sylvia Hotel
1154 Gilford St.
Tel:(604) 681-9321
$60 to $85

Waterfront Centre Hotel
900 Canada Place
Tel:(604) 691-1991
$145

Wedgewood Hotel
845 Hornby St.
Tel:(604) 689-7777
$180 to $230

Westin Bayshore
1601 W. Georgia St.
Tel:(604) 682-3377
$180 to $230

Victoria
Admiral Motel
257 Belleville St.
Tel:(604) 388-6267
$79 to $115

Best Western Carlton Plaza
Hotel
642 Johnson St.
Tel:(604) 388-5513
$98 to $140

Best Western Inner Harbour
412 Quebec St.
Tel:(604) 384-5122
$99 to $109

Canterbury Inn
310 Gorge Rd. E.
Tel:(604) 382-2151
$75

Casa Linda Motel
364 Goldstream Ave.
Tel:(604) 474-2141
$55

Chateau Victoria
740 Burdett Ave.
Tel:(604) 382-4221
$126 to $189

Coast Victoria Harbourside
Hotel
146 Kingston St.
Tel:(604) 360-1211
$188 to $208

Crystal Court Motel
701 Belleville St.
Tel:(604) 384-0551
$65

Empress Hotel
721 Government St.
Tel:(604) 384-8111
$215 to $285

Hotel Grand Pacific
450 Quebec St.
Tel:(604) 386-0450
$170 to $190

Ocean Pointe Resort
45 Songhees Rd.
Tel:(604) 360-2999
$135 to $195

Royal Scot Inn
425 Quebec St.
Tel:(604) 388-5463
$98 to $195

Whistler
Blackcomb
4220 Gateway Dr.
Tel:(604) 932-4155
$85 to $160

Chateau Whistler Resort
4599 Chateau Blvd.
Tel:(604) 938-8000
$195 to $250

Delta Mountain Inn
4050 Whistler Way
Tel:(604) 932-1982
$295

Mountainside Lodge
4417 Sundial Pl.
Tel:(604) 932-4511
$85 to $160

MANITOBA
Winnipeg
Best Western Carlton Inn
220 Carlton St.
Tel:(204) 942-0881
$60

Charter House Hotel
330 York Ave.
Tel:(204) 942-0101
$53

Delta Winnipeg
288 Portage Ave.
Tel:(204) 956-0410
$130

Holiday Inn Crowne Plaza
350 St. Mary Ave.
Tel:(204) 942-0551
$141

Sheraton
161 Donald St.
Tel:(204) 942-5300
$120 to $130

Travelodge
360 Colony St.
Tel:(204) 786-7011
$71

Westin Hotel
2 Lombard Pl.
Tel:(204) 957-1350
$136 to $153

NEW BRUNSWICK
Fredericton
Auberge Wandlyn Inn
58 Prospect St. W.
Tel:(506) 452-8937
$62

Lord Beaverbrook Hotel
659 Queen St.
Tel:(506) 455-3371
$71

Sheraton Inn
225 Woodstock Rd.
Tel:(506) 457-7000
$69 to $99

Moncton
Best Western Crystal Palace Hotel
499 Paul St.
Tel:(506) 858-8584
$95

Hotel Beausejour
750 Main St.
Tel:(506) 854-4344
$102

Keddy's Brunswick Hotel
1005 Main St.
Tel:(506) 854-6340
$69

St. Andrews
The Algonquin
184 Aldophus St.
Tel:(506) 529-8823
$99 to $150

Best Western Shiretown Inn
218 Water St.
Tel:(506) 529-8877
$70 to $85

Tara Manor Inn
559 Mowat Dr.
Tel:(506) 529-3304
$90 to $94

Saint John
Country Inn & Suites By Carlson
1011 Fairville Blvd.
Tel:(506) 635-0400
$64

Delta Brunswick
39 King St.
Tel:(506) 648-1981
$89

Howard Johnson Hotel
400 Main St.
Tel:(506) 642-2622
$92

Keddy's Fort Howe Hotel
10 Portland St.
Tel:(506) 657-7320
$62 to $65

Saint John Hilton
1 Market Square
Tel:(506) 693-8484
$120

NEWFOUNDLAND
St. John's
Battery Hotel
100 Signal Hill Rd.
Tel:(709) 576-0040
$65

Best Western Travellers Inn
199 Kentmount Rd.
Tel:(709) 722-5540
$77

Holiday Inn
180 Portugal Cove Rd.
Tel:(709) 722-0506
$75

Hotel Newfoundland
Cavendish Square
Tel:(709) 726-4980
$164

Journey's End Hotel
Cavendish Square
Tel:(709) 754-7788
$96

Radisson Plaza Hotel
120 New Gower St.
Tel:(709) 739-6404
$140

NORTHWEST TERRITORIES
Yellowknife
Discovery Inn
P.O. Box 784
4701 Franklin Ave.
Tel:(403) 873-4151
From $90

Explorer Hotel
P.O. Box 7000
Highway 4
Tel:(403) 873-3531
$137 to $250

NOVA SCOTIA
Annapolis Royal
Garrison House
350 St. George St.
Tel:(902) 532-5750
$68

Baddeck
Inverary Inn Resort
Route 205
Tel:(902) 295-3500
$89 to $160

Silver Dart Lodge
Route 205
Tel:(902) 295-2340
$79

Dartmouth
Future Inns
20 Highfield Park Dr.
Tel:(902) 465-6555
$57

Holiday Inn-Halifax/Dartmouth
99 Wyse Rd.
Tel:(902) 463-1100
$110

Ramada Renaissance Hotel
240 Brownlow Ave.
Tel:(902) 468-8888
$140

Halifax
Chateau Halifax
1990 Barrington St.
Tel:(902) 425-6700
$120

Citadel Inn Halifax
1960 Brunswick St.
Tel:(902) 422-1391
$95

Delta Barrington
1875 Barrington St.
Tel:(902) 429-7410
$95 to $125

Econo Lodge
560 Bedford Highway
Tel:(902) 443-0303
$58

Halifax Hilton
1181 Hollis St.
Tel:(902) 423-7231
$135 to $155

Holiday Inn Halifax Centre
1980 Robie St.
Tel:(902) 423-1161
$109 to $140

Keddy's Motor Inn
20 St. Margaret's Bay Rd.
Tel:(902) 477-5611
$73

Prince George Hotel
1725 Market St.
Tel:(902) 425-1986
$95

Sheraton Halifax Hotel
1919 Upper Water St.
Tel:(902) 421-1700
$125 to $135

Wedgewood Motel
374 Bedford Highway
Tel:(902) 443-1576
$55 to $61

Ingonish
Keltic Lodge
Ingonish Beach
Tel:(902) 285-2880
$233 to $248

Shelburne
Cape Cod Colony Motel
Route 3
Tel:(902) 875-3411
$46

Wildwood Motel
Minto St.
Tel:(902) 875-2964
$45

Sydney
Best Western Cape Bretoner Motel
560 Kings Rd.
Tel:(902) 539-8101
$76

Delta Sydney
300 Esplanade
Tel:(902) 562-7500
$79 to $104

Holiday Inn
480 Kings Rd.
Tel:(902) 539-6750
$79 to $83

Keddy's Inn
600 Kings Rd.
Tel:(902) 539-1140
$68

ONTARIO
Kingston
Ambassador Hotel
1550 Princess St.
Tel:(613) 548-3605
$95 to $135

Holiday Inn
1 Princess St.
Tel:(613) 549-8400
$125 to $140

Howard Johnson Hotel
237 Ontario St.
Tel:(613) 549-6300
$115

Seven Oakes Motor Inn
2331 Princess St.
Tel:(613) 546-3655
$64 to $68

Kitchener
Best Western Conestoga Inn
1333 Weber St. E.
Tel:(519) 893-1234
$60 to $85

Holiday Inn
30 Fairway Rd. S.
Tel:(519) 893-1211
$109

Valhalla Inn
Corner of King & Benton Sts.
Tel:(519) 744-4141
$100 to $110

London
Best Western Lamplighter Inn
591 Wellington Rd.
Tel:(519) 681-7151
$64 to $85

Econo Lodge
1170 Wellington Rd.
Tel:(519) 681-1550
$45 to $50

Howard Johnson Hotel
1150 Wellington Rd.
Tel:(519) 681-0600
$67 to $85

Radisson Hotel London Centre
300 King St.
Tel:(519) 439-1661
$88

Ramada Inn
817 Exeter Rd.
Tel:(519) 681-4900
$68

Sheraton Armouries Hotel
325 Dundas St.
Tel:(519) 679-6111
$145 to $165

Midland
Highland Inn Resort Hotel
& Conference Centre
Junction Highway 12 & King St.
Tel:(705) 526-9307
$60 to $89

Niagara Falls
Canuck Motel
5334 Kitchener St.
Tel:(905) 358-8221
$49 to $69

Days Inn Overlooking The Falls
6361 Buchanan Ave.
Tel:(905) 357-7377
$84 to $139

Holiday Inn By the Falls
(not a member of the chain)
5339 Murray Hill
Tel:(905) 356-1333
$85 to $144

Howard Johnson By the Falls
5905 Victoria Ave.
Tel:(905) 357-4040
$60 to $160

Liberty Inns
6408 Stanley Ave.
Tel:(905) 356-5877
$48 to $98

Michael's Inn By the Falls
5599 River Rd.
Tel:(905) 354-2727
$55 to $148

Old Stone Inn
5425 Robinson St.
Tel:(905) 357-1234
$85 to $130

Ramada Renaissance Hotel
Fallsview
6455 Buchanan Ave.
Tel:(905) 357-5200
$139 to $249

Sheraton Fallsview Hotel & Conference Centre
6755 Oakes Dr.
Tel:(905) 374-1077
$145 to $295

The Skyline Brock
5685 Falls Ave.
Tel:(905) 374-4445
$95 to $169

Niagara-on-the-Lake
Prince of Wales Hotel
6 Picton St.
Tel:(905) 468-3246
$115 to $234

Queen's Landing Inn
115 Byron St.
Tel:(905) 468-2195
$145 to $350

Ottawa
Chateau Laurier
1 Rideau St.
Tel:(613) 241-1414
$199

Delta Ottawa
361 Queen St.
Tel:(613) 238-6000
$160

Holiday Inn
350 Dalhousie St.
Tel:(613) 236-0201
$110 to $125

Journey's End Hotel
290 Rideau St.
Tel:(613) 563-7511
$87

Les Suites Hotel
130 Besserer St.
Tel:(613) 232-2000
$115

Lord Elgin Hotel
100 Elgin St.
Tel:(613) 235-3333
$89

Novotel Hotel
33 Nicholas St.
Tel:(613) 230-3033
$79 to $140

Parkway Motel
475 Rideau St.
Tel:(613) 789-3781
$58

Radisson Hotel
100 Kent St.
Tel:(613) 238-1122
$115 to $165

Town House Motor Hotel
319 Rideau St.
Tel:(613) 789-5555
$59

Westin Hotel
11 Colonel By Dr.
Tel:(613) 560-7000
$175 to $200

Stratford
Majer's Motel
Rural Road 4
Tel:(519) 271-2010
$55 to $60

Stone Maiden Inn
123 Church St.
Tel:(519) 271-7129
$110 to $160

Toronto
Bond Place Hotel
65 Dundas St. E.
Tel:(416) 362-6061
$69

Clarion Essex Park Hotel
300 Jarvis St.
Tel: (416) 977-4823
$85 to $136

Days Inn Carlton
30 Carlton St.
Tel:(416) 977-6655
$79

Delta Chelsea Inn
33 Gerrard St. W.
Tel:(416) 595-1975
$170

Four Seasons Hotel
21 Avenue Rd.
Tel:(416) 964-0411
$220 to $295

Holiday Inn City Hall
89 Chestnut St.
Tel:(416) 977-0707
$115

Hotel Ibis
240 Jarvis St.
Tel:(416) 593-9400
$69

Hotel Inter-Continental
220 Bloor St. W.
Tel:(416) 960-5200
$199 to $244

Hotel Selby
592 Sherbourne St.
Tel:(416) 921-3142
$60

L'Hotel
225 Front St. W.
Tel:9416) 597-1400
$115 to $270

Radisson Plaza Hotel Admiral
249 Queen's Quay W.
Tel:(416) 364-5444
$105

Ramada Renaissance
90 Bloor St. E.
Tel:(416) 961-8000
$165 to $210

Royal York Hotel
100 Front St. W.
Tel:(416) 368-2511
$155 to $219

Sheraton Centre
123 Queen St. W.
Tel:(416) 361-1000
$120 to $260

SkyDome Hotel
45 Peter St. S
Tel:(416) 360-7100
$130

Toronto Marriot Eaton Centre
525 Bay St.
Tel:(416) 597-9200
$145

The Westin Harbour Castle
1 Harbour Square
Tel:(416) 869-1600
$164

Waterloo
Journey's End Motel
190 Weber St. N.
Tel:(519) 747-9400
$64

Waterloo Inn
475 King St. N.
Tel:(519) 884-0220
$95

Windsor
Comfort Inn & Conference
Centre
1855 Church Rd.
Tel:(519) 966-1200
$59 to $83

Compri Hotel
333 Riverside Dr. W.
Tel:(519) 977-9777
$80

Hilton International
277 Riverside Dr. W.
Tel:(519) 973-5555
$102 to $126

Royal Marquis Hotel
980 Grand Marais E.
Tel:(519) 966-1900
$80 to $175

Travelodge Hotel Windsor
Downtown
33 Riverside Dr. E.
Tel:(519) 258-7774
$73

PRINCE EDWARD ISLAND

Cavendish

Cavendish Beach Cottages
52 Prince Charles Dr.
Tel:(902) 963-2025
$90

Cavendish Motel
Cavendish Beach
Tel:(902) 963-2244
$70 to $76

Lakeview Lodge
Route 6
Tel:(902) 963-2436
$60 to $90

Sundance Cottages
Rural Road 1
Tel:(902) 963-2149
$100 to $150

Charlottetown

Best Western MacLaughlan's Motor Inn
238 Grafton St.
Tel:(902) 892-2461
$105 to $115

Charlottetown Hotel A-Rodd
Classic Hotel
Kent & Pownal Sts.
Tel:(902) 894-7371
$95 to $132

Journey's End Motel
112 Trans-Canada Highway
Tel:(902) 566-4424
$73

Kirkwood Motor Hotel
455 University Ave.
Tel:(902) 892-4206
$65 to $88

Prince Edward Hotel & Convention Centre
18 Queen St.
Tel:(902) 566-2222
$175

Summerside

Best Western Linkletter Inn & Convention Centre
311 Market St.
Tel:(902) 436-2157
$63 to $104

Loyalist Country Inn
195 Harbour Dr.
Tel:(902) 436-3333
$93 to $104

Quality Inn Garden of the Gulf
618 Water St.
Tel:(902) 436-2295
$59 to $94

Sunny Isle Motel
720 Water St.
Tel:(902) 436-5665
$36

QUEBEC

Gaspe

Motel Adams
Adams & Jacques Cartier Sts.
Tel:(418) 368-2244
$57 to $77

Montebello

Le Chateau Montebello
392 Notre Dame
Tel:(819) 423-6341
$151 to $191

Montreal

Delta Montreal
450 Sherbrooke St. W.
Tel:(514) 286-1986
$99

Four Seasons Hotel
1050 Sherbrooke St. W.
Tel:(514) 284-1110
$205 to $250

Holiday Inn - Crowne Plaza Metro Centre
505 Sherbrooke St. E.
Tel:(514) 842-8581
$99

Holiday Inn Downtown Convention Centre
99 Viger Ave.
Tel:(514) 878-9888
$125 to $140

Hotel Chateau Versailles
1659 Sherbrooke St. W.
Tel:(514) 933-3611
$115 to $155

Hotel des Gouverneurs-Place Dupuis
1415 St. Hubert St.
Tel:(514) 842-4881
$89

Hotel Inter-Continental Montreal
360 St. Antoine St. W.
Tel:(514) 987-9900
$139 to $280

Hotel Vogue
1425 rue de la Montagne
Tel:(514) 285-5555
$255 to $305

Le Centre Sheraton
1201 Rene Levesque Blvd. W.
Tel:(514) 878-2000
$135

Chateau Champlain
1050 Lagauchetiere St. W.
Tel:(514) 878-9000
$125

Le Meridien Montreal
4 Complexe Desjardins
Tel:(514) 285-1450
$180 to $190

Queen Elizabeth Hotel
900 Rene Levesque Blvd. W.
Tel:(514) 861-3511
$125

Le Riche Bourg
2170 Lincoln Ave.
Tel:(514) 935-9224
$75

L'Hotel de la Montagne
1430 rue de la Montagne
Tel:(514) 288-5656
$129

Montreal Bonaventure Hilton
1 Place Bonaventure
Tel:(514) 878-2332
$139

Days Inn Downtown
2060 rue St. Dominique
Tel:(514) 844-4268
$59

Radisson Gouverneurs Montreal
777 University St.
Tel:(514) 879-1370
$115

Ritz-Carlton Kempinski
1228 Sherbrooke St. W.
Tel:(514) 842-4212
$150 to $250

Mont Ste. Anne Condominiums Val des Neiges
203 rue Val des Neiges
Tel:(418) 827-5721
$75 to $175

Hotel Chateau Mont Ste. Anne
500 boul. Beau-Pre
Tel:(418) 827-5211
$130

Mont Tremblant
Mount Tremblant Resort
3005 Chemin Principal
Base of the ski hill
Tel: 1-800-461-8711
Ski packages $157 and up

North Hatley
Auberge Hatley Inn
Magog & Virgin Sts.
Tel:(819) 842-2451
$200 to $350

Hovey Manor
Route 108 E.
Tel:(819) 842-2421
$255 to $340

Quebec City
Chateau Grande-Allee
601 Grande-Alle E.
Tel:(418) 647-4433
$79 to $99

Holiday Inn Centreville
395 rue de la Couronne
Tel:(418) 647-2611
$79

Hotel Manoir Victoria
44 Cote du Palais
Tel:(418) 692-1030
$95 to $135

Le Chateau Frontenac
1 rue des Carrieres
Tel:(418) 692-3861
$154 to $240

Loews Le Concorde
1225 Place Montcalm
Tel:(418) 647-2222
$125 to $185

Manoir La Fayette
661 Grande-Alle E.
Tel:(418) 522-2652
$69 to $94

Quebec Hilton
3 Place Quebec
Tel:(418) 647-2411
$115

Radisson Gouverneurs Quebec
690 boul. St. Cyrille E.
Tel:(418) 647-1717
$99

Val David
Hotel La Sapiniere
1244 Chemin La Sapiniere
Tel:(819) 322-2020
$240 to $328

SASKATCHEWAN
Regina
Delta Regina
1818 Victoria Ave.
Tel:(306) 569-1666
$79

Hotel Saskatchewan
2125 Victoria Ave.
Tel:(306) 522-7691
$94

Journey's End Motel
3221 E. Eastgate Dr.
Tel:(306) 789-5522
$55

Ramada Renaissance Hotel
1919 Saskatchewan Dr.
Tel:(306) 525-5255
$78

Regina Travelodge
4177 Albert St. S.
Tel:(306) 586-3443
$65

Saskatoon
Best Western Yellowhead Inn
1715 Idylwyld Dr. N.
Tel:(306) 244-5552
$48

Delta Bessborough
601 Spadina Cr. E.
Tel:(306) 244-5521
$60 to $128

Ramada Renaissance Hotel
405 29th St. E.
Tel:(306) 665-3322
$78 to $150

Sheraton-Cavalier
612 Spadina Cr. E.
Tel:(306) 652-6770
$100

YUKON
Dawson City
Downtown Hotel
Queen & 2nd
Tel:(403) 993-5346
$119

Eldorado Hotel
3rd & Princess
Tel:(403) 993-5451
$115

Whitehorse
Best Western Gold Rush Inn
411 Main St.
Tel:(403) 668-4500
$155

Westmark Whitehorse
201 Wood St.
Tel:(403) 668-4700
$148

EMBASSIES, CONSULATES AND OTHER DIPLOMATIC REPRESENTATIONS

Embassy of Algeria
435 Daly Avenue
Ottawa, ON K1N 6H3
Tel:(613) 789-8505

High Commission for Antigua and Barbuda
Place de Ville, Tower B, Suite 205
112 Kent St.
Ottawa, ON K1P 5P2
Tel:(613) 234-9143

Consulate of Antigua and Barbuda
60 St. Clair Ave. East, Suite 304
Toronto, ON M4T 1N5
Tel:(416) 961-3143

Embassy of Argentina
90 Sparks St., Suite 620
Ottawa, ON K1P 5B4
Tel:(613) 236-2351

Australian High Commission
50 O'Connor Street, Suite 170
Ottawa, ON K1P 6L2
Tel:(613) 236-0841

Consulate of Australia
175 Bloor St. E., Suite 314
Toronto, ON M4W 3R8
Tel:(416) 323-1155

Embassy of Austria
445 Wilbrod Street
Ottawa, ON K1N 6M7
Tel:(613) 789-1444

High Commission of the Bahamas
360 Albert Street, Suite 1020
Ottawa, ON K1R 7X7
Tel:(613) 232-1724

Consulate of Bahrain
1869 Rene Levesque Blvd. W.
Montreal, PQ H3H 1R4
Tel:(514) 931-7444

Bangladesh High Commission
85 Range Road, Suite 402
Ottawa, Ontario
K1N 8J6
Tel:(613) 236-0138

High Commission for Barbados
124 O'Connor Street, Suite 603
Ottawa, ON K1P 5MP
Tel:(613) 236-9517

Embassy of Belgium
80 Elgin Street
Ottawa, ON K1N 8J6
Tel:(613) 236-7267

Consulate of Belgium
999 Maisonneuve Blvd. W., Suite 850
Montreal, PQ H3A 3L4
Tel:(514) 849-7394

High Commission of Belize
112 Kent St., Suite 2005
Ottawa, ON K1P 5P2
Tel:(613) 232-7389

Embassy of Benin
58 Glebe Ave.
Ottawa, ON K1S 2C3
Tel:(613) 233-4429

Embassy of Bolivia
130 Albert St., Suite 504
Ottawa, ON K1P 5G4
Tel:(613) 236-8237

Consulate of Bolivia
11231 Jasper Ave.
Edmonton, AB T5K 0L5
Tel:(403) 488-1525

Embassy of Brazil
450 Wilbrod Street
Ottawa, ON K1N 6M8
Tel:(613) 237-1090

Consulate of Brazil
2000 Mansfield St., Suite 1700
Montreal, PQ H3A 3A5
Tel:(514) 499-0968

Consulate of Brazil
77 Bloor St., Suite 1109
Toronto, ON M5S 1M2
Tel:(416) 922-2503

Consulate of Brazil
1140 W. Pender St.
Vancouver, BC V6E 4G1
Tel:(604) 687-4589

British High Commission
80 Elgin St.
Ottawa, ON K1P 5K7
Tel:(613) 237-1530

Consulate of Britain
1155 University St., Suite 901
Montreal, PQ H3B 3A7
Tel:(514) 866-5863

Consulate of Britain
777 Bay St., Suite 1910
Toronto, ON M5G 2G2
Tel:(416) 593-1290

Consulate of Britain
1111 Melville St., Suite 800
Vancouver, BC V6E 3V6
Tel:(604) 683-4421

Embassy of Bulgaria
325 Stewart Street
Ottawa, ON K1N 6K5
Tel:(613) 789-3215

Consulate of Bulgaria
65 Overlea Blvd., Suite 406
Toronto, M4H 1P1
Tel:(416) 696-2420

Embassy of Burkina Faso
48 Range Rd.
Ottawa, ON K1N 8J4
Tel:(613) 238-4796

Embassy of Burundi
151 Slater St., Suite 800
Ottawa, ON K1P 5H3
Tel:(613) 236-8483

Embassy of Cameroon
170 Clemow Ave.
Ottawa, ON K1S 2B4
Tel:(613) 236-1522

Embassy of Chile
151 Slater St., Suite 605
Ottawa, ON K1P 5H3
Tel:(613) 235-4402

Consulate of Chile
1010 Sherbrooke St. W., Suite
710
Montreal, PQ H3B 2R7
Tel:(514) 499-0405

Embassy of China
515 St. Patrick St.
Ottawa, ON K1N 5H3
Tel:(613) 789-3434

Consulate of China
240 St. George St.
Toronto, ON M5R 2P4
Tel:(416) 964-7260

Consulate of China
3380 Granville St.
Vancouver, BC V6H 3K3
Tel:(604) 736-3910

Embassy of Columbia
360 Albert St., Suite 1130
Ottawa, ON K1R 7X7
Tel:(613) 230-3760

Consulate of Colombia
1010 Sherbrooke St. W., Suite
420
Montreal, PQ H3A 2R7
Tel:(514) 849-4852

Embassy of Costa Rica
135 York St., Suite 208
Ottawa, ON K1N 5T4
Tel:(613) 234-5762

Consulate of Costa Rica
894 Bellerive,
Longueuil, PQ J4J 1A7
Tel:(514) 651-0472

Embassy of the Czech Republic
541 Sussex Dr.
Ottawa, ON K1N 6Z6
Tel:(613) 562-3875

Embassy of Denmark
85 Range Rd., Suite 702
Ottawa, ON K1N 8J6
Tel:(613) 234-0704

Consulate of Denmark
151 Bloor St. W., Suite 310
Toronto, ON M5S 1S4
Tel:(416) 962-5661/2

**Consulate of the Dominican
Republic**
1650 Maisonneuve Blvd. W.,
Suite 302
Montreal, PQ H3H 2P3
Tel:(514) 933-9008

**High Commission for the
Countries of the Eastern
Caribbean States**
112 Kent St., Suite 1610
Ottawa, ON K1P 5P2
Tel:(613) 236-8952

Embassy of Ecuador
50 O'Connor St., Suite 1311
Ottawa, ON K1P 6L2
Tel:(613) 563-8206

Consulate of Ecuador
1010 St. Catherine St. W., Suite
625
Montreal, PQ H3B 3R3
Tel:(514) 874-4071

Consulate of Ecuador
151 Bloor St. W., Suite 470
Toronto, ON M5S 1S4
Tel:(416) 968-2077

Embassy of Egypt
454 Laurier Ave. E.
Ottawa, ON K1N 6R3
Tel:(613) 234-4931

Consulate of Egypt
3754 Cote des Neiges
Montreal, PQ H3H 1V6
Tel:(514) 937-7781

Embassy of El Salvador
209 Kent St.
Ottawa, ON K2P 1Z8
Tel:(613) 238-2939

Consulate of El Salvador
292 Sheppard Ave. W., Suite
200
Willowdale, ON M2N 1N5
Tel:(416) 512-8196

Embassy of Ethiopia
151 Slater St., Suite 210
Ottawa, ON K1P 5H3
Tel:(613) 235-6637

**Commission of the European
Communities**
350 Sparks St., Suite 1110
Ottawa, ON K1R 7S8
Tel:(613) 238-6464

Embassy of Finland
55 Metcalfe St., Suite 850
Ottawa, ON K1P 6L5
Tel:(613) 236-2389

Consulate of Finland
1200 Bay St., Suite 604
Toronto, ON M5R 2A5
Tel:(416) 964-0066

Embassy of France
42 Sussex Dr.
Ottawa, ON K1M 2C9
Tel:(613) 789-1795

Consulate of France
Highfield Place, Suite 300
10010 106th St.
Edmonton, AB T5J 3L8
Tel:(403) 428-0232

Consulate of France
736 Granville St., Suite 1201
Vancouver, BC V6Z 1H9
Tel:(604) 681-4345

Embassy of Gabon
4 Range Rd.
Ottawa, ON K1N 8J5
Tel:(613) 232-5301/02

Embassy of Germany
275 Slater St., 14th floor
Ottawa, ON K1P 5H9
Tel:(613) 232-1101

High Commission for Ghana
1 Clemow Ave.
Ottawa, ON K1S 2A9
Tel:(613) 236-0871/3

Embassy of Greece
76-80 MacLaren St.
Ottawa, ON K2P 0K6
Tel:(613) 238-6271

High Commission of Grenada
See Eastern Caribbean States

Consulate of Grenada
439 University Ave., Suite 820
Toronto, ON M5G 1Y8
Tel:(416) 595-1343

Embassy of Guatemala
885 Meadowlands Dr., Suite 504
Ottawa, ON K2C 3N2
Tel:(613) 224-4322/4780

Embassy of Guinea
483 Wilbrod St.
Ottawa, ON K1N 6N1
Tel:(613) 789-8444

High Commission for Guyana
151 Slater St., Suite 309
Ottawa, ON K1P 5H3
Tel:(613) 235-7249

Embassy of Haiti
Place de Ville, Tower B
112 Kent St., Suite 212
Ottawa, ON K1P 5P2
Tel:(613) 238-1628

Consulate of Haiti
Place Bonaventure
CP 187
Montreal, PQ H5A 1A9
Tel:(514) 871-8993

Embassy of the Holy See
724 Manor Ave.
Ottawa, ON K1M 0E3
Tel:(613) 746-4914

Embassy of Honduras
151 Slater St., Suite 300A
Ottawa, ON K1P 5H3
Tel:(613) 233-8900

Hong Kong Trade Development Council
347 Bay St., Suite 1100
Toronto, ON M5H 2R7
Tel:(416) 366-3594

Embassy of Hungary
7 Delaware Ave.
Ottawa, ON K2P 0Z2
Tel:(613) 232-1711/3209

High Commission of India
10 Springfield Rd.
Ottawa, ON K1M 1C9
Tel:(613) 744-3751

Consulate of India
2 Bloor St. W., Suite 500
Toronto, ON M4W 3E2
Tel:(416) 960-0751/2377

Embassy of Indonesia
287 MacLaren St.
Ottawa, ON K2P 0L9
Tel:(613) 236-7403

Embassy of Iran
245 Metcalfe St.
Ottawa, ON K2P 2K2
Tel:(613) 235-4726

Embassy of Iraq
215 McLeod St.
Ottawa, ON K2P 0Z8
Tel:(613) 236-9177

Embassy of Ireland
170 Metcalfe St.
Ottawa, ON K2P 1P3
Tel:(613) 233-6281

Embassy of Israel
50 O'Connor St., Suite 1005
Ottawa, ON K1P 6L2
Tel:(613) 567-6450

Embassy of Italy
275 Slater St., 21st floor
Ottawa, ON K1P 5H9
Tel:(613) 232-2401

Jamaican High Commission
275 Slater St., Suite 800
Ottawa, ON K1P 5H9
Tel:(613) 233-9311

Consulate of Jamaica
214 King St. W., Suite 400
Toronto, ON M5H 3S6
Tel:(416) 598-3008

Embassy of Japan
255 Sussex Dr.
Ottawa, ON K1N 9E6
Tel:(613) 236-8541

Embassy of Jordan
100 Bronson Ave., Suite 701
Ottawa, ON K1R 6G8
Tel:(613) 238-8090

High Commission for Kenya
415 Laurier Ave. E.
Ottawa, ON K1N 6R4
Tel:(613) 563-1773

Embassy of Korea
151 Slater St., 5th floor
Ottawa, ON K1P 5H3
Tel:(613) 232-1715

Embassy of Lebanon
640 Lyon St.
Ottawa, ON K1S 3Z5
Tel:(613) 236-5825

High Commission for Lesotho
202 Clemow Ave.
Ottawa, ON K1S 2B4
Tel:(613) 236-9449

Embassy of Liberia
160 Elgin St., Suite 2600
Ottawa, ON K1N 8S3
Tel:(613) 232-1781

Embassy of Madagascar
282 Somerset St. W.
Ottawa, ON K2P 0J6
Tel:(613) 563-2506

High Commission for Malawi
7 Clemow Ave.
Ottawa, ON K1S 2A9
Tel:(613) 236-8931

High Commission of Malaysia
60 Boteler St.
Ottawa, ON K1N 8Y7
Tel:(613) 237-5182

Embassy of Mali
50 Goulburn Ave.
Ottawa, ON K1N 8C8
Tel:(613) 232-1501

Consulate of Malta
1 St. John's Rd., Suite 305
Toronto, ON M6P 4C7
Tel:(416) 767-4902/2901

Embassy of Mexico
130 Albert St., Suite 1800
Ottawa, ON K1P 5G4
Tel:(613) 233-8988/9272

Embassy of Morocco
38 Range Rd.
Ottawa, ON K1N 8J4
Tel:(613) 236-7391

Consulate of Morocco
1010 Sherbrooke St. W., Suite
1510
Montreal, PQ H3A 2R7
Tel:(514) 288-8750

Embassy of Myanmar
85 Range Rd., Suite 902
Ottawa, ON K1N 8J6
Tel:(613) 232-6434

Embassy of the Netherlands
275 Slater St., 3rd floor
Ottawa, ON K1P 5H9
Tel:(613) 237-5030

New Zealand High Commission
99 Bank St., Suite 727
Ottawa, ON K1P 6G3
Tel:(613) 238-5991

Consulate of New Zealand
888 Dunsmuir St., Suite 1200
Vancouver, BC V6C 3K4
Tel:(604) 684-7388

Embassy of Nicaragua
170 Laurier Ave. W., Suite 908
Ottawa, ON K1P 5V5
Tel:(613) 234-9361

Embassy of Niger
38 Blackburn Ave.
Ottawa, ON K1N 8A2
Tel:(613) 232-4291

High Commission for Nigeria
295 Metcalfe St.
Ottawa, ON K2P 1R9
Tel:(613) 236-0521

Embassy of Norway
90 Sparks St., Suite 532
Ottawa, ON K1P 5B4
Tel:(613) 238-6571

Consulate of Norway
1208 Wharf St., Suite 401
P.O. Box 577
Victoria, BC V8W 2P5
Tel:(604) 384-1174

High Commission for Pakistan
151 Slater St., Suite 608
Ottawa, ON K1P 5H3
Tel:(613) 238-7881

Consulate of Pakistan
3421 Peel St.
Montreal, PQ H3A 1W7
Tel:(514) 845-2297

Consulate of Pakistan
4881 Yonge St., Suite 810
Willowdale, ON M2N 5X3
Tel:(416) 250-1255

Consulate of Panama
1425 Rene Levesque Blvd. W.,
Suite 304
Montreal, PQ H3G 1T7
Tel:(514) 874-1929

Embassy of Paraguay
1300 Dowler Ave.
Ottawa, ON K1H 7S1
Tel:(613) 523-9306

Embassy of Peru
179 Laurier Ave. W., Suite 1007
Ottawa, ON K1P 5V5
Tel:(613) 238-1777

Consulate of Peru
550 Sherbrooke St. W., Suite
376
Montreal, PQ H3A 1B9
Tel:(514) 844-5123

Consulate of Peru
10 St. Mary St., Suite 301
Toronto, ON M4Y 1P9
Tel:(416) 963-9696

Consulate of Peru
505 Burrard St., Suite 1770
Vancouver, BC V7X 1M6
Tel:(604) 662-8880

Embassy of the Philippines
130 Albert St., Suite 606
Ottawa, ON K1P 5G4
Tel:(613) 233-1121

Consulate of the Philippines
151 Bloor St. W., Suite 365
Toronto, ON M5S 1S4
Tel:(416) 922-7181

Consulate of the Philippines
470 Granville St., Suite 301
Vancouver, BC V6C 1V5
Tel:(604) 685-7645

Embassy of Poland
443 Daly Ave.
Ottawa, ON K1N 6H3
Tel:(613) 789-0468

Consulate of Poland
1500 Pine Ave. W.
Montreal, PQ H3G 1B4
Tel:(514) 937-9481

Consulate of Poland
2603 Lake Shore Blvd. W.
Toronto, ON M8V 1G5
Tel:(416) 252-5471

Consulate of Poland
1177 W. Hastings St., Suite 1600
Vancouver, BC V6E 2K3
Tel:(604) 688-3530

Embassy of Portugal
645 Island Park Dr.
Ottawa, ON K1Y 0B8
Tel:(613) 729-0883

Consulate of Portugal
2020 University St., Suite 1725
Montreal, PQ H3A 2A5
Tel:(514) 487-4322

Consulate of Portugal
121 Richmond St. W., 7th floor
Toronto, ON M5H 2K1
Tel:(416) 360-8260

Consulate of Portugal
700 W. Pender St., Suite 904
Vancouver, BC V6C 1G8
Tel:(604) 688-6514

Consulate of Portugal
228 Notre Dame Ave., Suite 902
Winnipeg, MB R3B 1N7
Tel:(204) 943-8941

Embassy of Romania
655 Rideau St.
Ottawa, ON K1N 6A3
Tel:(613) 789-5345

Consulate of Romania
1111 St. Urbain St.
Montreal, PQ H2Z 1X6
Tel:(514) 876-1792

Consulate of Romania
111 Peter St., Suite 530
Toronto, ON M5V 2H1
Tel:(416) 585-5802

Embassy of the Russian Federation
285 Charlotte St.
Ottawa, ON K1N 8L5
Tel:(613) 235-4341

Consulate of the Russian Federation
3685, av du Musee
Montreal, PQ H3G 2C9
Tel:(514) 843-5901

Embassy of Rwanda
121 Sherwood Dr.
Ottawa, ON K1Y 3V1
Tel:(613) 722-5835

High Commission of Saint Lucia
See Eastern Caribbean States

Consulate of Saint Lucia
3 Dewberry Dr.
Markham, ON L3S 2R7
Tel:(905) 472-1423

High Commission of Saint Vincent and the Grenadines
See Eastern Caribbean States

Consulate of Saint Vincent and the Grenadines
210 Sheppard Ave. E., ground floor
Willowdale, ON M2N 3A9
Tel:(416) 222-0745

Embassy of Saudi Arabia
99 Bank St., Suite 901
Ottawa, ON K1P 6B9
Tel:(613) 237-4100

Embassy of Senegal
57 Marlborough Ave.
Ottawa, ON K1N 8E8
Tel:(613) 238-6392

Embassy of Slovakia
50 Rideau Terrace
Ottawa, ON K1M 2A1
Tel:(613) 749-4442

Embassy of Slovenia
150 Metcalfe St., Suite 2101
Ottawa, ON K2P 1P1
Tel:(613) 565-5781

Embassy of South Africa
15 Sussex Dr.
Ottawa, ON K1M 1M8
Tel:(613) 744-0330

Consulate of South Africa
1 Place Ville Marie, Suite 2615
Montreal, PQ H3B 4S3
Tel:(514) 878-9217

Consulate of South Africa
2 First Canadian Place, Suite 2515
P.O. Box 424
Toronto, ON M5X 1E3
Tel:(416) 364-0314

Embassy of Spain
350 Sparks St., Suite 802
Ottawa, ON K1R 7S8
Tel:(613) 237-2193

Consulate of Spain
1 Westmount Square, Suite 1456
Montreal, PQ H3Z 2P9
Tel:(514) 935-5235

Consulate of Spain
1200 Bay St., Suite 400
Toronto, ON M5R 2A5
Tel:(416) 967-4949

High Commission for Sri Lanka
85 Range Rd., Suite 102
Ottawa, ON K1N 8J6
Tel:(613) 233-8440

Embassy of the Sudan
85 Range Rd., Suite 407
Ottawa, ON K1N 8J6
Tel:(613) 235-4000

High Commission for Swaziland
130 Albert St., Suite 1204
Ottawa, ON K1P 5G4
Tel:(613) 567-1480

Embassy of Sweden
377 Dalhousie St.
Ottawa, ON K1N 9N8
Tel:(613) 236-8553

Consulate of Sweden
1155 Rene Levesque Blvd. W.,
Suite 800
Montreal, PQ H3B 2H7
Tel:(514) 866-4019

Consulate of Sweden
1 Queen St. E., Suite 2010
P.O. Box 85
Toronto, ON M5C 2W5
Tel:(416) 367-8768

Embassy of Switzerland
5 Marlborough Ave.
Ottawa, ON K1N 8E6
Tel:(613) 235-1837

Consulate of Switzerland
1572, av Dr. Penfield
Montreal, PQ H3G 1C4
Tel:(514) 932-7181

Consulate of Switzerland
154 University Ave., Suite 601
Toronto, ON M5H 3Y9
Tel:(416) 593-5371

Consulate of Switzerland
World Trade Centre, Suite 790
999 Canada Place
Vancouver, BC V6C 3E1
Tel:(604) 684-2231

High Commission for Tanzania
50 Range Rd.
Ottawa, ON K1N 8J4
Tel:(613) 232-1500

Embassy of Thailand
180 Island Park Dr.
Ottawa, ON K1Y 0A2
Tel:(613) 722-4444

Embassy of Togo
12 Range Rd.
Ottawa, ON K1N 8J3
Tel:(613) 238-5916/17

High Commission for Trinidad & Tobago
75 Albert St., Suite 508
Ottawa, ON K1P 5E7
Tel:(613) 232-2418

Consulate of Trinidad & Tobago
2005 Sheppard Ave. E., Suite 303
Willowdale, ON M2J 5B4
Tel:(416) 495-9442

Embassy of Tunisia
515 O'Connor St.
Ottawa, ON K1S 3P8
Tel:(613) 237-0330

Embassy of Turkey
197 Wurtemburg St.
Ottawa, ON K1N 8L9
Tel:(613) 789-4044

High Commission for Uganda
231 Cobourg St.
Ottawa, ON K1N 8J2
Tel:(613) 233-7797

Embassy of the Ukraine
331 Metcalfe St.
Ottawa, ON K2P 1S3
Tel:(613) 230-2961

Embassy of the United States
100 Wellington St.
P.O. Box 866, Stn. B
Ottawa, ON K1P 5T1
Tel:(613) 238-5335

Consulate of the United States
615 Macleod Trail SE., Suite 1050
Calgary, AB T2G 4T8
Tel:(403) 266-8962

Consulate of the United States
910 Congswell Tower, Scotia Square
Halifax, NS B3J 3K1
Tel:(902) 429-2480

Consulate of the United States
455 Rene Levesque Blvd. W.
CP 65, Stn. Desjardins
Montreal, PQ H2Z 1Z2
Tel:(514) 398-9695

Consulate of the United States
1075 W. Georgia St.
Vancouver, BC V6E 4E9
Tel:(604) 685-4311

Embassy of Uruguay
130 Albert St., Suite 1905
Ottawa, ON K1P 5G4
Tel:(613) 234-2727

Embassy of Venezuela
32 Range Rd.
Ottawa, ON K1N 8J4
Tel:(613) 235-5151

Consulate of Venezuela
2055 Peel St., Suite 400
Montreal, PQ H3A 1V4
Tel:(514) 842-3417

Consulate of Venezuela
2 Carlton St., Suite 703
Toronto, ON M5B 1J3
Tel:(416) 977-6809

Embassy of Vietnam
25B Davidson Dr.
Gloucester, ON K1J 6L7
Tel:(613) 744-4963

Embassy of Yemen
350 Sparks St., Suite 1100
Ottawa, ON K1R 7S8
Tel:(613) 232-8525

Embassy of Yugoslavia
17 Blackburn Ave.
Ottawa, ON K1N 8A2
Tel:(613) 233-6289

Embassy of Zaire
18 Range Rd.
Ottawa, ON K1N 8J3
Tel:(613) 236-7103

High Commission for Zambia
130 Albert St., Suite 1610
Ottawa, ON K1P 5G4
Tel:(613) 563-0712

High Commission of Zimbabwe
332 Somerset St. W.
Ottawa, ON K2P 0J9
Tel:(613) 237-4388

GOVERNMENT DEPARTMENTS

Agriculture and Agri-Food
Sir John Carling Bldg.
930 Carling Ave.
Ottawa, ON K1A 0C5
Tel:(613) 995-8963

Canadian Heritage
Terasses de la Chaudiore
25 Eddy St.
Hull, PQ K1A 0C5
Tel:(819) 997-0055

Environment
Terasses de la Chaudiore
10 Wellington St.
Hull, PQ K1A 0H3
Tel:(819) 997-2800

Federal Office of Regional Development (Quebec)
800 Tour de la Place Victoria
P.O. Box 247, Bureau 3800
Montreal, PQ H4Z 1E8
Tel:(514) 283-6412

Finance
Esplanade Laurier
140 O'Connor St.
Ottawa, ON K1A 0G5
Tel:(613) 992-1573

Fisheries and Oceans
200 Kent St.
Ottawa, ON K1A 0E6
Tel:(613) 993-0600

Foreign Affairs and International Trade
Lester B. Pearson Bldg.
125 Sussex Dr.
Ottawa, ON K1A 0G2
Tel:(613) 996-9134

Health
Jeanne Mance Bldg.
Tunney's Pasture
Ottawa, ON K1A 0K9
Tel:(613) 957-2991

Human Resources Development
Ottawa, ON K1A 0J9
Tel:(819) 997-2617

Indian Affairs and Northern Development
Terasses de la Chaudiore
10 Wellington St.
Hull, PQ K1A 0H4
Tel:(819) 997-0380

Industry
C.D. Howe Bldg.
235 Queen St.
Ottawa, ON K1A 0H5
Tel:(613) 952-4782

Intergovernmental Affairs
155 Queen St.
Ottawa, ON K1A 1K2
Tel:(613) 943-1838

Justice
Justice Bldg.
Kent at Wellington St.
Ottawa, ON K1A 0H8
Tel:(613) 957-4222

National Defence
National Defence Headquarters
101 Colonel By Dr.
Ottawa, ON K1A 0K2
Tel:(613) 992-4581

National Revenue
Ottawa, ON K1A 0L5
Tel:(613) 995-2960

Natural Resources
580 Booth St.
Ottawa, ON K1A 0E4
Tel:(613) 995-0947

Public Works and Government Services
Place du Portage, Phase III
11 Laurier St.
Hull, PQ K1A 0S5
Tel:(819) 997-6363

Transport
Tower C, Place de Ville
28th floor
Ottawa, ON K1A 0N5
Tel:(613) 990-2309

Treasury Board
Esplanade Laurier
140 O'Connor St.
Ottawa, ON K1A 0R5
Tel:(613) 957-2400

Veterans Affairs
66 Slater St.
Ottawa, ON K1A 0P4
Tel:(613) 992-4237

Western Economic Diversification
Canada Place, 15th floor
9700 Jasper Ave.
Edmonton, AB TJ5 4H7
Tel:(403) 495-4164

HOSPITALS

ALBERTA
Calgary
Calgary District Hospital
1035 7th Ave. SW.
Calgary, AB T2P 3E9
Tel:(403) 541-2700

Calgary General Hospital
841 Centre Ave. E.
Calgary, AB T2E 0A1
Tel:(403) 268-9111

Foothills Provincial General Hospital
1403 29th St. SW.
Calgary, AB T2N 2T9
Tel:(403) 270-1110

Edmonton
Charles Carnsell General Hospital
12804 114th Ave.
Edmonton, AB T5M 3A4
Tel:(403) 453-5311

General Hospital of Edmonton
1100 Youville Dr. W.
Edmonton, AB T6L 5X8
Tel:(403) 450-7000

Royal Alexandra Hospital
10240 Kingsway Ave.
Edmonton, AB T5H 3V9
Tel:(403) 477-4111

BRITISH COLUMBIA
Vancouver
St. Paul's Hospital
1081 Burrard St.
Vancouver, BC V6Z 1Y6
Tel:(604) 682-2344

U.B.C. Hospital
4500 Oak St.
Vancouver, BC V6H 3N1
Tel:(604) 228-7121

Vancouver General Hospital
855 12th Ave. W.
Vancouver, BC V5Z 1M9
Tel:(604) 875-4111

Victoria
Gorge Road Hospital
63 Gorge Rd. E.
Victoria, BC V9A 1L2
Tel:(604) 386-2464

Royal Jubilee Hospital
1900 Fort St.
Victoria, BC V8R 1J8
Tel:(604) 595-9200

Victoria General Hospital
841 Fairfield Rd.
Victoria, BC V8V 3B6
Tel:(604) 389-6300

MANITOBA
Winnipeg
Grace General Hospital
300 Booth Dr.
Winnipeg, MB R3J 3M7
Tel:(204) 837-8311

St. Boniface General Hospital
409 Tache Ave.
Winnipeg, MB R2H 2A6
Tel:(204) 233-8563

Seven Oaks General Hospital
2300 McPhillips St.
Winnipeg, MB R2V 3M3
Tel:(204) 632-7133

NEW BRUNSWICK
Saint John Regional Hospital
P.O. Box 2100
Saint John, NB E2L 4L2
Tel:(506) 648-6000

NEWFOUNDLAND
General Hospital Health Sciences Centre
Prince Philip Dr.
St. John's, NF A1B 3V6
Tel:(709) 737-6300

NOVA SCOTIA
Victoria General Hospital
1278 Tower Rd.
Halifax, NS B3H 2Y9
Tel:(902) 428-2110

SASKATCHEWAN
Regina
Regina General Hospital
1400 14th Ave.
Regina, SK S4P 0W5
Tel:(306) 359-4444

Pasqua Hospital
4101 Dewdney Ave.
Regina, SK S4T 1A5
Tel:(306) 359-2497

Saskatoon
St. Paul's Hospital
1702 20th St. W.
Saskatoon, SK S7M 0Z9
Tel:(306) 382-3220

Saskatoon City Hospital
Queen St. & 7th Ave.
Saskatoon, SK S7K 0M7
Tel:(306) 242-6681

ONTARIO
Niagara Falls
Greater Niagara General Hospital
5546 Portage Rd.
Niagara Falls, ON L2E 6X2
Tel:(905) 358-0171

Ottawa
Ottawa Civic Hospital
1053 Carling Ave.
Ottawa, ON K1Y 4E9
Tel:(613) 761-4201

Ottawa General Hospital
501 Smyth Rd.
Ottawa, ON K1G 8L6
Tel:(613) 737-8449

Riverside Hospital
1967 Riverside Dr.
Ottawa, ON K1H 7W9
Tel:(613) 738-7100

Toronto
Doctors' Hospital
45 Brunswick Ave.
Toronto, ON M5S 2M1
Tel:(416) 923-5411

Mount Sinai Hospital
600 University Ave.
Toronto, ON M5G 1X5
Tel:(416) 586-5080

St. Michael's Hospital
30 Bond St.
Toronto, ON M5B 1W8
Tel:(416) 360-4000

Toronto General Hospital
220 Elizabeth St.
Toronto, ON M5G 2C4
Tel:(416) 595-3111

Wellesley Hospital
160 Wellesley St. E.
Toronto, ON M4Y 1J3
Tel:(416) 926-7002

**PRINCE EDWARD
ISLAND**
Charlottetown
Queen Elizabeth Hospital
P.O. Box 6600
Charlottetown, PE C1A 8T5
Tel:(902) 566-6111

QUEBEC
Montreal
Montreal General Hospital
1650, av Cedar
Montreal, PQ H3G 1A4
Tel:(514) 937-6011

Royal Victoria Hospital
687, av des Pins ouest
Montreal, PQ H3A 1A1
Tel:(514) 842-1231

**Sir Mortimer B. Davis Jewish
General Hospital**
3755, ch C>te Ste-Catherine
Montreal, PQ H3T 1E2
Tel:(514) 340-8222

Quebec
Quebec General Hospital
260, boul. Langelier
Quebec, PQ G1K 5N1
Tel:(418) 529-0931

MUSEUMS

The larger museums are usually open seven days a week, closing only on Christmas and New Year's Day. Opening times vary during the year, so check before you go. As a rule, museums are open from 9:00 a.m. or 10:00 a.m. until 5:00 p.m., with extended hours on Thursday night. Some museums offer free admission at certain times of the

week.

NIGHTLIFE

Most cities have an interesting and vibrant nightlife. An eclectic range of clubs host live bands playing everything from jazz, blues, rock, country, West Indian music, heavy metal to alternative music. Cover charges range from nothing to $30 for the most popular bands.

If you just want a drink, there are taverns and quiet cafes where you can soak up the local atmosphere.

If you desire something a little more culturally enriching, you can attend a play, orchestra, opera or a ballet.

PLACES OF WORSHIP

The larger cities, with their multicultural populations, offer services for a wide range of religious faiths. Check a local phone book or contact the city's tourist information centre for more details.

POLICE

In an emergency, you can contact the police by dialling 911 in some of the larger cities, otherwise dial 0 to ask the operator for help.

The Royal Canadian Mounted Police (RCMP) is Canada's national police force. They often act as local and provincial police in jurisdictions without their own police forces.
Canadian cities and the provinces of Ontario and Quebec have their own police forces.

SHOPPING CENTRES

The larger shopping centres usually have one or two department stores, a grocery store and a large number of small retail shops selling everything under the sun. These large shopping

centres are mainly located in the suburbs.

The most famous shopping centres in Canada are Toronto's Eaton Centre and the West Edmonton Shopping Mall which, incidentally, has a submarine fleet larger than the Canadian Navy's fleet.

PHOTO CREDITS

INDEX